International Media Development

Mass Communication and Journalism

Lee B. Becker
GENERAL EDITOR

Vol. 23

The Mass Communication and Journalism series is part of the Peter Lang Media and Communication list. Every volume is peer reviewed and meets the highest quality standards for content and production.

PETER LANG
New York • Bern • Berlin
Brussels • Vienna • Oxford • Warsaw

International Media Development

Historical Perspectives and New Frontiers

EDITORS

Nicholas Benequista, Susan Abbott,
Paul Rothman, and Winston Mano

PETER LANG
New York • Bern • Berlin
Brussels • Vienna • Oxford • Warsaw

Library of Congress Cataloging-in-Publication Data

Names: Benequista, Nicholas, editor. | Abbott, Susan, editor.
Rothman, Paul, editor. | Mano, Winston, editor.
Title: International media development: historical perspectives and new frontiers /
edited by Nicholas Benequista, Susan Abbott, Paul Rothman, and Winston Mano.
Description: New York: Peter Lang, 2019.
Series: Mass communication and journalism; vol. 23 | ISSN 2153-2761
Includes bibliographical references.
Identifiers: LCCN 2018038522 | ISBN 978-1-4331-5147-7 (hardback: alk. paper)
ISBN 978-1-4331-5148-4 (paperback: alk. paper) | ISBN 978-1-4331-5149-1 (ebook pdf)
ISBN 978-1-4331-5150-7 (epub) | ISBN 978-1-4331-5151-4 (mobi)
Subjects: LCSH: Mass media.
Classification: LCC P90 .I567 2019 | DDC 302.23—dc23
LC record available at https://lccn.loc.gov/2018038522
DOI 10.3726/b14700

Bibliographic information published by **Die Deutsche Nationalbibliothek**.
Die Deutsche Nationalbibliothek lists this publication in the "Deutsche Nationalbibliografie"; detailed bibliographic data are available on the Internet at http://dnb.d-nb.de/.

The paper in this book meets the guidelines for permanence and durability of the Committee on Production Guidelines for Book Longevity of the Council of Library Resources.

Peter Lang Publishing, Inc.
29 Broadway, 18th floor, New York, NY 10006
www.peterlang.com

Printed in the United States of America

Contents

Figures

Tables

Acknowledgments

This volume is the result of a tremendous collective effort. The editors of this book are most grateful to the many contributing authors—for their ideas, hard work, patience, and commitment to building knowledge in our field.

Ideas about media development are put to the test by the practitioners who work on the frontlines of media development every day. In this regard, we are thankful for the encouragement and support of Center for International Media Assistance (CIMA), which created several opportunities to gather scholars and practitioners around the table. The editors of this book are especially grateful to Mark Nelson, Senior Director at CIMA, for his patience, mentorship, and overall guidance in making this book a possibility. In addition, Guy Berger and his team at UNESCO offered early support and insights to the book and our interest in forming a knowledge community of scholars and practitioners on the topic of media development. The views and opinions of Tara Susman-Peña from IREX, and her continual push to bridge the worlds of academic and practitioner research, were also vital to our efforts. In addition, the opportunity to partner with the Global Forum for Media Development (GFMD) and the support we received from Mira Milosevic, GFMD's Director, and Ricardo Corredor, GFMD's Chairman and the Executive Director of the Gabriel García Márquez New Journalism Foundation in Colombia, has been extremely fruitful.

The volume also benefitted tremendously from the occasions we had to come together with the contributors at the conferences organized by the International Association for Media and Communication Research (IAMCR) in Leicester in 2016 and Cartagena in 2017. We would like to thank the organizers of IAMCR, namely Bruce Girard, for his support and assistance in helping us bring our ideas to life. We would also like to thank the many scholars who helped us along the way, including Monroe Price of the Annenberg School for Communication, University of Pennsylvania, Silvio Waisbord at George Washington University, Martin Scott at the University of East Anglia, Robin Mansell from the London School of Economics and Political Science, and Colin Sparks from Hong Kong Baptist University. We are also grateful to the University of Leeds, especially Professors Chris Paterson and Jairo Lugo-Ocando for their assistance with the Cartagena and London workshops. For helping us to get involved with the IAMCR and guiding us through its complexities, we thank Arne Hintz at Cardiff University, Marc Raboy at McGill University, and Tom Jacobson from Temple University. We would also like to thank the University of Westminster, especially Karen Foster, Fauzia Ahmad, and CAMRI Director Professor Christian Fuchs.

Finally, we are indebted to Lee Becker, Professor at the University of Georgia and Series Editor on Mass Communication and Journalism for Peter Lang. Without his support, this book would not have been published.

About This Volume

The idea to put together an edited volume on media development research and scholarship began in spring 2016 as a simple conversation between a small but lively group of scholars, journalists, NGO representatives, and donors at an event organized by the Center for International Media Assistance at the National Endowment for Democracy. While discussing the ideas, theories, and literature that has guided the study and practice of media development, the group identified a common interest in building a knowledge community that could bridge research and practice in the field.

This goal later motivated a series of conferences and workshops convened by the Center for International Media Assistance and the University of Westminster, most notably two pre-conferences at the International Association for Media and Communication Research's annual gatherings in Leicester, England (2016), and Cartagena, Colombia (2017). In fall 2018, the editors and contributors also participated in a two-day workshop held simultaneously in London and Washington, D.C.. These gatherings were important for a number of reasons. They brought together researchers, monitoring and evaluation specialists, academics, media development practitioners, and donors who support media development work. These collaborative gatherings offered space to debate the key issues facing media development and offered an opportunity to reflect, probe, and unpack the history of ideas that have shaped efforts to stimulate media development. Out of these conferences and workshops has emerged a budding network of scholars and applied researchers with a common purpose and strategic goals. This volume is a contribution to that network's objectives, and we hope that the efforts that went into the book and the contents herein will contribute to more research collaboration and knowledge exchange on how to orient media systems towards democracy and development.

CHAPTER ONE

Introduction

NICHOLAS BENEQUISTA, SUSAN ABBOTT, PAUL ROTHMAN, AND WINSTON MANO

Those interested in understanding the dynamic interplay of forces either in hindering or propelling social progress could previously be excused for giving only a passing attention to the role of media, but no longer. The spread of digital communication technologies over the last three decades has had profound positive and negative impacts on the world, with much still resting on how media will continue to develop globally, nationally, and locally.[1]

Unfortunately, there remains a significant risk that the future of media, at all these levels, will not be determined by those who care about human rights, democracy, pluralism or driven by the needs and interests of citizens. The development of media that serves these values and interests will require concerted, strategic action by local activists, reform-minded governments and their unwavering international allies. To be effective, this action must be supported by learning and knowledge and bolstered by a commitment to human rights and democratic values that give more space to the needs of local communities.

As a modest contribution to the knowledge required, we have assembled in this volume a wide-ranging set of essays from both researchers and practitioners on the question of media development: how does media change, preferably for the better, and with what implications for the broader social, economic, and political development? By media, we mean the technologies and infrastructure that enable communication at a distance, the content of that communication, and the institutions and individuals engaged in creating both. Media, in that respect, is best thought of as the entire system of components that shape how citizens witness the world beyond their immediate, everyday lives and how they can communicate and engage in turn with the wider world. Admittedly, it can be difficult to differentiate changes in the "connective tissue" of media from political, economic, or social changes simultaneously going on around it, but that is the point. Media's current transition is integral to broader transformations, as it has been in the past.

In the 18th century, the rapid growth of books and newspapers, enabled by a combination of the printing press and the expansion of open markets, produced a new sense of emotional attachment among people living in dispersed villages and cities. This new sense of distant attachment produced by the advent of mass media—*the imagined community*—was integral to the rise of nationalism in Europe (Anderson 1983). Later, as undersea cables and satellites expanded connections even further, mass media became entwined with a larger pattern of globalization that has seen authority and power dispersed from state to global actors (Held and McGrew 2002).

Today, scholars argue that we are in the midst of another sea change. Relatively new communication technologies such as the internet and mobile phone are now deepening and intensifying our mediated relationships in an age of unprecedented connectivity. We are witnessing media infiltrate more and more of our daily lives, and more and more economic and social activities (consider how even a small non-governmental organization now must be a competent user of media to be effective) in what some scholars describe as *mediatization*—a concept that explains how media strongly impacts and shapes today's society (Krotz 2009).

While there are many lofty questions to be explored about the moral, social, and political significance of these changes in the media sphere, the editors and contributors to this volume are especially concerned with the implications of these changes for citizenship and democracy. Historically, the media's role in providing news and information has been considered the most prominent feature of its public service function, and ensuring that media provide citizens with reliable news and information remains a vital part of media's development today—and a salient issue throughout this volume. But media's development must also contend with how digital media has changed the nature of the public's connection to the media (see chapters by O'Maley and Susman-Peña on this question). Whereas newspaper, radio, and television underpinned a system of one-to-many communication, the internet enables many-to-many communication (Meier 2011); once passive media consumers can now be producers (Rosen 2006). Media development must contend with digital media's capabilities to allow citizens to speak for themselves, distribute and analyze information, and organize collectively.

The seemingly inherent democratic affordances of digital media initially ushered in optimistic talk of "liberation technologies" (Diamond and Plattner 2010). The lower barriers to entry created by digital technology also stirred hope that media markets controlled by a few rich and powerful individuals would soon be more plural and competitive, with citizens benefitting from this by receiving more information, more diverse perspectives, and higher quality news. But the early hopes placed in "liberation technologies" have given way to growing anxieties about on-line echo chambers and political polarization, social media-fueled disinformation campaigns, and surveillance and the loss of privacy. At the same time, the digital age of media has since proven to be commercially devastating for local and independent media, and a boon for large corporations and politically-driven oligarchs seeking inexpensive broadcasting assets (See chapter by Dragomir). Adding to the anxiety is the concomitant backsliding into authoritarianism in once promising democracies such as the Philippines, Turkey, and Hungary. Meanwhile, even consolidated democracies are experiencing a dramatic decline in public support for democratic institutions, including the media (Hanitzsch, Dalen, Steindl 2017), and stoking concerns about what has been called democratic *de-consolidation* (Mounk 2018).

While the trend toward more intensive connectivity may be inevitable, the negative social and political consequences associated with it are not. Rather, the social and political impact of media will be determined by innumerable decisions—large and small, local and global—about market regulations, tax policies, criminal laws, organizational procedures, technological standards, codes of ethics, and international development targets, among other enactments of collective will.

Some of these decisions, including in the sphere of internet governance, will have global effects, but most will be far narrower in scope. While it is tempting to believe that digital technologies and the internet have made us all part of the same media system—one global public sphere (Volkmer 2014)—that is simply not the case. Media systems are notoriously uneven, with citizens of different countries, and even within countries, having dramatically different kinds of access to knowledge about the wider world and the resources to make themselves heard.

For many of the world's population, access to quality news and information and free and independent media is out of reach. According to recent Freedom House research "only 13 percent of the world's population enjoys a free press—that is, a media environment where coverage of political news is robust, the safety of journalists is guaranteed, state intrusion in media affairs is minimal, and the press is not subject to onerous legal or economic pressures." Their research goes on to note that 45 percent of the population lives in countries where the media environment is considered "not free."[2]

These inequities are of particular concern to the study of media development. The contributors to this volume offer diverse and sometimes conflicting views on what explains the unevenness, and how it should be resolved. At the core of these debates, however, is a shared interest in understanding how media development takes place within a society, how it is supported and advocated, what developed media looks like, and *whose interests* different conceptions of media development serve (see chapters by Price, Stremlau, Segura, Kalathil, and Deane for different perspectives on how competing visions for media development play out in politics and practice).

Media Development in Theory and Practice

Media development sits at the intersection between the world of theory and the world of action, with all the tensions that arises from that position. The contributions to this volume frequently reflect those tensions, and students and scholars are invited to use these chapters to further explore the emerging issues.

In the different contributions to this volume, you will find *media development* treated as a normative concept of what media ought to look like (e.g., chapters by Jain and Jacobson), as the process by which media systems are shaped (e.g. chapters by Freedman and Obar, and Nelson), as a field of international assistance (e.g., chapters by Price and Abbott), and as a field of research (e.g. Waisbord's chapter). In some chapters, several of these ways of thinking about media development may be present simultaneously, though we have tried, as the editors of this volume, to encourage as much clarity as possible. Some disagreement, however, is inevitable, as the term itself bears the marks of its history.

The term "media development" was first used following the collapse of the Berlin Wall in 1989, when there was a sudden increase in foreign aid monies devoted to the media—most intended to help countries in transition to reconstruct and transform their media sectors into institutions supportive of democratic governance. Media organizations, reform-minded civil society groups, and even governments that wanted to join Western institutions and participate in global markets requested this support. What started out as part of efforts aimed at supporting the transition to democracy in Central and Eastern Europe (see chapter by McCormack) and areas of the former Soviet Union later spread throughout Africa (see chapter by Mano), Asia (see chapter by Jain), Latin America (see chapter by Segura), and the Middle East. Today, assistance to media development is a small global enterprise, with a relatively meager $600 million or so in annual funding scattered around the world from government aid agencies, multilateral donors, and private philanthropies.[3] These efforts can take many forms, from funding the establishment of an entirely new media outlet to funding freedom of speech movements to formulating policies for media regulatory bodies. While support to media development does frequently come from the international community, it is important to acknowledge that media development activities include efforts by organizations, people, and sometimes governments to develop the capacity and quality of the media sector within a specific country or region. Several different approaches to media development are highlighted in this volume, including the support for investigative journalism conducted by the Organized Crime and Corruption Reporting Project (see chapter by Sullivan), efforts to blunt disinformation with media literacy (see chapters by Griffin and Ljubic), examples of media reform movements (chapters by Freedman and Obar, and Byerly), and support to public sector broadcasting (chapter by Aslama and Marko).

Unfortunately, as many of the chapters in volume will attest, the organizations associated with international assistance to media development have dominated thinking and approaches on the topic, with varied consequences for its practice. In particular, the international organizations that first popularized the term frequently treated media development as something that is done to other countries. This conceptualization of media development has become its Achilles heel, alienating and disempowering the actors most essential to the media's development. Rather than being understood as an endogenous process of change that takes place among the diverse players in the media environment of a country or region, it has often been seen as supply-driven service performed and funded by outsiders. This donor-driven approach to development work, generally, has not only drawn academic scorn, but also failing marks from independent evaluators. Many donor reviews of media development programs have found it difficult to establish that these efforts—especially when focused on training journalists—have been effective (Arsenault and Powers 2010, Nelson 2012, Norris 2010, Phiri and Fourie 2011).

Media development has not been spared scholarly criticism either. A long-standing critique of the internationally funded effort to promote media development is that it has been driven by assumptions and received wisdom of the modernization paradigm, which is associated with seminal figures in Western communication theory such as Lerner, Rogers and Schramm (Lerner, 1958; Rogers, 1962; Schramm, 1964). These scholars have argued that media development assistance has pushed Western blueprints for media and news journalism that may not be the most appropriate for a given context (Nyamnjoh 2005). While this critique is well founded, it does not always offer constructive insight into how media development can be supported through bottom-up, demand-driven processes. We've challenged authors in this volume to think beyond that critique, to consider how a different paradigm of media development might look, both normatively and in practice.

On the other hand, practitioners of media development have also been reluctant to acknowledge scholarly critique of the field. Amid a competitive environment for funding, there has been a disincentive for practitioners to communicate doubts or failures. Furthermore, much of the research or data collection conducted expressly for the purposes of media development assistance has been limited in scope, owing to funding constraints, and generally focused on the outcomes of specific interventions at the neglect of the bigger picture (See Phiri and Fourie 2011 and also Abbott, this volume). Now in an era marked by severe strains on budgets and repeated calls to show "value for money," media development organizations are under serious pressure to substantiate their programs and put forward a compelling case for how donor money gets used and what impact it has had. This has led to a scurry of activity by donors, NGOs, academics, and others to come up with better monitoring and evaluation schemes, toolkits, best practices, and frameworks for proving to the world that media do matter, and that they really do all the things that the media development community likes to purport. The applied researchers and practitioners contributing to this volume were also encouraged to bring forward thinking on this issues to their chapters.

Knowledge for Media Development

Media development has a knowledge problem. Unlike in other sectors of development, such as governance and public health, media development has no cohesive community of scholars dedicated to understanding and addressing new challenges or develop new ways of thinking in the quickly evolving and complex media space. The weak linkages to scholarship around media development issues are not because such scholarship does not exist, but rather because the scholarship is scattered across academic disciplines. One can find important research related to media development at academic conferences for communications, political science, anthropology, and many more. Furthermore, many of the assumptions that researchers and practitioners make about the role of media in supporting democratic processes and development are based largely on theories and conjecture.

Empirical evidence and rigorous testing of the relationship between media and developmental outcomes is scant (Norris 2010, World Bank 2017). The evidence of impact so necessary to continue justifying assistance to media development is often difficult to demonstrate due to limitations of time, money, staff, and methodological know-how. Funding for and inclusion of plans for program evaluation is rarely adequate, although this gap is starting to be closed, or at least addressed, as monitoring and evaluation becomes something of a cause *du jour* in international development circles. But the data from these evaluations must inform broader learning objectives and engage with scholarly ideas about media's role in the future of social progress.

In short, media development as a field must come of age, and in doing so, evolve and put into practice research methods and techniques that employ sound results-based monitoring and evaluation systems. In addition, more robust and action-oriented research is needed on the issues at the intersection media systems, politics, social identity, and development.

Still, while more research and improved techniques for monitoring and evaluation are important, they are just a small part of the greater effort required to solve media development's knowledge problem, as many of the chapters in this volume attest. Media development's greater knowledge challenge is to create the possibility of concerted, strategic, and global action that is driven by the needs and desires of local communities. Media's development is too important a topic to be the prerogative of a privileged few; thinking on the topic needs to be revitalized with multiple and diverse perspectives at every level. Civil society organizations and social movements everywhere that are struggling to win political freedoms or strengthen social inclusion need to be engaged in shaping the future of media systems (see Freedman and Obar, this volume). Policy-makers, regulators, and think tanks, particularly in the Global South, need the capacity to assess the weaknesses in the broader enabling environment for media pluralism in their countries, and to prescribe tailored solutions for their countries. Journalists and publishers who have sought to adapt their work and business model to the changing media environment around them must begin to see themselves as makers and shapers of that very environment (see Betz and Foster, this volume). Perhaps most importantly, those who are making and shaping the internet—the environment that is likely to be most consequential for the future of media—must be accountable for the consequences of their decisions on citizenship and social cohesion (see O'Maley, this volume). Finally, the international community, which is largely blind on this issue without global comparable data or guiding principles for the enormity of the challenge, also has a serious knowledge gap when it comes to media development (see Raboy, this volume). And, as Shanthi Kalathil writes in her chapter, media development is also becoming a site of competing international interests with consequences that have not been yet fully understood.

This may sound daunting, but much progress is already occurring on all these fronts as actors of every type become more aware of the great stakes at play in the changing nature of media systems around the world. As this book goes to press, the challenges to media are formidable and growing. New strategies and thinking about how to manage these problems will require a new generation of scholars and practitioners who will need to learn from the mistakes of the past and invent the approaches for the future.

This book aspires to provide some inspiration for this challenge. With a first-of-its-kind collection of chapters from both scholars and practitioners of media development, *International Media Development: Historical Perspectives and New Frontiers* provides advanced undergraduate and graduate students, international development practitioners, and policymakers with a diverse collection of contributions from academics and practitioners on the role of media in international development. It takes stock of the history of ideas and theories related to media development, surveys current issues in the field, presents different regional perspectives, offers a sample of different approaches to media development, and examines some of the implications of digital communication for media development. The final chapter, an epilogue by Guy Berger, provides further reflection on the cross-cutting issues in the volume.

We hope that you enjoy this book and that it will be a useful resource for innovative thinking and approaches in the field of media development.

Notes

1. For a comprehensive summary of the research on media's contribution to social progress globally, see Couldry, N., & Rodriguez, C. (2018). Media and Communications. In International Panel on Social Progress (Ed.), *Rethinking Society for the 21st Century: Report of the International Panel on Social Progress* (pp. 1–132). Cambridge: Cambridge University Press.
2. https://freedomhouse.org/report/freedom-press/freedom-press-2017.
3. This average calculated from official aid figures available from the OECD-DAC database for the years 2010–2015, together with an estimated $150 million in annual private funding derived from the Media Impact Funders database. The full report from that analysis is Mary Myers and Linet Juma, "Defending Independent Media: A Comprehensive Analysis of Aid Flows," Washington, D.C.: Center for International Media Assistance, 2018.

References

Anderson, Benedict. 1983. *Imagined communities: Reflections on the origin and spread of nationalism*. London: Verso.

Arsenault, Amelia, and Shawn Powers. 2010. "The Media Map Project: Review of Literature (Version 2)." Washington, D.C.: Internews and the World Bank Institute.

Diamond, Larry Jay, and Marc F. Plattner. 2012. *Liberation Technology: Social Media and the Struggle for Democracy*. Journal of Democracy Book. Baltimore, MD: Johns Hopkins University Press.

Hanitzsch, Thomas, Arjen Van Dalen, and Nina Steindl. 2017. "Caught in the Nexus: A Comparative and Longitudinal Analysis of Public Trust in the Press." *The International Journal of Press/Politics* 23(1): 3–23. doi:10.1177/1940161217740695.

Held, David, and Andrew McGrew, eds. 2002. *Governing Globalization: Power, Authority and Global Governance*. Cambridge: Polity Press.

Krotz, Friedrich. 2009. "Mediatization: A Concept with Which to Grasp Media and Societal Change." In *Mediatization: Concept, Changes, and Consequences*, edited by K. Lundby, 19–38. New York: Peter Lang Publishing.

Lerner, Daniel. 1958. *The Passing of Traditional Society: Modernizing the Middle East*. New York, NY: The Free Press.

Meier, Patrick Philippe. 2011. "Do 'Liberation Technologies Change the Balance of Power Between Repressive States and Civil Society." PhD dissertation, The Fletcher School of Law and Diplomacy, Medford, MA. Available at http://irevolution.files.wordpress.com/2011/11/meier-dissertation-final.pdf.

Mounk, Yascha. 2018. *The People vs. Democracy: Why Our Freedom Is in Danger and How to Save It*. Cambridge, MA: Harvard University Press.

Nelson, Mark with Tara Susman-Peña. 2012. "Rethinking Media Development: A Report on the Media Map Project." Washington, D.C.: Internews.

Norris, Pippa, ed. 2010. *Public Sentinel: News Media and Governance Reform*. Washington, D.C.: The World Bank.

Nyamnjoh, Francis. 2005. *Africa's Media, Democracy and the Politics of Belonging*. London: Zed Books.

Phiri, Sam and Pieter J. Fourie. 2011. "Media Development Aid and the Westernisation of Africa: The Case of the Open Society Initiative for Southern Africa (OSISA). *Communicatio: South African Journal for Communication Theory and Research*, 37, no. 1: 80–99.

Rogers, Everett. 1962. *Diffusion of Innovations*. New York: The Free Press.

Rosen, Jay. 2006. "The People Formerly Known as the Audience." *PressThink*, June 27, 2006. http://archive.pressthink.org/2006/06/27/ppl_frmr.html (accessed 26 April 2018).

Schramm, Wilbur. 1964. *Mass Media and National Development: The Role of Information in the Developing Countries*. Standford, CA: Stanford University Press and UNESCO.

Volkmer, Ingrid. 2014. *The Global Public Sphere: Public Communication in the Age of Reflective Interdependence*. Cambridge, MA: Polity Press.

World Bank. 2017. *Governance and the Law: World Development Report 2017*. Washington D.C.: The World Bank Group.

PART ONE

Theories and Histories

CHAPTER TWO

Global Media

New Issues, Old Story

MARC RABOY

Is there anything left to know about the state of communication in the world? To ask the question is to answer it: of course, there is. Human society has never been so extensively equipped in technologies of communication, and yet we can confidently assert that people are arguably not much farther ahead in their capacity to *communicate*.

Contemporary media contribute at least as much to keeping us apart as they do to bringing us together. Media frame issues and debates in arcane and perplexing ways, perpetuate prejudice and stereotypes, provoke unproductively divisive confrontations and conflicts.

And yet, the emancipatory *promise* of media remains. If only the power of media could be harnessed and shared, we would be a big step closer to using media for the greater common good, for equity and social justice, for *development* in the broadest, most generous, sense.

In order to take that step we need to understand what separates the promise from the reality. This is not new. The problem is as old as the media themselves. The efforts at understanding media are legion. But it may be time to change the lens.

There is nothing new about the unequal development of communication technologies. Nonetheless, well-meaning people everywhere continue to believe that if the latest technologies can be harnessed for the public good, things will be different. This remains to be seen.

I will illustrate this point with a historical anecdote about the origins of China's contemporary television infrastructure. In 1972, the Canadian economist Dallas Smythe—one of the pioneers of the political economy of communication—visited the People's Republic of China. "At that time in China, politics was said everywhere to be in command," Smythe later wrote, using a Maoist slogan. "At the same time, it was emphasized that China lagged behind the West and must 'catch up.'" Mao was still at the helm, and China was planning a national television system, among many other things. Smythe—no wide-eyed idealist but a rigorous Marxist—suggested that China had a tremendous opportunity to break with "the one-way TV system capitalism had developed to make possible the production of audiences which would market commodities to themselves. I said that [the one-way TV system] was an implicitly authoritarian system in which influence was transmitted from the top down ..." (Smythe 1981, 226).

What would be more fitting for China's "socialist road," Smythe suggested, than a two-way system in which TV receivers were equipped with a built-in video response capacity? "My hosts asked me why I thought it was desirable in China for the TV system to be two-way ... Now when China was still not committed to a Western-style one-way TV system, China could design a TV industrial art which would serve its ideological purposes rather than adopt uncritically a capitalist industrial art for TV which embodies capitalist ideology." Smythe had essentially the same conversation with specialists in Beijing, Shanghai, Nanjing, Wuhan, and Guangzhou "and in every instance the suggestion was received with interest, and the comment that they would think about it." The reaction of a group of economists and philosophers at the University of Beijing was most illuminating; here Smythe was told that technology was "universal and politically neutral; that socialism could use one-way TV without ideological danger." China proceeded to introduce the Western model of one-way TV (Smythe 1981, 227), establishing the infrastructure for what has since become one of the world's most authoritarian media systems.

Of course technology is not politically neutral, and its universality depends on the uses to which it is put. If we have learned anything since the 1970s, it is that it is not sufficient to change the media's ideological viewpoint for a desired effect to occur. Technologies *can* be put to radically different uses. Once past the initial stage of innovation, however, those uses tend to be driven by a combination of political and commercial agendas.

This reality about technological uptake has been understood by the purveyors of "media development" since the term originated in the first decade or so after the end of the Second World War. Media development, as a concept and a field, emerged in the wake of the consolidation of ideas about freedom of expression and their crystallization, in distilled form, in the most important, most consensual human rights document of the 20th century, the Universal Declaration of Human Rights. The idea that "everyone has the right to freedom of opinion and expression" was explicitly tied to *media*. Freedom of expression was no longer "simply" an individual human right, the UDHR recognized that it encompassed the right "to seek, receive and impart information and ideas through any media and regardless of frontiers." As the Cold War developed in the 1950s, a lot of attention was paid to "frontiers"—U.S. Secretary of State John Foster Dulles famously stated: "If I were to be granted one point in foreign policy and no other, I would make it the free flow of information" (quoted in Schiller 1976, 30). In parallel, however, great efforts were made by state agencies, particularly in the West, to promote and establish media—in a range of forms of technologically mediated communication—in the soft conflict for human loyalties.

By the early 1970s, parts of the world with less developed media systems—led by countries emerging from colonization—were beginning to tire of what they increasingly saw as "cultural imperialism" coming from the West. Countries such as Egypt and India may have been interested in modernizing media, but they were less sanguine about the supposed benefits of Western media models. Media inequalities were characteristic of the broader problem of development, but the solutions were not seen to be more of the same. In 1978, the newly-emerging nations of the Non-Aligned Movement, or NAM, pushed through a Mass Media Declaration at UNESCO on the role of media for the promotion of international peace and human rights.

The Mass Media Declaration was grounded in a debate within UNESCO aimed at establishing a New World Information and Communication Order (NWICO), and was immediately followed by the creation of an International Commission for the Study of Communication Problems, chaired by the Irish statesman Sean MacBride. When the Commission reported in 1980, Western governments were shocked at the tone as well as the substance of its Report (International Commission for the Study of Communication Problems 1980).

The recommendations of the MacBride Report were, in retrospect, relatively mild. Its most telling section was a brief "comment," published in an appendix by the two Latin American members of the Commission, Colombian Nobel laureate Gabriel García Márquez and Chilean diplomat Juan Somavía. After praising how the report highlighted the need for more democratic communication structures, nationally and internationally, they took a critical dissenting position:

> "There is a tendency in different parts of the report to 'glorify' technological solutions to contemporary communication problems. We want to emphasize that the 'technological promise' is neither neutral nor value-free. Decisions in this field have enormous political and social implications. Each society has to develop the necessary

> instruments to make an evaluation of alternative choices and their impact" (International Commission for the Study of Communication Problems 1980, 281).

This was the nub of the issue. "The insistence on the need to develop communication infrastructures in third world countries is correct and necessary, but it should not be overstated." Western aid—described in the Report as "a 'Marshall Plan' for the development of third world communications"—was inappropriate as it would tend to reproduce Western values and transnational corporate interests in third world societies.

According to one commentator, the Finnish scholar and media activist Kaarle Nordenstreng, the MacBride experience "was not primarily a scientific exercise of discovering the state of communication in the world, but first and foremost a political exercise in taking stock of the socio-economic forces in the world at that time" (Nordenstreng 2010, 1). The two go hand in hand, and this is the first thing we need to keep in mind. Not only has communication changed dramatically in the last forty years, the socio-economic forces in the world have changed possibly even more dramatically.

The post-war order, dominated by the east-west "cold war" and the historic movement of decolonization, gave way to the collapse of communism, the rise of neoliberalism, the emergence of strong new economies (The so-called "BRICS": Brazil, Russia, India, China, and South Africa), and the worldwide expansion of communication technologies. Arguably, the global internet would not have emerged in the bipolar atmosphere of the Cold War. Forty years on, the internet is the platform for both progressive civil society and the resurgence of racist, authoritarian, neo-fascist populist movements.

The NWICO debate led to the withdrawal of the United States and United Kingdom from UNESCO in 1984 and 1985 respectively, citing a view that the organization had become "a forum for Soviet and radical Third World initiatives against a free press, human rights, and Western positions on arms control" (Associated Press, 1985). For most of the next two decades, these dominant members of the Western alliance—and arguably the leading exporters of Western media and communication technologies and their accompanying ideologies—were absent from the debates within the UN's lead agency on issues in education, science, culture, and communication.

The United Kingdom returned to UNESCO in 1997, the United States in 2003, but more than the high-profile diplomatic fallout from the NWICO—"a capricious gallery of forces rather than a solid coalition" (Nordenstreng 2010, 4)—the question of aid for development has continued to dog North-South relations in communication. There was an unanticipated crucial change in the 80s and 90s, however, the emergence of global civil society as a major new player in international relations. By the turn of the new millennium, states and corporations were no longer the only actors on the scene.

In the wake of the adoption of the UN's Millennium Development Goals in September 2000, the UN General Assembly called for a World Summit on the Information Society (WSIS), with an explicit invitation to civil society to take part. An important coalition of NGOs, academics, and civil society activists campaigned to place the issue of communication rights on the Summit agenda. The campaign met with a limited success in the formal outcomes of the Summit, but succeeded in raising broad international awareness of the limitations of the conventional approaches to dealing with issues such as the global "digital divide," as inequality in North-South relations were then known. The efforts to bring a civil society vision to the debate also re-emphasized the broad question of democratization of communication, while tying together the whole gamut of communication issues. The culmination was an unprecedented Civil Society Declaration, published at the end of the Summit's first phase in 2003.[1]

Since that time, a range of "WSIS+" implementation and follow-up activities have characterized media and communication development undertakings in the multinational sphere. Today we recognize that this challenge must address not only the imbalance between regions and countries but between sectors of society and communities within countries—what I have referred to elsewhere as "media divides" (Raboy and Shtern 2010). The WSIS process underscored the absence of a global venue for discussion of policy issues regarding media and technology issues. Despite its important symbolic value, the internet Governance Forum established in 2006 has so far been a half-hearted effort with no concrete outcomes. The withdrawal, once again, of the United States from UNESCO announced in October 2017 did not augur well for a multilateral approach to these issues in the short term.[2]

It is worth considering whether discussion around the UN's Agenda for Sustainable Development, adopted by the General Assembly in 2015, could provide a high-level context for addressing new issues in media and communication. Like so many UN documents before it, the Agenda does not prioritize media and communication per se, while implicitly assuming the importance of "good" communication in achieving its sustainable development goals.

The essential starting point would have to be recognizing that one crucial element remains underdeveloped: research. The impact of the Internet and new web-based platforms (social media), and the possible alternative uses to which these technologies could be put remains highly speculative—although there is no shortage of emerging best practices. Can we imagine a UN agency, or even the United Nations Development Group (UNDG) consortium undertaking such a project?

Whatever the shortcomings of the MacBride Report ("a negotiated document," in the words of Gabriel García Márquez and Juan Somavía), its 100 research reports comprised an evidence base that served national and international media policy advocates for the next twenty years. We need a similar evidence base today to address the challenges of the digital media environment. The challenges are different in different parts of the world, and the solutions will be correspondingly different. But the first step is to clearly understand and define the problems.

Notes

1. See "Shaping Information Societies for Human Needs," https://www.itu.int/net/wsis/docs/geneva/civil-society-declaration.pdf.
2. The stated reason for the U.S. withdrawal was UNESCO's "continuing anti-Israel bias", presumably referring to the admission of Palestine to the organization in 2011. The U.S. said it would "remain engaged with UNESCO as a non-member observer state in order to contribute U.S. views, perspectives and expertise on some of the important issues undertaken by the organization, including the protection of world heritage, advocating for press freedoms, and promoting scientific collaboration and education." ("Press Statement," U.S. Department of State, October 12, 2017). However, given the Trump Administration's general dim view of both multilateralism and media freedom, the latest U.S. move can only mean more stagnation.

Recommended for Further Reading

Buckley, Steve, Kreszentia Duer, Toby Mendel, and Seán Ó Siochrú. 2008. *Broadcasting, Voice and Accountability: A Public Interest Approach to Policy, Law, and Regulation*. Ann Arbor, MI: University of Michigan Press.

International Commission for the Study of Communication Problems (UNESCO). 1980. *Many Voices, One World*. London: Kogan Page.

Mansell, Robin and Marc Raboy. 2011. *The Handbook of Global Media and Communication Policy* Malden, MA: Wiley-Blackwell.

Raboy, Marc and Jeremy Shtern, et al. 2010. *Media Divides: Communication Rights and the Right to Communicate in Canada*, Vancouver: UBC Press.

References

Associated Press. December 5, 1985. "Britain Following Lead of U.S., Will Withdraw from UNESCO." *Los Angeles Times*, accessed December 12, 2017. http://articles.latimes.com/1985-12-05/news/mn-371_1_unesco-membership.

International Commission for the Study of Communication Problems (UNESCO). 1980. *Many Voices One World*. London: Kogan Page.

Nordenstreng, Kaarle. January 27, 2010. "MacBride Report as a Culmination of NWICO." Keynote at International Colloquium "Communication et changement social en Afrique," Université Stendhal, Grenoble.

Raboy, Marc and Jeremy Shtern, et al. 2010. *Media Divides Communication Rights and the Right to Communicate in Canada*. Vancouver: UBC Press.

Schiller, Herbert I. 1976. *Communication and Cultural Domination*, White Plains, NY: International Arts and Science Press.

Smythe, Dallas. 1981. *Dependency Road: Communications, Capitalism, Consciousness, and Canada*. Norwood, NJ: Ablex.

CHAPTER THREE

Media Development and the Market for Loyalties

MONROE E. PRICE

My goal in this chapter is to place media development efforts within a specific frame: namely the actions of great strategic communicators (states, religions, transnational corporations, for example) as they seek to increase support for their general positions in the world. Development efforts can be, and often are pursued for altruistic purposes, and they are often couched within an altruistic frame. The altruistic impulse and justification is significant and praiseworthy; but enduring development efforts in the long run are perceived to serve national economic and political interests as well. Happily, values and interests are often in sync, but not always. No government, even that of the United States or Great Britain, can sustain investment efforts over decades without convincing arguments (and maybe proof) that the expenditures benefit the investor society as well as that of the target recipient.

How does one parse this all out? If it is the case that societies act out of values and interests, can one describe a scaffolding of decision-making? Over the years, I have tried to build a frame for thinking about these questions through the concept of a *market for loyalties*, a process of analysis aimed at rendering competing interests more transparent as media systems are contemplated and funded, both within states and transnationally. In general, according to this framing, regardless of the rhetoric in which they are embedded, development efforts have preferred outcomes in terms of the structure of the target society in terms of how inclusive or democratic the society should be, and which entities gain and which lose or have the potential to gain or lose influence. This framing effort is helpful if it assists policy makers and stakeholders to understand how various forces seek to expand, contract, alter, and manipulate investments in media development.

What Is the Market for Loyalties Approach?

I start with expanding on the approach I sought to develop in *Television, the Public Sphere, and National Identity* and later in *Media and Sovereignty* (Price 1995; Price 2002). In those books, I postulated a market for loyalties, in which large-scale competitors for power, in a shuffle for allegiances, use the regulation of communications to organize a cartel of imagery and identity among themselves. Government is usually the mechanism that allows the cartel to operate and is often part of the cartel itself. Usually, management of the market yields the collection of ideas and narratives employed by a dominant group or coalition to maintain power. For that reason alone, control over participation in the market has been, for many countries, a condition of political stability. These markets, I contended, have existed everywhere and at all times. What differs in today's counterparts is the range of participants, the scope of its boundaries, and the nature of the regulatory bodies capable of establishing and enforcing rules for participation and exclusion.[1] Contemporary markets for loyalties are less resistant to entry and require more monitoring and attention by states, fearful of the consequences.

> The "sellers" in these markets are all those for whom myths and dreams and history can somehow be converted into power and wealth—classically states, governments, interest groups, businesses, and others. The "buyers" are the citizens, subjects, nationals, consumers—recipients of the packages of information, propaganda, advertisements, drama, and news propounded by the media. The consumer "pays" for one set of identities or another in several ways that, together, we call "loyalty" or "citizenship." Payment, however, is not expressed in the ordinary coin of the realm: It includes not only compliance with tax obligations, but also obedience to laws, readiness to fight in the armed services, or even continued residence within the country. The buyer also pays with his or her own sense of identity. (Price 1994, 669–70)

Understanding this structure of these markets is key to understanding what we are calling "media development." Media development encompasses the efforts of major stakeholders in these markets to improve or adjust those markets, to increase their own impact. As such, this chapter does not make normative claims about particular interventions; nor does it distinguish—as other chapters in this volume do—between the subfield of international aid known as media development, and other actions by international and national actors aiming to influence the media systems.

It is easiest to understand the functioning of such a market for loyalties in the traditional context of a single state. One can make the general and expansive claim that much domestic broadcast regulation is an effort, within a society, to maintain or adjust media narratives to adjust the distribution of power among those who are dominant or purposely to give greater sway to subsidiary groups, or to become more or less inclusive, depending on social and technological changes.

Media globalization creates new tensions in existing markets for loyalties. States that considered that they had effective cartelization or control suddenly find that new legal regimes or new technologies weaken or eliminate existing arrangements. The coming into effect of the Television Without Frontiers Directive of the European Union, meant that states within Europe could no longer so completely control what material reached their citizens. Satellite and internet not only disrespected frontiers, they transcended the arrangements that existed in the world of terrestrial licensing.

Some Examples

I have always been fascinated by the Dutch example of the market for loyalties and its implications for thinking about media development. Early radio and then television policy in the Netherlands established a system of broadcasting based on Dutch ideas of "pillarization" in which segments of society (the pillars) had their own churches, schools, protected societies, political parties, and newspapers and ultimately allocated television time. Dutch society was "pillarized" and the function of media development was to adapt media to this style of political participation and representation. Each pillar (the Dutch Reformed Church, the Socialist Party, vegetarians, etc.) was enabled to gain segments of air time on a nationally organized system captured by the pillar and programmed by its representatives. Media development of this sort required protection from unauthorized competitors. This was a system that worked, as indicated, until the European Union's rules altered the capacity to achieve this mode of protection. Programming originating in the EU but outside the Netherlands was innovative and winning; cable operators could not be protected from carrying these outside channels, and the cartel was broken.[2]

One could say that media development in Singapore reflected similar concerns but with a different outcome. Singapore's media development efforts sought an information-rich environment that could support rapid business growth, but in ways that maintained substantial controls over programming that the government considered potentially destabilizing or hostile (or even insulting). Media development in Singapore meant designing a satellite and related cable television system that could maintain the state's hold over its market for loyalties (Cherian 2012).

Media development in the post-conflict Balkans meant dealing with the components of Bosnia-Herzegovina in ways that attempted a radio and television of unity, but one which reflected and recognized the sharp differences and autonomy of such components—a project of enormous difficulty (Thompson and De Luce 2002).

In Ukraine, and the Baltics generally, media development must cope with harshly intensified relations with Russia where "competition for allegiances" is sharpened by national security concerns and propaganda, and challenges to existing political arrangements are considered dangerously tangible. In these cases, media development encompasses a much more emergent approach threatening compliance with international norms. Among the specific questions are how to deal with broadcasters sponsored by the Russian government, signals from abroad reaching into Ukraine, the status and regulation of who is a journalist, what to do about fake news and how to manage social media where there is a field for complex strategies of intervention (Pikulicka-Wilczewska and Sakwa 2016).

Put differently, a market-for-loyalties perspective allows much media development to be understood as related to efforts to adjust a specific market for loyalties in ways that are integrated in part to the interests of the intervenor. Media development becomes significant at its most ambitious because its implementation can affect or hope to affect the very infrastructure of how information is distributed in a society. Media development may be so designed as to facilitate entry for voices that have been excluded. It may seek to contribute to stability—an outcome that might be widely desired. Or media development, as in many more authoritarian settings, can yield a structure that simplifies control and reinforces existing barriers to entry. It can help in shaping a system in which chances for moderation are increased or that "extremist" recruitment can be more readily identified. Those deeply engaged in the process of information distribution within and outside a state's border are, of necessity, preoccupied with this question of platforms and infrastructure, and regularly hold strong, often conflicting, views on desirable outcomes.

Implications for Media Development

How can understanding a markets-for-loyalties analysis help clarify and refresh media development approaches or research opportunities related to media development? Great competitors have such a stake in aspects of media development efforts that they often seek stability by informally organizing (or trying to organize) an arrangement, perhaps a conceded sphere of influence, perhaps a pacted settlement in which media development reflects an agreement about how powers to communicate are distributed among vying forces. I have called this process of seeking consensus and some version of stability an effort by competitors to achieve a cartel of imagery and identity among themselves. Especially at the national level, government is usually the mechanism that allows the cartel to operate and is often part of the cartel itself. Media development thus involves internal or external efforts to reinforce, break or strengthen existing understandings. In some instances, media development can be designed, for example, to make it easier for new voices to gain traction, for new political parties to establish themselves. Indeed, in some instances, for example in the settlement of civil wars or other outcomes of polarization, it can assure a new system that is politically planned to be more inclusive.

It is a characteristic of contemporary discourse to reserve the term "media development" for techniques that advance democratization—and fortunately, much media development is directed at that set of political results. But media development can reflect many goals. The neutral enveloping of the term can shroud specific desired political outcomes. Some traditions of media development facilitate stability over further openness; or favor one set of interests over another. Often, management of a market yields the collection of ideas and narratives employed by a dominant group or coalition to maintain power and media development efforts can reinforce that.

Control over participation in the market has been, for many countries, a manner of holding to the status quo. Media development efforts must be cognizant of the many overlapping dynamics that characterize these markets. Any architect of a media development effort must first understand the nature of the market they seek to affect or improve. They must understand the structure of "sellers" and "buyers" in the struggle for allegiances. And this is no minor task: a diagnostic should have an informed sense of the range of participants, the scope of the market's boundaries, and the nature of the regulatory bodies. These bodies are capable of establishing and enforcing rules for participation and exclusion and the ways in which governments or others can create and enforce a cartel of interests.[3] Media development efforts are applauded where they strengthen the infrastructure of the production and distribution of information in ways designed to bolster democratic outcomes. But even when the hope is media for democratization, good intentions find realization difficult producing disappointing echoes of ancient promises (Price 1975). And, especially in a time of fear of terror, media architectures contain the seeds for a return to scarcity and control (Mozur 2017).

Media development must be sensitive to the stated and unstated desires of consumers, the evolved audience. In a world of increasing propaganda and fake news, media development must encompass media literacy. The measure of efficacy must be more than how effectively sellers can reach buyers. Strategic communicators may have other goals such as facilitating particular forms of journalism or enriching a public sphere. In a new world of user-generated content and citizen journalism the very fixedness of the categories needs to be considered. Media development affects where new voices can originate and how unburdened or constricted they are.

Understanding the complexity of these markets can be key to predicting how media development will develop in the future and what steps will be taken or resisted in media development efforts. The main players—the somewhat simplified "sellers," as described above, will be committed to their own strategy for media development. Certainly, if they are major participants, including the state itself or interested foreign entities, they will seek a media development strategy that makes it more likely that their message, their view of the world, their myths and dreams will be furthered. And, similarly, they will make efforts to shape media development to limit opportunities for those with sharply competing and antagonistic approaches.

The incentive to change media law and policy occurs as part of media development. One example, of course, is when conflict intensifies. But another, within a state, occurs when the cartel of political allegiances can no longer maintain its position of civil dominance. For example, the pressures of globalization lead to changes in domestic media laws and structures if either (1) existing domestic broadcasting laws are inadequate at protecting the cartel, or (2) circumstances have changed and action is necessary to be more inclusive, to legitimate new players, and to protect them, in turn, against unregulated challenge. In Colombia, the settlement with the FARC required revisiting political arrangements, and, undoubtedly, related media habits. In Syria, whatever political circumstances evolve, there will also be explicit and implicit media development consequences.

Much of the early writing about markets for loyalties took place in a pre-internet era, although the debates surrounding satellite communication foreshadowed many of the issues that would emerge with the internet. Further media globalization and new information technologies yielded a crisis of domestic law and policy. If barriers to entry became low for those excluded from the old political cartel, especially if the new entrants could be threats to the control of the ancient regime, the option of cartelization became more distant. This reflected limitations on affecting who can enter, who can be excluded and with what repercussions.

New Justifications for Media Development?

All of this leads to a second order aspect of current media development efforts. A less recognized task of many of those proposing or encouraging particular genres of media development is to provide a narrative that helps garner support for that specific effort. There are at least two venues where narratives of support are needed: support in the originating state (where a state is the agent or funder of media development) and the society where media development is to be implemented. The justifying narratives may be different in the two contexts (the originating and the implementing context); it may be different depending on the state or origin (China or the United States or Sweden, for example). And the narratives may differ if the implementer is a state, itself, or a non-government organization.

Though it may not be immediately obvious, narratives of justification may be widely different because strategies of media development may themselves range across a wide spectrum. Those who advocate "media development" in the United States may consider that the term primarily covers systems or approaches that further greater democratization and in some cases greater pluralism. Media development, to be worthy of the term, requires a maximum of independence; independence of the media and independence of the regulator that provides such oversight as is consistent with international norms. Media development efforts that are designed to meet these objectives come wrapped in their own elegant bank of justification.

There is a range of "media development" efforts, which is relatively clear comparing efforts by China, for example, to influence media development in Africa (there is a small body of scholarship on this contrast). One can see throughout Central Asia, the influence of Russia, but distinctions are present within Western efforts as well. In the 1990s, as the former Yugoslavia became broken into states, each with an appetite for media development, somewhat different strategies were adopted by European consultants, U.S. consultants, and often by experts from within the region. One interesting example involved public service broadcasting (PSB). European consultants considered PSB efforts to be central to constituting a new political environment. Often advisors financed by USAID or similar sources took a very different approach. There are interconnected points here. First, media development is not unitary. Second, different approaches generate different justifications or result from different philosophies. Finally, and this is the Market for Loyalties issue: all these differences in strategies, (e.g., United States and European in the Balkans, China in Africa, Russia in Central Asia) reflect, to some extent, an architecture of how state-centered, how controlled, or how open a media system should be.[4]

Understanding these various components is increasingly important. States and other strategic communicators are more and more sophisticated about flows of information and their relationship to power. Global information space is being transformed, media structures altered, and the role of the state, simultaneously, redefined.[5] Information, it is said to the point of cliché, is increasingly key to stability and fragility of governance. More sophistication about structuring media development and how to articulate its architecture will be essential in the years ahead. Older arguments may no longer be persuasive at home.

International norms like Article 19 of the Universal Declaration of Human Rights, domestic constitutional rules like the First Amendment in the United States, and regional constraints like the European Convention on Human Rights, have a special role in limiting the cartelization of the market for loyalties. These provisions are usually considered curbs on the power of local political cartels to use law and regulation to screen out voices that seek to alter the current power structure, and especially those who seek to use broadcasting and other means despite lacking the power to force such change. Increasingly, these norms are used swordlike by those external to the state, often foreign NGOs and media corporations with existing global power, to encourage a more favorable legal regime within a state.[6] To be sure, such expansion often serves the honorable principle of the right to receive and impart information, and the assistance frequently is granted at the request of local civil society groups operating within repressive environments, but it is about the extension of power and influence as well.

Due to markets for loyalties being so varied and because the politics and technologies of reshaping these markets are so dynamic, implications for media development are subtle and varying. In a period of increasing cynicism, pragmatism and manipulation, the old formulae of justifications may not be so hardy. Recognizing shifts in the structure of informational power may become more salient and more frequently invoked. The advocates of media development to create stronger, more robust societies will need to internalize these massive changes in technology, in geopolitics and in the interior contests in much contested markets for loyalties.

Notes

1. In developing a framework for comparative analysis of European media, Karen Siune et al. defined policy making as "a reaction to a challenge, a reaction that is intended to find a reasonable balance between 'forces of change' and 'forces of preservation.'" The authors also stated that "[i]n the current process of adaptation to technological progress public action strategies in most European countries may seem to be a reaction to the risk of disintegration, especially in cultural matters, in the broadest sense." See chapter 2 of Denis McQuail

and Karen Siune, eds., New Media Politics: Comparative Perspectives in Western Europe (London: Sage, 1986).

2. The story is nicely told in Arend Lijphart, The Politics of Accommodation, Pluralism and Democracy in the Netherlands (University of California Press, 1975).
3. In developing a framework for comparative analysis of European media, Karen Siune et al. defined policy making as "a reaction to a challenge, a reaction that is intended to find a reasonable balance between 'forces of change' and 'forces of preservation.'" The authors also stated that "[i]n the current process of adaptation to technological progress public action strategies in most European countries may seem to be a reaction to the risk of disintegration, especially in cultural matters, in the broadest sense." See chapter 2 of Denis McQuail and Karen Siune, eds., New Media Politics: Comparative Perspectives in Western Europe (London: Sage, 1986).
4. The narratives may consciously or unconsciously mask underlying objectives (sometimes masking such objectives from the makers of the narratives themselves).
5. See, for example, Jerry Everard, *Virtual States: The Internet and the Boundaries of the Nation-State* (Oxford: Routledge, 1999).
6. See Margaret A. Blanchard's *Exporting the First Amendment: The Press-Government Crusade.*

Recommended for Further Reading

Deane, James. 2013. "Fragile States: The Role of Media and Communication." BBC Media Action Policy Briefing 10. http://downloads.bbc.co.uk/mediaaction/policybriefing/fragile_states_policy_briefing.pdf

Price, Monroe. 2015. *Free Expression, Globalism and the New Strategic Communication.* Cambridge: Cambridge University Press.

Voltmer, Katrin. 2011. *The Media in Transitional Democracies*, Cambridge: Polity Press.

References

Blanchard, Margaret A. 1986. *Exporting the First Amendment: The Press-Government Crusade of 1945–1952.* New York: Longman.

Cherian, George. 2012. *Freedom from the Press: Journalism and State Power in Singapore.* Singapore: NUS Press.

Lijphart, Arend. 1975. *The Politics of Accommodation: Pluralism and Democracy in the Netherlands.* University of California Press.

Mozur, Paul. 2017. "China's Top Ideologue Calls for Tight Control of Internet." *New York Times, Dec. 3, 2017.* https://www.nytimes.com/2017/12/03/world/asia/china-internet-censorship-wang-huning.html?_r=1&module=ArrowsNav&contentCollection=Asia%20Pacific&action=keypress&region=FixedLeft&pgtype=article.

Pikulicka-Wilczewska, Agnieszka and Richard Sakwa. 2016. *Ukraine and Russia: People, Politics, Propaganda and Perspectives*. Bristol: E-International Relations Publishing.

Price, Monroe. 1975. "Requiem for the Wired Nation: Cable Rulemaking at the FCC." *Virginia Law Review* 61(3): 541–77.

———. 1994. "The Market for Loyalties: Electronic Media and the Global Competition for Allegiances." *Yale Law Journal* 104(3): 667–705.

———. 1995. *Television, the Public Sphere, and National Identity*. Oxford: Clarendon Press.

———. 2002. *Media and Sovereignty: The Global Information Revolution and Its Challenge to State Power*. Cambridge, MA: MIT Press.

Thompson, Mark and Dan De Luce. 2002. "Escalating to Success? The Media Intervention in Bosnia and Herzegovina." In *Forging Peace: Intervention, Human Rights and the Management of Media Space*, edited by Monroe Price and Mark Thompson. Bloomington: Indiana University Press.

CHAPTER FOUR

Redefining Media Development

A Demand-Driven Approach

MARK M. NELSON

Amidst the flowering of freedoms in Central Europe and the former Soviet Union in 1990s, media development had its brief but exhilarating heyday.

New publications, television stations, and websites emerged to chart the changing course of a vast swath of humanity. Reformist governments knocked repressive media laws off the books, and Central Europeans raced to join the European Union. Investigative and political journalism flourished. An exciting, colorful media industry emerged, fueled by double-digit annual growth rates in advertising revenue. International donors and media consultants played a critical role in the media boom, offering training, advice, and international partners.

Even as journalists and media industries grew in numbers and technical sophistication, however, the specter of the past refused to lower its head. The informal rules and practices of many of the formerly communist regimes failed to adjust. Journalistic disclosures about corruption went unpunished. New forms of government censorship emerged. Public broadcasting reforms went nowhere. Oligarchs worked with governments to buy up media enterprises and control public debate. Foreign investors left or were kicked out. When Vladimir Putin came to power in 1999, Russia's brief experiment with media freedom began to collapse, with barely a whimper from Russian citizens. Today, prodigious media reformers of that period such as Poland and Hungary are likewise sliding back into old habits of media control and state propaganda.

Before penning the obituary for the whole concept of media development, however, we should take stock of what we have learned. The moral of the media development story in Central and Eastern Europe applies almost everywhere: strengthening the media in itself is not enough. Power and politics matter, and failure to build political will and support for the role of independent media in society can unravel the whole effort.

At a time when the media everywhere is undergoing rapid globalization and momentous changes in the way it is delivered and produced, we need to redefine media development for a new, uncertain era. Media development specialists and activists need a concept of media development that understands and addresses the deeply political nature of the media as an institution. We also need a way to cope with rapidly changing technology and the media's increasingly global nature. Media development is as much about building strong political foundations for independent media as it is about high-quality journalism. It also requires integration and scaling up within broader democratic governance reforms.

This type of media development depends on engaging with a wider group of actors at the country level, not just journalists, editors and other media agents, but also civil society, private sector, and government representatives. It requires activists to develop more sophisticated analysis and policy positions that consider the broader institutional and governance framework for the media. For the purposes of this essay, I will refer to this effort to engage with a wider group of change agents in society on media reforms as a *demand-driven approach*.

Media reform efforts that fail to engage with local actors and build consensus and sustainable structures within their societies can actually impede media development and the critical freedoms and responsibilities on which it rests. While journalistic skills and business models for the news media are critically important, sustainable reforms in media systems require an environment that produces two outcomes: (1) political acceptance of open debate, vigorous fact-finding, and open dissent; and (2) quality journalism based on fairness, high ethical standards, and accuracy.

Defining Demand-Driven Media Development

Understanding media development from the standpoint of the "demand side" is an essential way to address many of the shortcomings in the way media development has been defined and practiced in the past, whether by country-level professionals and activists, or by international donors who support media development through foreign aid budgets. Those efforts have relied mainly on "supply-side" interventions, relying mostly on training journalists and editors or directly supporting journalism and program production. These efforts have been important, and often successful, at least in the short term. They have rarely been enough, however, to foster long-term improvements in the enabling conditions or to produce sustainable changes in the political environment for media. In today's fast-changing, technology-driven media environment—where business models are failing, and the old blueprints are no longer working—a new, more adaptive approach is needed.

The concept of demand-driven media development is, however, more than a simple pledge not to force foreign blueprints. It is a much broader commitment about the design, leadership, and implementation of media development processes. It entails assuring local—though not necessarily government—leadership and ownership of a vision that enjoys popular support, or, when that support is lacking, a process led by local actors to build the needed coalitions and political backing for the needed reforms. While foreign representatives can play important and even catalytic roles in this work, success depends on local leadership.

Such an approach requires analyzing the enabling conditions, examining shortcomings, and prioritizing solutions. It entails deep understanding of local institutions, behaviors, customs, and governance practices. It can seek solutions from within the society or from elsewhere, learning from the successes and mistakes of other countries. It often requires building knowledge among a wide community of stakeholders, not just media practitioners, but also lawmakers, regulators, and business leaders. Investors and funders of media enterprises also have to be part of the process, along with public service media organizations. It usually requires constructing coalitions of activists who see the cross-cutting and political nature of media reforms, who recognize how media affects other aspects of society, and who band together to convince others that certain changes are needed to maximize the media's contribution to society.

It takes time, even decades. The Media Sustainability Index has charted the development of media systems for some countries for close to two decades, tracking five key dimensions of media systems—free speech, journalistic professionalism, plurality of news sources, business management, and supporting institutions. That data suggests that media development is a constantly-changing battlefield, with many countries managing to improve in some areas while falling behind in others. As of 2017, none of the 21 countries in Europe and Eurasia tracked by MSI had managed to establish themselves in the "sustainable" category (IREX 2017, xiv–xv).

One way of visualizing this broad concept of media development is to disaggregate the change process into a two-dimensional matrix. In Figure 4.1 below,

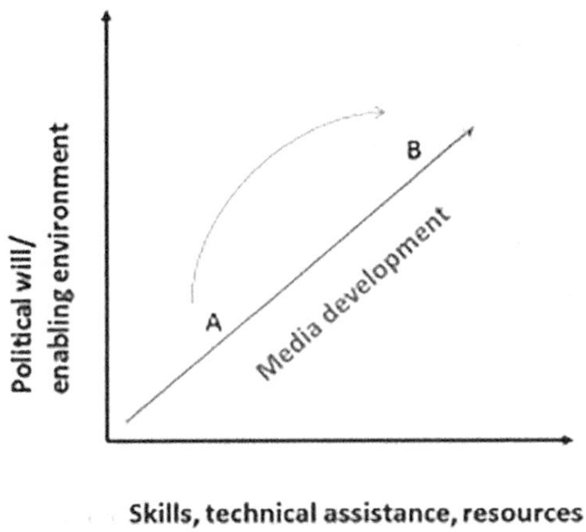

Figure 4.1. Media development requires increases in both skills and enabling conditions.

the horizontal axis represents the "supply" or level of skills, technical know-how, and resources within the media system; an increase in these factors means moving from right to left from any given point on the line. The vertical axis represents the "demand side," the extent to which the media system is supported by high quality laws, regulations, practices, and political support for independent media and its role within the society; increasing these enabling factors means moving up the vertical scale from bottom to top. Media development occurs along the intersection of these two dimensions, moving in this idealized example along the hypothetical intersection line from point A to point B.

In the real world, it rarely works like this, of course. Most countries struggle to develop along the optimal trajectory, going through many twists and turns. In Figure 4.2, three points show hypothetical countries in their media development process. Country 1 enjoys strong media laws and enabling conditions, but its journalists and media actors suffer from a low level of skills and material resources. One might think of a country such as Mali in the early part of the millennium: it had strong press laws and a culture that supported freedom of expression, but a poorly trained and resourced media sector. Country 2 has highly educated journalists and material resources but weak enabling conditions, a situation that roughly describes Russia. Country 3 has a more balanced situation but still has room to improve along both dimensions, which would apply to many promising emerging economies like Colombia, Indonesia, or Ghana. The key to successful media development is to move from any given location closer to an upward trajectory on

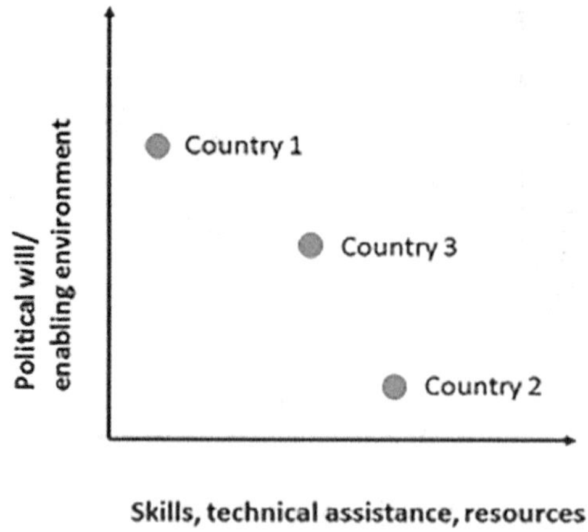

Figure 4.2. Hypothetical country examples of degree of media development.

the A-to-B line as shown in Figure 4.1. Country 1 would need to move mainly to the "east," for example, increasing skills and resources, while country 2 would need to move "north" by improving enabling conditions. Country 3 would move to the "northeast," aiming to increase both dimensions of media development in a balanced way.

The problem with a "one-sided" process of media development—especially moving higher on the skills and resources axis without matching progress in political will and institutional development—is that it can lead to systemic failure. Journalists with strong skills uncover corruption, government mismanagement, and other shortcomings, but nothing happens to follow up on their disclosures. Society becomes cynical about the daily drumbeat of media scandals and even starts to blame the media itself for societies' broader shortcomings. In response, government cracks down on media freedom rather than addressing the problems highlighted by media coverage.

External donors who have delivered media development support have tended to put much more emphasis on the horizontal axis, mainly by training journalists, offering technical assistance to media organizations, and other supply-driven activities. This could be a function of cost, since interventions that address the vertical axis require more planning, longer-term engagement, and a level of knowledge of local conditions that may be in short supply. I address approaches to dealing with weaknesses on the vertical axis later in this essay.

The lessons for improving media development mirror insights from other areas of development practice, such as from the reform of sectors such as health or education. The findings of evaluations of what people have called "capacity development activities" over the past decades have shown that practitioners have often approached sector-level weaknesses through input-driven interventions, increasing the quantity of training, or technical assistance. This has been done with the expectation that increasing such factors would lead to an increased capacity or performance in the given sector. The well-documented failure of this approach in the absence of enabling conditions has led to a broader concept that sees capacity development as a function of both the supply-side inputs, as well as the demand-side environment in which a sector functions. More recently, development experts have begun to promote more adaptive solutions embodied in the so-called "*Doing Development Differently Movement*," which emphasizes problem-driven approaches, building coalitions, and politically-savvy design and implementation rather than rigid blueprints.[1]

A large 2011 World Bank study, "Stimulating the Demand for Good Governance," examined the evidence of impact for demand-side interventions. Reviewing project evaluations, anecdotal evidence, and data from cross-country analyses, that study found that demand-side work is "a powerful instrument to combat corruption, engage citizens to demand improved governance, and provide incentives for transparency and accountability, among other benefits" (Bhargava et al., 2011, XIII). In several of the cases highlighted, researchers were able to quantify the benefits. For example, supporting civil society organizations in their efforts to monitor the delivery of textbooks in the Philippines resulted in increasing the delivery rate to 95 percent, from 60 percent before the program, resulting in a $3.6 million impact on a $30 million program. While the study found no single worldwide study of effectiveness of such programs, the evidence was clear that a focus on demand-side actors "has considerable potential for improving development outcomes and fighting corruption," (Bhargava et al., 2011, 10).

Civil Society Coalitions for Media Development

Countries that have moved from low to higher levels of media development have generally been pushed in the direction of reform either by a political shock—such as the simultaneous jolts in the 1990s of the end of communism in the former Soviet bloc and the collapse of apartheid in South Africa—or by active, highly engaged multi-stakeholder coalitions. While some governments have led the process, more often civil society leaders chart the course by identifying critical reform issues, building coalitions with other groups from civil society and the private sector, and then pushing entrenched interests towards legal and regulatory reform. Such coalitions also help build wider public acceptance of the change process.

Several cases of successful media development driven by civil society coalitions have been documented, particularly in Latin America.[2] These movements may take many years to reach their goals. In Uruguay, activists organized behind the scenes for more than a decade, building allies in parliament and with other NGOs, when a change in government gave them an opportunity to push forward successful media laws. In India, the struggle to pass the 2015 Right to Information Act took 10 years and involved multiple actors from civil society and government.

Civil society plays a number of critical roles in the difficult process of media development:

- Creating coordinated activity among diverse groups and interests and creating coalitions for reform
- Unleashing reformers within government, giving leaders political cover, and helping to tilt the balance towards reform
- Improving media policy by increasing the stock of knowledge, experience, and perspectives reflected in the policy
- Improving implementation: knowledge gained through advocacy can be useful to monitor implementation
- Building capacity within broader society to improve the policy or its impact.[3]

In practical terms, areas of reform include strengthening freedom of expression, improving the transparency and regulatory framework for broadcast spectra allocation, government advertising, and media ownership. Reform may imply transformation of state media into public service media. It also may require improving the ability of the government to respond to media information requests through access to information laws and improving the quality of government information services.

More important than the "what" of reform, however, is the "how." Figure 4.3 describes examples of activities that can foster coalitions and consensus on reform measures. These activities, which can be carried out at the country level or among multi-country groups, can be instrumental not only in improving the atmosphere for reform, but also in helping to refine possible reform measures into locally workable solutions that ensure a more effective media system.

The aims of this more integrated approach to media reform and development is to increase incentives for better media outcomes, that is, creating a news and information environment deeply embedded within society that favors the public interest. Such an environment requires corporate social responsibility among media owners, and high quality, trusted government information systems that provide citizens with accurate, verifiable information, data, and

Figure 4.3. Examples of demand-side media development activities.

statistics. While such systems do not inoculate a society from "fake news," conspiracies, or rumors, it does make it harder for them to thrive. A 2017 survey in Ukraine showed that audiences weary of scandal and hype from the media are increasingly asking for more media coverage of economic reforms and other current affairs topics affecting their lives (see sidebar on Ukraine below).

The international community has begun to recognize the importance of media as a critical element within the debate about governance. The Organization for Economic Cooperation and Development in 2017 launched a learning process aimed at articulating the critical role of media, and the OECD's Governance Network, which includes governance experts from the 30 major Western donors, has included media as a part of its ongoing dialogue on governance polices. Another important development was the agreement in 2015 by members of the United Nations to include a governance dimension in the Sustainable Development Goals, a set of global targets for the year 2030. While agreeing on the highly-contested goals entailed many compromises, three elements of goal no. 16, which focuses on governance, included a commitment to measure governments' efforts to include demand-side actors and media in their governance reforms. (See Figure 4.4)

The next frontier will be to convince more aid-recipient governments to include media reform in their country-led development programs, which are the principle means that donor governments allocate $146 billion a year in overseas development assistance. The Open Governance Partnership—a multilateral initiative with more than 75 members that aims to secure concrete commitments from governments to promote multi-stakeholder governance—is also working to

From supply-side to demand-side in Ukraine

Since its declaration of independence from the Soviet Union in 1991, Ukraine has been a focus of many attempts at media reform and a major recipient of donor support. Much of that support has been in the form of training, technical assistance and other supply-side approaches. By most measures, it produced disappointing results.

After the so-called Maidan Revolution in 2014, Ukraine got another chance to tackle its daunting governance challenges, and activists decided to take a new approach to media development and other governance reforms. Over time, a group of think tanks and civil society organizations banded together to build a broader coalition with media as an integral part of needed reforms. The coalition brought together 65 non-governmental organizations that agreed on a common set of goals. Along with media reform, the coalition's "Roadmap for Reforms for Ukraine" included action plans for the judiciary, the public sector, budget and tax system, and local government. The approach was successful in passing legislation on transparency of media ownership, and introducing new laws for independent public service broadcasting. "We realized that we had to combine our forces," says Taras Shevchenko, Director of the Center for Democracy and the Rule of Law, which is part of the coalition.

[Interview with the author, 12 October 2017]

Organizations funded by foreign governments also expanded their demand-side media development work in Ukraine. The U.S.-based media development organization Internews, active in Ukraine since 1993, moved beyond its traditional role of providing technical assistance and training and increasingly focused on enabling conditions for independent media, working with civil society, governments, and citizens. The 2017 Media Consumption Survey carried out for Internews by InMind with U.S. Agency for International Development funding, portrayed a growing demand in Ukrainian society for high quality news and information, increased knowledge about the underlying problems of the media sector, and stronger support and confidence in regional newspapers, at the expense of television and internet.

[https://internews.org/story/ukrainians-grow-critical-news-consumers-accessed 30 Oct 2017]

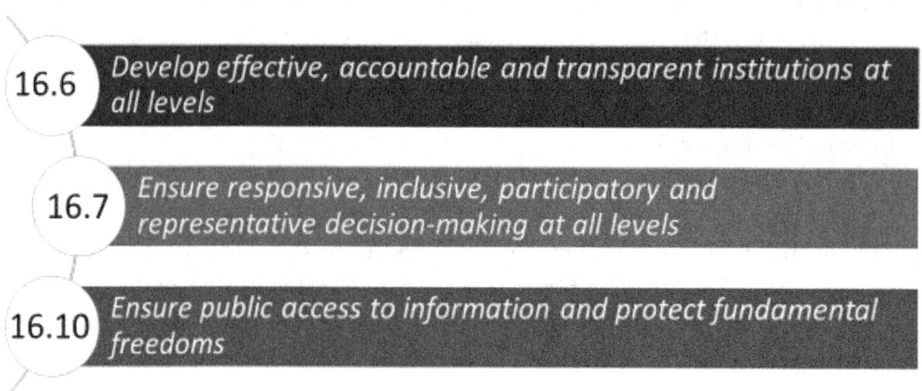

Figure 4.4. Key SDG targets for civil society and media.

increase the commitments for media reforms. Yet, less than 0.5 percent of Official Development Assistance was being allocated to media reforms as of 2017.[4]

Internet Governance and Media Development

At the global level, demand-side actors are critical to defining how internet governance will affect media development. While traditional media, especially television and radio, continue to be the dominant platforms for media in the developing world, the future of the media worldwide will increasingly depend on the healthy development of the internet. Media advocates in the Global South have a clear interest in engaging in the debate about the emerging "rules of the game" on the internet. This means defending an internet and global digital space that maintains universal human rights commitments like freedom of expression, that incentivizes truth over deception, and that offers a level playing field for new competitors in the news business.

Globalization of the media, the internet, and platforms like Google, Facebook and Twitter means that media governance has an important international dimension over which no individual nation has total control or sovereignty. Nor is it desirable that governments alone control this system, particularly in a world where few governments have shown the capacity to manage the complex technical and governance challenge that the global media system now embodies. Much like the country level, global media governance requires a multi-stakeholder structure that gives as wide a voice as possible to all participants in the system and decision-making founded on universal democratic values and principles. A key challenge in this context is to strengthen the capacity of civil society and other actors from less developed parts of the world to participate fully in the governance structures and articulate their interests.

Conclusion

Good journalism and independent news and information systems are powerful forces that can deliver important benefits to society. Unleashing these forces in a way that does good rather than harm requires a complex system of democratic governance that ensures those benefits are produced and delivered productively, and that the system itself is sustainable. While the private sector can play a constructive role in the media environment, a supportive government role, backed up and checked by an engaged society, is critical to creating effective enabling conditions. Getting constructive outcomes for and from the media system requires thinking about media development more as a governance challenge than as a technical one.

A demand-driven approach to media development is necessary because producing such a system requires a high level of political will, sustained support, and vigilance from a wide array of institutions as well as from citizens. At a time of massive transition in the media environment worldwide, existing blueprints are inadequate. The path forward requires engaging widely with agents of change to help steer societies toward workable solutions and to check the power of autocrats, oligarchs, and corporate monopolies who are constantly trying to control media. It requires integration of media reform measures into country development and reform programs. It also requires alliances not only within countries, but also at the global level, with sustained funding from donors. As media rely increasingly on the internet and social media, a much wider global alliance of well-informed people, organizations, and country leaders is essential to tackling these crucial challenges.

Notes

1. For a review of literature on capacity development and new thinking on development approaches, see Lucas, Brian. 2013. "Current thinking on capacity development," Governance and Social Development Resource Centre. http://www.gsdrc.org/docs/open/hdq960.pdf and http://doingdevelopmentdifferently.com/.
2. See for example, Mauersberger, Christof. 2016. *Advocacy Coalitions and Democratizing Media Reforms in Latin America: Whose Voice Gets on the Air?* (Heidelberg: Springer International Publishing AG Switzerland) and Segura, Maria Soledad, and Silvio Waisbord. 2016. *Media Movements: Civil Society and Media Policy Reform in Latin America.* London: Zed Books
3. For a comprehensive overview of how civil society helps countries solve problems and strengthen governance, see Development Research Centre on Citizenship, Participation and Accountability. 2011. "Blurring the Boundaries: Citizen Action Across States and Societies." https://assets.publishing.service.gov.uk/media/57a08aea40f0b64974000854/cdrc.2011-blurring.pdf and World Bank. *World Development Report 2017: Governance and the Law.* Washington DC, 2017.
4. For a discussion of media development funding as a component of official development assistance, see Mary Myers and Linet Angaya Juma, 2018. "Defending Independent Media: A Comprehensive Analysis of Aid Flows." Center for International Media Assistance, Washington DC.

Recommended for Further Reading

Lucas, Brian. 2013. "Current thinking on capacity development." London: Governance and Social Development Resource Centre.

Segura, Maria Soledad, and Silvio Waisbord. 2016. *Media Movements: Civil Society and Media Policy Reform in Latin America.* London: Zed Books.

World Bank. 2017. *World Development Report 2017: Governance and the Law.* Washington D.C.

References

Bhargava, Vinay, Kit Cutler and Daniel Ritchie. 2011. "Stimulating the Demand for Good Governance: An Agenda for Enhancing the Role of the World Bank." Washington D.C.: Partnership for Transparency Fund.

Development Research Centre on Citizenship, Participation and Accountability. 2011. "Blurring the Boundaries: Citizen Action Across States and Societies," Brighton: Institute of Development Studies. https://assets.publishing.service.gov.uk/media/57a08aea40f0b64974000854/cdrc.2011-blurring.pdf

Doing Development Differently Community. 2014. "The Manifesto." http://doingdevelopmentdifferently.com/the-ddd-manifesto/

IREX. 2017. *Media Sustainability Index 2017.* Washington D.C.

Lucas, Brian. 2013. "Current thinking on capacity development." London: Governance and Social Development Resource Centre. http://www.gsdrc.org/docs/open/hdq960.pdf

Mauersberger, Christof. 2016. *Advocacy Coalitions and Democratizing Media Reforms in Latin America: Whose Voice Gets on the Air?* Heidelberg: Springer International Publishing AG Switzerland.

Myers, Mary and Linet Angaya Juma. 2018. "Defending Independent Media: A Comprehensive Analysis of Aid Flows." Washington, D.C.: Center for International Media Assistance.

Nelson, Mark, with Tara Susman-Peña. 2012. "Rethinking Media Development: A Report on the Media Map Project." Washington, D.C.: Internews and World Bank. http://www.internews.org/sites/default/files/resources/Internews_1-9_Rethinking_Media_Dev-2014-01.pdf.

Segura, Maria Soledad, and Silvio Waisbord. 2016. *Media Movements: Civil Society and Media Policy Reform in Latin America.* London: Zed Books.

World Bank. 2017. *World Development Report 2017: Governance and the Law.* Washington D.C.

CHAPTER FIVE

Evaluating Success

What Should We Be Measuring?

SUSAN ABBOTT

The challenge of measuring the impact of media development assistance is largely attributable to the uncertainty about what it is that we are measuring, and towards what ends.[1] To put it a different way, there is a lingering question about whether there is a measurable theory of media development, and one that is evaluable. The core argument that I would like to make is that not everything that can be measured should be measured, and similarly, many of the areas that we would like improved measurement around often defy measurement (at least in quantitative terms). Media development doesn't suffer from a monitoring and evaluation (M&E) problem as much as it does from an inadequate body of research on the connections between media, development, and democracy. The shortcoming of M&E tools used in the field of support to media development certainly merit further exploration, but it is important to first ask a broader question about how proponents of media development—at every level from the local to the global—have the right capabilities and approaches to make use of the massive amount of data generated by projects. This more serious shortcoming will continue to hamper the ability of those engaged in media development efforts to learn, to improve, and ultimately to make the case for their goals and ambitions.

Media development practitioners, through their M&E efforts, seek to better understand how the inputs from media assistance—trainings, grants, policy work and the like—lead to improvements in a specific media environment, which in turn strengthen democratic governance. The presumed connection between these inputs and the expected impact rests on the ideas and philosophy associated with the liberal democratic ideals of media as a so-called Fourth Estate (Norris 2008), unbeholden to interests of the state, the church, the military, or any group of elites. If there exists such a free and independent media—which can represent public interest and speak truth to power—then a robust, flourishing, and stable democracy is more likely to prosper. The influence of the ideals of the Fourth Estate thinking are clearly noticeable in a USAID policy paper from 1999 that for all intents and purposes offers the prevailing paradigm for why media development matters:

> Within the context of supporting democratic transitions, the goal of media development generally should be to move the media from one that is directed or even overtly controlled by government or private interests to one that is more open and has a degree of editorial independence that serves the public interest. If the media is to have any meaningful role in democracy, then the ultimate goal of media assistance should be to develop a range of diverse mediums and voices that are credible, and to create and strengthen a sector that promotes such outlets. ... A media sector supportive of democracy would be one that has a degree of editorial independence, is financially viable, has diverse and plural voices, and serves the public interest. (USAID, 1999)[2]

In recent years, the ideal of the Fourth Estate as an independent body that fosters democracy has been challenged.[3] Critics of the ideal have, for example, questioned the relationship between the Fourth Estate and media owners, politicians and market economics (see chapters in this volume by Freedman, Peterson, Stremlau, Price). At the same time, other critiques, emerging particularly from Latin America and Africa, have challenged the presumptions of how a democratic system should work that come with the Fourth Estate (Mano and Segura, this volume).

However, M&E as it currently stands is not being used in a way that can test either the paradigm of the Fourth Estate or models that are more antagonistic to it.

M&E and Media Development

The ultimate purpose of M&E (as aptly summarized by the UN Women Virtual Knowledge Center) is to build a strong, global evidence base, provide evidence on what kinds of strategies are most effective, track project level implementation and outputs, provide data that demonstrates that program efforts have had a measurable impact on expected outcomes, and assess for overall effectiveness.[4] What's important to note is that M&E is always conducted in reference to a specific program or initiative, but good M&E should help to answer larger questions.

Up until the past decade or so media development practitioners struggled with how to best pursue M&E: what indicators to track, how to ascertain where assistance has had the greatest impact, and how best to map the data collected to the ultimate purpose of making the case for why media development matters.[5] The media development sector as a whole has made enormous strides in improving its M&E systems, and the professional know-how of doing M&E has been mainstreamed throughout the sector, but the enduring shortcomings of M&E in the field are evident when compared to sectoral, macro-level research. Unlike these broader research efforts in the field, M&E in the sector still fails to inform general knowledge about what works, what doesn't, or to inform a higher-level analysis of what media development has achieved and contributed to in terms of developmental goals, including economic and political outcomes.

For the media development sector to truly advance in terms of research and learning there is a need to better leverage M&E data towards improved sectoral research and learning. The insights, data and findings from M&E attached to specific projects needs to be shared out, compared and analyzed in aggregate. The next section looks at the gaps in knowledge about media development that more coordinated M&E efforts could usefully address.

Media Development's Elusive Questions

Two major questions continue to elude the efforts of M&E and research on the issue of media development (Price, Abbott and Morgan 2011; Scott 2014; and Noske-Turner 2017). The first is the more immediate question of what kinds of interventions and forms of support are most effective in a given context for promoting the development of a vibrant and independent media sector that serves the public interest. A second, and more difficult question to answer, relates to the role of media in broader developmental and democratic outcomes—what practitioners of media development might refer to as *impact.*

Effectiveness

Indeed, one of the core questions evaluators of media development assistance are often asked is whether the media development program in question has been an effective or not. While there is presently not an agreed upon definition of what counts as an "effective program" in media development circles, the OECD DAC definition of effectiveness is commonly used in program evaluation. According to this definition, effectiveness is defined as a measure of the extent to which an aid activity attains its objectives. In evaluating the effectiveness of a program or a project, it is useful to consider the following questions: To what extent were the objectives achieved / are likely to be achieved? What were the major factors influencing the achievement or non-achievement of the objectives?[6] While there are macro-level studies about media development related trends or interests, i.e. IREX's Media Sustainability Index, Reporters Without Borders Press Freedom Survey, and Freedom House's Annual Survey on Press Freedom, these studies offer useful diagnostic research, but stop short of explaining what works and what doesn't in media development and how media assistance more broadly contributes to and supports broader development goals and objectives.

The premise of much media development evaluation work is largely based on finding evidence to understand and interrogate the link between development aid designed to help "evolve a free and independent media"[7] and any number of different types of programmatic activities deemed vital to the function of democracy, for example, as noted by USAID:

> A free press plays a vital role in democratic societies, enabling the open exchange of information and opinions among ordinary citizens, businesses, citizen associations, political parties, and governments. Free and open media systems give voice to citizens, truth test candidates and political parties during elections, inform policy debates in legislatures, investigate corruption, hold public officials accountable, enable democratic governance and facilitate more effective development.[8]

Going back to the first Global Forum for Media Development in Amman, Jordan in 2005, and a publication that came out of it—*Media Matters*—both scholars and practitioners lamented the challenge of measuring media development in meaningful ways.[9] The difficulty of measuring the impact and results of media development was also detailed in a 2005 USG General Accounting Report called "Independent Media Development Abroad: Challenges Exist in Implementing U.S. Efforts and Measuring Results." Some of the reasons given were inconsistency of program indicators, the relevance or appropriateness of using media freedom related indices (like the Freedom House Freedom of the Press Survey or the IREX Media Sustainability Index) to measure programmatic impact of specific media development initiatives, challenges in accessing core data and information about media development programs, changing circumstances and volatility on the ground in the environments where media assistance takes place, and very wide ranging number of goals, strategies, and objectives of the different types of media development programs that could be studied.[10] It would not be unfair say that as a sector international support to media development has not made a lot of progress in overcoming the types of concerns and obstacles to measurement and evaluation that are outlined in the GAO report.

Impact

In subsequent years there have been sporadic scholar and practitioner-led efforts which have sought to both advocate for and critically reflect upon the importance of independent media as a key component good governance and democracy as well as essential for rooting out corruption and jumpstarting economic reforms (see for example, the World Bank/Internews Media Map Project, and Pippa Norris' *Public Sentinel: News Media and Governance Reform*, also published by the World Bank). What seems clear is that in the nearly 30 years since the fall of the Berlin Wall, and the period of long-sustained media assistance that has followed, those who study and research international media development remain uncertain about how to best study media development's impact, and argue that while the work may be justified, the evidence base that supports media development's impact is still lacking. Martin Scott writes about one aspect of this evidence challenge (the theory to practice disconnect) in his book *Media and Development*:

> However, as with all claims about the direct links between media and democracy/good governance, there are a number of ways in which seemingly logical theoretical arguments can be quite easily problematized. (Scott 2014, 120)

Scott continues further on:

> Despite indicating the existence of a strong and significant positive correlation between media development and good governance and democracy, the results of such studies have very real limitations. Most importantly, such statistical analysis cannot account for why or how media development is linked to these particulate aspects to development. (Scott 2014, 123)

The evidence for the impact of media development is somewhat compounded by a consistent decline in global measures of press freedom over the past decade. How is it that some 30 years of support to improving press freedom and democratic media systems around the world that on global scale press freedom, and democracy, are not only under threat, but on the decline. Similarly, proxy measures of journalism's importance to democracy and healthy state institutions are also cause for concern. Globally, trust in media has also been on the decline. In some countries, media registers as the least trusted institution.[11] This seems more than cause for concern for those engaged in media development; it puts the entire enterprise in peril, and certainly presents a significant area of interest for media development researchers.

Theoretical Problems of Media Development

So, where does the problem lie in this media development research and evidence deficit? Part of the problem is that many of the claims that media developers like to make—that free media are important for political stability and democratic reforms, that media play a pivotal role in alleviating poverty and enabling economic development, and that media serve as springboard for many of the other human rights and freedoms that are associated with democratic ideals—are largely based on normative values and rooted in a human rights discourse about development. Simply put, this is just very hard to measure. And while political theory and philosophy compellingly make the case for why a free and independent media is vital to support economic development and political reforms, the connection between the state and quality of a country's media system and the hopeful development outcomes that NGOs and donors hope to support is notoriously difficult to quantify or write about in an evaluative manner. Considering recent concerns about backsliding democracies and the trend towards an illiberal state, political scientists are starting to grapple more with press freedom issues, indicating that it is one of the most important pre-conditions for democracy, and vital to the survival of the democratic system. Still, the need to show proof of impact and value for money is a very real concern for NGOs and donors who fund media development, which form the root of the problem for media development researchers and M&E practitioners alike.

The media development impact problem is one that scholars Anya Schiffrin and Ethan Zuckerman discuss in their analysis of whether the contributions of media and journalism to society can be measured. They write: "Just because journalists have exposed people to information doesn't mean that people will take action or demand policy changes in response to that information."[12] In their analysis of approaches to gauging whether and how news organizations make a difference in the world, Schiffrin and Zuckerman make reference to the "last mile problem" in journalism—the question of how does journalism actually reach people, and does it cause them to make better decisions, and will it lead to overall improvements to quality of governance, and the state of society. If media development researchers could help provide better ways to gauge and understand this "last mile problem" this would certainly help in future media development efforts—both in the so-called developed north, and the so-called developing world of the global south.

The Way Forward

Media development presents many unique challenges and difficulties when it comes to understanding seemingly simple issues like unit of measurement, indicators of success, and selecting a research framework or methodology to assess impact. One reason for this is that media development constitutes a vast range of activities, programs and types of support. Indeed, there remains after 30 years of media development a continued uncertainty about what it is that we are measuring, and towards what ends—is it democracy, accountability, poverty reduction, social change, or any number of other development agenda related goals? Another really vexing problem for media development researchers is what exactly to focus on in terms of what are the most salient aspects of media development, and how to best articulate its theory of change. Put in another way, to understand media development and its importance you must understand the sum of all the parts, i.e. the whole media systems and all its interconnections and nuances. It's problematic to study one aspect of a media system in isolation without thinking of a myriad of other issues and concerns.

In thinking about possible ways forward, media development research would benefit from a greater infusion with and linkages to academic researchers, and the expansive range of theory, studies, and ideas housed in school of journalism, communication and other social sciences. Increasingly in this regard, fields of study like the political economy of communication, digital anthropology, and legal aspects of communication are particularly important.

In addition, the media development sector is in serious need of updating its theoretical foundations related to media and development for the 21st century. The reigning paradigm of media development as a field of study has been rooted in the ideas of the modernization theories of the 1950s and 1960s. For the media development sector to flourish, and for new impact models to emerge, the sector would benefit from forward thinking ideas about the role of journalism and information systems in society, and how to safeguard the democratic and human rights potential they are historically linked to.

There's also a need to develop common learning agenda, one that includes key metrics for studying media development and democratization, and is based on case studies that take stock of what has happened with development funding tied to media in various contexts and environments—social, political, and economic. Part of this learning agenda could include ways to re-think and better use the "industry of indices" related to measures of press freedom and development. While there have been several efforts to mind the data of these indices, as Martin Scott (2014) noted in his analysis of these efforts they have a number of limitations. Still, the data is quite valuable, and indices like the Freedom House Freedom of the Press Survey, with its longitudinal data going back more than 30 years offers a valuable record and historical insight to the trends of press freedom that have impacted the ability of media development's progress. The media development sector, however, may need to think about what types of indices and macro-level studies would best help the field of media and information systems development in 21st century.

To move the media development research agenda forward, there are several issues that must be addressed. Among them:

(a) Coming to consensus in terms of when media has made a difference to development.
(b) Similarly, developing some generally agreed upon criteria (perhaps indicators) for when media development programs have contributed to democratization.
(c) Relatedly, the seemingly mundane discussion of indicators also bears upon the issue of what research methods should be used, and what literature and academic influences the media development sector can draw upon. This issue is most present in discussions around theories of change. Here the media development community would be well-served to have improved dialogue and interaction with social scientists working on the thorny problems of democracy, media, and development.
(d) When it comes to deciding on what to measure, and how to measure media development, should researchers look at the macro or micro level—or both? The importance of this question is nicely illustrative in thinking about "the last mile problem" in journalism, i.e. how does journalism reach people, and what difference does it make? In this regard, it's important to not dismiss the press freedom indices, and perhaps to think more critically why it is that there continues to be such a downward trend, and considering this, how and whether media development has the necessary approaches and tools to help improve how media systems and press freedom matter to democracy.
(e) Finally, the qualitative/quantitative data quandary gives rise to the need for the sector to think about new approaches to measurement, evaluation, research and learning, particularly in terms of how to best balance advances in the technological possibilities of data collection and analysis (like machine learning) with the need to continue to support and make use of human capacity, particularly in terms of delineating for context, cultural references, and social significance.

The purpose of this chapter was to make the case for research as a core priority of media development and to appeal to media development researchers and practitioners to better leverage programmatic M&E towards improved sectoral learning and knowledge about what works and why. The lack of a substantial body of research is often put forward as one of the key impediments hindering the advancement of the media development sector. The reasons for this are many: the sheer number of topics and issues a researcher could focus on is quite daunting; there's a need to simultaneously look at factors of technology, business and finance, legal and regulatory models as well as the economic, social and political conditions that media development programs exist in; and, rather obviously, the resources to pay for research are often lacking. There's also a data problem in that there's a perennial debate as to whether qualitative or quantitative research will best support the needs of the media development sector and help make the case for its place amongst many other competing international development priorities. The latter problem has long been a thorn in the side of the media development sector, but in this era of 'value for money' donors and development institutions tend to favor quantitative, hard data that shows correlation, causation, and proof of impact. Thus, for media development to thrive and to contribute to the economic, political and social development affecting countries where media assistance takes place, there's a need to reassess and reflect on commonly used theories of change and to make better use of individual programmatic M&E to better inform sectoral thinking and understanding of how and why media matters to development and democratization.

Notes

1. In this chapter, I am using the terms "media development" and media assistance interchangeably. For a useful discussion on these terms and the various history of the idea of media development as media assistance, see Jessica Noske-Turner, Rethinking Media Development through Evaluation: Beyond Freedom, Palgrave, 2017.
2. See: USAID, *The Role of Media and Democracy, A Strategic Approach*, 1999, available at: https://www.usaid.gov/sites/default/files/documents/2496/200sbc.pdf
3. See for instance, Julianne Schultz, *Reviving the Fourth Estate: Democracy, Accountability and the Media*, Cambridge University Press, 1998, wherein the author explores in detail many of the inherent contradictions and tensions in modern day media systems, and how pressure from the state, market, and commercial forces creates challenges to the idea of "watchdog journalism" and exposes the many threats to democratic media due ownership concentration, and abusive practices of media power.
4. See UN Women Virtual Knowledge Center, and their summarization of some key M&E literature at http://www.endvawnow.org/en/articles/331-why-is-monitoring-and-evaluation-important.html.

5. The problem of indicators and which ones are best to use for assessing impact of media development programs has been the subject of much debate and reflection at numerous conferences, workshops and gatherings of both media development practitioners and researchers. One of the best background papers on the challenges posed by indicators for assessing media development was written by Andrew Puddephatt for UNESCO: Defining Indicators of Media Development, available at http://unesdoc.unesco.org/images/0016/001600/160017eb.pdf.
6. See DAC Criteria for Evaluating Development Assistance: https://www.oecd.org/dac/evaluation/daccriteriaforevaluatingdevelopmentassistance.htm.
7. See the definition of international media development offered by CIMA: The term media development refers to evolution and change in the fields of news media and communications. Such change relates to a range of institutions, practices, and behaviors including the rule of law, freedoms of expression and press, education systems for journalists, business environments, capacities of journalists and managers, as well as support for a diversity of views in society. This evolution can be stimulated by donor support, private investment, or local processes of change led by media owners, managers, journalists, media industry associations, and other collective efforts. https://www.cima.ned.org/what-is-media-development/.
8. Jill Moss and Mark Koenig, Free Press: The Cornerstone of Democracy, USAID, Center of Excellence on Democracy, Human Rights and Governance, May 3, 2013, available at: https://blog.usaid.gov/2013/05/free-press-the-cornerstone-of-democracy/
9. See Media Matters: Perspectives on Advancing Governance & Development from the Global Forum for Media Development, Creative Commons, 2008.
10. See Independent Media Development Abroad: Challenges Exist in Implementing U.S. Efforts and Measuring Results, Jess Ford (author), available at http://www.gao.gov/new.items/d05803.pdf.
11. Edelman, 2018 Edelman Trust Barometer: Global Report (2018), Available at https://cms.edelman.com/sites/default/files/2018-01/2018%20Edelman%20Trust%20Barometer%20Global%20Report.pdf.
12. See: Anya Schiffrin and Ethan Zuckerman, "Can We Measure Media Impact? Surveying the Field," Fall 2015, Stanford Social Innovation Review. Available at https://ssir.org/articles/entry/can_we_measure_media_impact_surveying_the_field.

Recommended for Further Reading

Escalera, Carolina, Ruizhi Li, HoCheol Shin, and Paulo Uebel, with Julie Poncelet (Advisor). 2013. *Measuring Outcomes of Impact, Investing in Independent Media: Developing a Media Impact Index: The Case Study of El Periódico in Guatemala*. Columbia, SIPA/ Media Development Investment Fund Report. https://www.mdif.org/wp-content/uploads/2013/09/MDIF-SIPA-EL-Periodico-Impact-Report-Final.pdf.

Roy, Sanjukta. 2011. *Overview Report: Measuring Media Development*. Washington D.C.: Inernews and World Bank.

Susman-Peña, Tara. 2012. *Making Media Development More Effective*. A Special Report to the CIMA.

References

Norris, Pippa. 2008. "The Fourth Estate." In *Driving Democracy: Do Power-Sharing Institutions Work?*, 186–208. Cambridge, NY: Cambridge University Press.

Noske-Turner, Jessica. 2017. *Rethinking Media Development through Evaluation: Beyond Freedom*. Basingstoke: Palgrave Macmillan.

Price, Monroe, Susan Abbott, and Libby Morgan, eds. 2011. *Measures of Press Freedom and Media Contributions to Development: Evaluating the Evaluators* (Mass Communication and Journalism). New York, NY: Peter Lang.

Scott, Martin. 2014. *Media and Development* (Development Matters). New York, NY: Zed Books.

CHAPTER SIX

A Sketch of Media Development

From Meeting Point to Field?

SILVIO WAISBORD

Since its early days during the post-war period, international development has included specific components related to media and press issues that fell under the rubric of "media development" (or "media assistance"). Despite some ambiguity in the field, media development remains associated with initiatives to promote media democracy and pluralism around the world, with an array of programs focused on media legislation, journalism skills, and "independent" media (Norris 2009). These programs are frequently designed, supported, and implemented by a range of actors besides donors and other international aid groups, including government and inter-government agencies, private philanthropic donors, local organizations, and activists (see Price, Abbott and Morgan 2011). As such, media development, as a topic, has been a meeting point for scholars and practitioners with common interests, but diverse perspectives. In academia, media development sits at the junction of several streams in communication studies: media systems, media policy, media activism/advocacy, journalism studies, communication for social change/development, and public diplomacy. The broad range of thematic interests, lines of research, and programmatic goals subsumed under the topic of media development makes for an unwieldy area of practice and research.

Notwithstanding a long and rich tradition of reflection and practice, it is unclear whether media development is and could (or should) be a distinctive and cohesive field of specialization in academia. What it should be called remains a matter of debate, too. Both "media" and "development" have multiple meanings and include myriad issues. To become a distinctive field of study, media development would need the essential building blocks: a common object of study and solid theoretical frameworks that lay down analytical foundations, conceptual apparatus, questions, and propositions. Media development will almost certainly remain a meeting point for research and programmatic interests, but scholars and researchers interested in this topic will need to do more to establish it as a unique field of enquiry.

Thematic Dispersion in Media Development

Thematic dispersion is the result of the fact that media development comprises a long list of issues variously associated with pluralism, democracy, and independence of the media. Also, it reflects the multiple agendas of public and private donors that have supported programs linked to democracy promotion, curbing violence/extremism, humanitarian emergencies, global health, and other developmental outcomes. Donors have wielded significant influence in shaping research and programs according to shifts in policy priorities and global circumstances. Also, the media, as institutions, are associated with different analytical and programmatic foci: structural issues (e.g., ownership, funding), practice (competencies/skills of media workers), legacy and digital platforms, companies and industries, media access, and media use and literacy.

No wonder, media development, as a topic, has become an aggregation of multiple interests at the intersection of various lines of research and programs. Despite persistent fogginess in terms of ontological focus and analytical scaffolding, it is a convenient label, a shorthand for research and practice, with currency both in the international aid industry and academic quarters.

No doubt, media development has also become more complex and nuanced than during its Cold War days. Back then, it was primarily identified with programs promoting Whiggish notions of media independence/freedom grounded in Western, particularly U.S.-centric, perspectives. This perspective infused programs for training reporters and promoting free speech legislation. It survived virtually untouched after the Berlin Wall came down and vast swaths of the world experienced a spring of liberal democracy in the 1990s.

Due to the combination of several factors, however, this vision eventually lost its former luster in the recent years. The multilayered realities of media systems across the globe demonstrated that regime change was not sufficient to promote better conditions for media performance and public expression. From "media capture" by business allied with governments to anti-press violence, the challenges were many, and could not be understood by conventional notions of media independence (from whom? for what?). Curbing or eliminating government intervention in the media was insufficient, incoherent and, improbable.

Also, it became harder to sustain Western confidence in traditional pillars of media independence as media systems in global North became dominated by runaway commercialism, clientelism, and partisanship. Ambitious programmatic goals rang hollow when conditions in donor countries were notably distant from ideals promoted worldwide. Media independence has been under assault in the same countries that believed they embodied it.

Finally, top-down programs that embraced the Holy Grail of press liberalism clashed against indigenous movements and local traditions that defined media, independence, and freedom in different ways. Questions about "what is development" and "for whom" became central in the redefinition of media development. Old truisms became challenged: are all forms of government interventions negative for public speech? Are markets necessarily the antidote to government censorship? Are community media suitable solutions? What media models are desirable and possible in conflict and post-conflict societies?

The former radiant optimism and self-assuredness of Western liberalism about media freedom gradually gave room to the notions of media pluralism and media democracy. The latter foregrounded the need to promote a range of media and voices instead of a narrow perspective that made governments as culprit of all evils. Gradually, a human rights perspective that underscored the importance of the right to expression and communication gained presence. This perspective underscored the importance of the communication rights of women, racial and ethnic groups, and linguistic minorities and their media. It emphasized a more holistic and institutional approach both to diagnose problems and promote solutions. It called attention to multiple obstacles, including the political, economic, and cultural realities of media systems. It brought up the importance of safe conditions to promote speech, especially considering massive violations of speech rights of journalists and citizens. It broadened the analytical and programmatic foci by identifying multiple legal and institutional reforms, from libel laws to public access to information, needed to sustain democratic speech and accountability.

As this transition was taking place, the digital revolution brought about unprecedented transformations in public expression and new challenges. Issues such as digital access (including quality and skills), the emergence of digital news and the diversification of business models, the growing power of digital corporations, government efforts to censor, monitor and influence digital communication, invasion of privacy, online harassment of political dissidents, and the dystopian realities of digital media (e.g. cyberbullying, hate speech, fake news) gained attention. Understandably, the issues added another thick layer of priorities for public expression on top of already complex and full thematic agenda.

Consequently, media development comprises a diverse set of issues, without obvious commonalities in terms of scholarly questions or programmatic objectives. What applies to consolidated democracies may not be relevant for fragile states. What makes sense for settings with healthy community media may not applicable in contexts rift with ethnic rivalries. Shaped by multiple considerations, donors' priorities do not always match local needs and priorities. Funding is generally tied to various streams of development money, such as humanitarian, health, education, security, and environmental programs not focused on media and communication goals.

What to Do?

How to turn a rich, vibrant yet chaotic body of research and practice into a somewhat defined field? How to bring coherence across research and programmatic agendas? What propositions can be advanced based on insights and evidence accumulated over years around the world? What are the common questions to inform future work? Where are the unifying interests among media assistance in post-conflict areas, support for digital startups, training of health journalists and the promotion of freedom of information legislation?

One option is to take the **programmatic route**: refine a research and programmatic agenda tied to the sustainable development goals (SDGs). Because the SDGs have become the common horizon of development initiatives, it would make sense to connect media development issues to them. The problem is that there are no specific goals related to media pluralism or the right to communication, a telling reminder that media development does not rank highly in development priorities. Media and public expression objectives remains secondary, instrumental to social, economic, and political goals.

Another option is the **research route**: identify central theoretical questions to be addressed by research and programs. A few quickly come to mind. How can we re-read the literature to identify effective actions to promote media democracy/pluralism? What are the similarities and the differences across different settings? How do international and local actions complement each other? How should media democracy and pluralism be understood given multiple challenges and the current communication chaos? What are the common threats among multiple ways of understanding media development and programmatic initiatives? (Segura and Waisbord 2016)

Whether one route or both are taken, it would be necessary to bring together various stakeholders. Scholars, practitioners, governments, activists, civil society organizations, and donors would need to agree on a common blueprint about media development, questions, goals, indicators, and interventions. Only then it would be possible to take full advantage of a trove of insights and experiences relevant to both academia and practice.

A broad-based, institutional alliance may contribute to developing a common vocabulary and to overcoming thematic and programmatic dispersion. This alliance could function globally, regionally and/or locally. It could persuade donors to commit to strengthening media development as a primary area of focus rather than as accessory to other equally important global goals. It would need common spaces (e.g. meetings, journals, programs, research) for sharing ideas and outlining future directions. It should nudge a shift from top-down priorities and perspectives, decided in cubicles and boardrooms in the global North, to bottom-up definition of problems, questions, and solutions. It would need to take risks by doing what is needed rather than what is easier, well-known, or tried and true. It would need to be sympathetic to theory-building grounded in a rich body of evidence (Noske-Turner 2015). It would need to be open-minded and humble by tapping into a reservoir of local experiences, energies, and demands.

Admittedly, this is a tall order, particularly at a time when geopolitical agendas limit imagination and creativity in the global aid industry. Yet no one ever said that media development is easy or that it should consist of rolling out well-worn ideas with the hope they would magically deliver results—produce media pluralism, cultivate informed citizens, or strengthen public speech. Doing business as usual may continue to keep everyone busy, but it will not necessarily advance better conditions, especially at a time of unprecedented political, social and communication transformations. Intellectual risk-taking and programmatic innovations are imperative to connect dispersed ideas and actions into a more cohesive field of research and practice. Otherwise, media development may remain a vibrant field of research and practice, but a Babel of ideas and projects with widely different intellectual goals and practical missions.

Recommended for Further Reading

Berger, Guy. 2010. "Problematizing 'Media Development' as a Bandwagon Gets Rolling." *International Communication Gazette* 72 (7): 547–65.

Deane, James. 2014. "Media Development." In *The Handbook of Development Communication and Social Change,* edited by Karin Gwinn Wilkins, Thomas Tufte, and Rafael Obregon. United Kingdom: Wiley.

Peters, Bettina. 2010. "The Future of Journalism and Challenges for Media Development: Are We Exporting a Model that No Longer Works at Home?" *Journalism Practice* 4 (3): 268–73.

Relly, Jeannine E. & Margaret Zanger. 2016. "The Enigma of News Media Development with Multi-Pronged 'Capture': The Afghanistan case." *Journalism* 18 (10): 1233–55.

References

Norris, Pippa, ed. 2009. *Public Sentinel: News Media and Governance Reform.* Washington, DC: World Bank.

Noske-Turner, Jessica. 2015. "10 Years of Evaluation Practice in Media Assistance: Who, When, Why and How?" *Nordicom Review* 36: 41–56.

Price, Monroe E., Susan Abbott and Libby Morgan. 2011. *Measures of Press Freedom and Media Contributions to Development: Evaluating the Evaluators.* New York, NY: Peter Lang.

Segura, Maria Soledad and Silvio Waisbord. 2016. *Media Movements: Civil Society and Media Policy Reform in Latin America.* London: Zed Books.

PART TWO

Democratic and Social Challenges

CHAPTER SEVEN

Media Development and the Political Marketplace

NICOLE STREMLAU

In the midst of the technological and political turbulence of today, it is opportune to reflect on the significance and potential of international support to media development. Is the field of media development assistance still relevant? And, if yes, how can it be steered to be more relevant given the present democratic challenges?

By adopting the metaphor of a political marketplace, a contemporary system of governance where loyalty may be bought or sold and political allegiances are negotiated, this chapter unpacks and elaborates a more realistic and reflective view of the role, and potential, media development may have in different contexts. A political marketplace, in this context, encompasses an important set of governance actors—political entrepreneurs, who may include career politicians, businesspeople, religious leaders, among others—and the rules, incentives, norms, and ethics that govern the way they interact with each other, their constituents or communities, and ordinary people (although the latter is not always a priority). This lens allows for greater focus on power, politics, and the role of money in media assistance.

While it is difficult to generalize about the varied media development efforts in different contexts, and indeed this chapter strongly argues for greater focus on local contexts, it draws on lessons and experiences from the Horn of Africa. This region is, in many respects, a periphery with examples that are often on the extreme. Looking to the edges can often provide deeper insight into more common cases, particularly given that media development is most often concerned with poorer countries and those engaged in, or emerging from, violent conflict. Ethiopia, for example, is the largest recipient of donor aid on the continent yet has historically had one of the most closed media systems and, apart from Eritrea, remains the outlier where the government has retained a complete monopoly over telecommunications in the name of socio-economic access and development. But it is also a country where ideology and definitive ideas about the role of a developmental state (or Revolutionary Democracy), and the role of media in such a state, has set trends for centralizing leadership, consolidating state power, and provided intellectual leadership in development theory in the region. Neighbouring Somalia contrasts significantly. Often described as a state that is "failed" or where nothing works, there have been dramatic investments in the ICT sector. Where Ethiopia is dominated by state infrastructure, Somalia is the opposite and is the only country on the continent where the telecommunications sector is comprised solely of local, national companies that have operated largely in the absence of effective state regulation. Companies such as MTN, Vodafone and others that are active across the continent have been unable to find a way to penetrate this market and navigate local business norms and security concerns. This has actually enabled tremendous local innovation including the most ambitious mobile money sector on the continent, and a relatively vibrant radio and online news environment. These cases are highlighted not for their generalizability, but rather for the particular insights and lessons they offer.

The chapter proceeds by elaborating on how a "political marketplace" helps us to better understand media development in a contemporary context, and how initiatives to support media development can better adapt to present circumstances. I then turn to three key factors that are central in the type of political marketplaces this chapter is concerned with, but too often overlooked or misinterpreted by media development actors. Bringing them to the center of our understanding of media development can potentially improve its relevancy in today's context. First is the central, but often misinterpreted, role of ideology or political thought, particularly as it relates to ideas of freedom of expression or development. Waving the flag of media freedom and human rights and allied with civil society actors, external media development actors often overlook local ideas, context, and experiences when designing support interventions. Second is the shifting but central role of new communications technologies in altering political marketplaces. It is not enough for media development actors to simply embrace new technology actors and try to leverage technology for their own projects and objectives. What is needed is a more "technopolitical" approach that considers both how technology is changing the dynamics between political entrepreneurs (and their constituents) as well as how these actors are also trying to shape technology for their political agendas. Finally, the third issue is money and the ways in which the influx of funds from media development organizations, and their associated donors, shapes and influences the political marketplace, elevating and empowering some actors, while marginalizing others. The chapter concludes by suggesting how a more realistic perspective about the politics of media development support might actually enable it to be more targeted and effective, whereby strengthening its position and relevance in contemporary times.

Understanding a Political Marketplace

Media development organizations often portray themselves as apolitical, working to support journalists, in some cases bloggers, and freedom of expression advocates, as well as encouraging government reform. The range of possible interventions, as this book highlights, is significant. Many organizations explicitly speak about their work in "fragile" states, "transitioning" countries, or "authoritarian" regimes but rarely do they describe interventions as political engineering. International Media Support, a Danish-NGO, is indicative of this mainstream approach. They describe their role in conflict situations to channel "objective" or "peacebrokering" information. In "democratic development countries" the emphasis is on "institution-building," particularly in terms of public service broadcasting, as well as support to encourage "the development of the media as a fourth estate, able to reinforce democratic processes and secure the state against non-democratic tendencies and forces." In "authoritarian countries and repressive democracies" interventions focus on supporting "pro-reform groups" and "providing direct support to professional independent media to circumvent state harassment and restrictions. This may include support to "illegal" and exiled media outlets."[1]

In this case, there is transparency about providing support to "illegal" or "exiled media outlets," but there appears to be strong assumptions about the independence and pro-reform (or press freedom) ideology for such groups. However, research suggests that diaspora media outlets tend to be more partisan, and often ethnically-based, than national media (Gagliardone and Stremlau 2011). The point is that International Media Support, like other organizations in this sector, is deeply engaged in politics. The provision of "peacebrokering" information and the support of "illegal" media are not necessarily "objective" or "independent." As this chapter will further elaborate, a wider dialogue about the type of political engineering media development organizations are attempting might better affect the political, social or cultural change to which they aspire.

The marketplace metaphor helps us to think about this and is often used to understand media systems. The "marketplace of ideas," the most well-known, typically refers to the potential role of the First Amendment in the United States in creating a space where the best ideas, and ultimately the "truth," will emerge through popular participation and engagement. The term was popularized by the Nobel Prize winning economist R. H. Coase, who argued "that, in the market for goods, government regulation is desirable whereas, in the market for ideas, government regulation is undesirable and should be strictly limited" (Coase 1974, 384). Critics have since argued that such a theory is based on "assumptions of rational decision-making that are implausible in modern society" where, in reality, "the market is severely skewed in favor of an entrenched power structure and ideology" (Ingber 1984, 1). Further critiques have emphasized that the promotion of unrestricted speech and idealistic notions of a somehow level and open public debate in newly democratizing states, or states emerging from violent conflict can further exacerbate nationalist tensions (Allen and Stremlau 2005; Snyder and Ballentine 1996). In such a context, when the state and other elites are engaged in struggles over power and resources, there are significant incentives for manipulating public opinion with potentially disastrous effects that a "marketplace of ideas" may be unable to address. This concern has parallels to some of the debates around electoral competition and a potential increase or return to violence in conflict and post-conflict settings (Brancati and Snyder 2013; Collier, Hoeffler, and Söderbom 2008; Paris 2004).

The "market for loyalties" is another marketplace metaphor that has been applied to understand the dynamics of media systems, particularly in transitioning countries. As Monroe Price describes it, the market for loyalties is a space in which "large-scale competitors for power, in a shuffle for allegiances, often use regulation of communication to organize a cartel of imagery and identity among themselves" (Price 1994, 667). In further writings he elaborates the complex and ambitious ways that actors, whether international governments, media assistance organizations, or diaspora media, also attempt to shape and compete in this marketplace in an effort to achieve their own political, cultural or economic goals (Price 1997; 2002). Sometimes this reflects the foreign policy of state actors but increasingly, as technology has changed, smaller actors are empowered to compete in many of the same ways as state or large actors.

A political marketplace is slightly different—in this context the emphasis is on the power dynamics between the actors that vie for influence. Some have referred to this as the "real politics" (De Waal 2015) which looks beyond the veneer of "democratic" transitions and state building to the actual price of loyalty and the realities of political budgets. Others discuss it (or similar phenomenon) in terms of local "public authorities" or "twilight institutions" (Booth 2009; Kelsall 2012; Lund 2006) and the relationship between money and power in such settings. While these approaches vary, the essence is somewhat similar—to look at how different political actors, often beyond the state though frequently in concert with actual authorities and constituencies within communities, navigate the "political marketplace," as well as those who attempt to regulate it, including international actors such as media development organizations (Dc Waal 2009; Ramseyer and Rosenbluth 2009). While there are different ways of attempting to analyze and assess the dynamics of a political marketplace, this chapter highlights three major drivers: the ideational background or the ideologies that characterize the marketplace; the ways in which new communications technologies are altering the political and economic dynamics of the political marketplace by changing the ways actors compete or cooperate; and the role of external funding, particularly in terms of monetary compensation (although other types of "gifts" such as trips or trainings could be considered).

Ideology and the Shifting of Values

Media assistance organizations typically offer a set of ideas about the values and norms media, or free expression, should have in political and economic processes. However, when it comes to understanding the political marketplace, taking local ideas and ideologies seriously is imperative. Ideas, and political ideology, can be seen as the boundaries of possible action undergirding the language, laws and symbols that give them form. In a marketplace analogy, ideas may be quickly categorized with umbrella concepts such as a "Marxist" or "free market" approach, but in the context of conflict environments, or areas where power is contested and the state might have limited reach, it can be seldom categorized in such normative categories. Ideologies are tied up with leadership and the architects or funders that may be seeking to justify and explain media and developmental projects. They tend to reflect the life histories of the leaders or parties that drive forward the ideas. In some cases, when a political project is strongly ideologically grounded, the importance of ideas trumps the development of institutions or even economic interests.

For some countries in the Horn of Africa, the role of ideology has been particularly salient in shaping the media system, yet its influence is often misunderstood or underestimated. In Ethiopia, for example, Revolutionary Democracy, or more recently ideas of a Developmental Democratic State, permeate all aspects of government and nation-building. This political thought has informed all projects when it comes to media policy and media development—from the government's insistence that it maintains a monopoly over the telecommunications sector to ambitious projects to connect all local government offices through satellite, enabling the "center" of the state, Addis Ababa, one-way communication with the "peripheries." Similarly, the Ethiopian government has been investing heavily in the "SchoolNet" project to provide standardized teaching using satellite technology. As schools have historically been involved with challenging the government and protests, there is a strong dimension of civic, or political, education. While Ethiopia may be one of the more extreme cases, it has set an example for other countries in the region. Paul Kagame of Rwanda, for example, has credited former Ethiopian Prime Minister Meles Zenawi of having "the intellectual ability to formulate and argue the case for a developmental democratic state … and the boldness to push it through," urging other Africans to "practice variations of the concept based on local conditions" and they may "get equally good results" (Kagame 2015).

The importance of such ideology in shaping and setting the direction of media policy and systems is often underestimated by external media development actors. Media assistance is often involved in attempting to shift these values and ideas towards more normative systems of media freedom. Looking at cases where ideology is central to politics, reminds us of the importance of seeing change as part of a larger historical process and context and cautions against the hubris of simply attempting to replace one set of ideas with another, whether in the name of freedom of expression, development, or peacemaking.

New Technologies

Media assistance actors have, in some cases, been quick to embrace new technologies and the agenda around digital rights. This often means supporting initiatives at tech hubs or projects that attempt to leverage ICTs for development or awareness raising around particular rights. Their focus has been on young elites in capital cities with questionable constituencies beyond elites and on trendy projects such as crisis mapping that have also had debatable impact.[2] But new technologies are changing how more traditional political marketplaces function, often in overlooked ways, with significant implications for media assistance organizations.

Longstanding means of mobilizing support or developing constituencies for particular political projects, including liberation struggles or even civil wars, have typically involved intensive efforts to build support, often over decades. Relationships are fashioned and negotiated; ideology and political objectives are debated. An example of this type of intensive coalition building is the student movement at Addis Ababa University in the 1960s and 1970s. This movement gave birth to the Tigrayan People's Liberation Front (TPLF), the insurgency that after decades in the bush eventually overthrew the Soviet-backed Derg government in the early 1990s. In this case, relationships were refined and cultivated over an extended period of time. There were significant barriers for external actors to enter the political marketplace and doing so was expensive, particularly in terms of time and loyalties.

Technologies have been lowering these barriers and enabling those that might not otherwise have access to the elites or powerful actors, or might not be in a strong position to negotiate their interests, to do so. Agreements and negotiations that once had to happen through face-to-face meetings or through intermediaries or even letter writing are now able to occur through phone calls or WhatsApp messages. This has increased accessibility of key actors and is forcing agreements, negotiations, and resolutions at a faster pace. The surge in access to elites and power brokers that new technologies have offered, has, in some respects, empowered protesters and activists seeking to publically organize against public authorities or issues. However, at the same time the long-term impact of weaker networked protest and efforts at political change remains debatable (e.g., the protests in Egypt).

Traditional media, particularly newspapers, which have often set the news agenda for other mediums, have been spaces for elites to negotiate power, often over long periods. Frequently politically aligned and tied with patronage networks, traditional media have been forums for building alliances and navigating conflicts. By recognizing the central role of media in brokering and forming political allegiances, particularly in transitions, rather than focusing on their aspired or potential role as "watchdogs" or as neutral information providers, media assistance actors can make more transparent and realistic assessments of the role of particular outlets, their journalists, and the possibilities of these outlets to contribute to meaningful political change. Supporting such media, however, often means taking an explicit side lending support and credibility to one set of political actors rather than another.

Money

While media assistance is just a small portion of development aid, it has significant impact on media systems. In many respects, viewing much of the support as political financing underscores how assistance organizations might privilege or elevate one political position over another. Direct financing, opportunities for travel to international conferences and the granting of international awards for recognition as media or free speech defenders are all important mechanisms for raising an individual or group's profile. In some cases these monetized modes of endorsement offer some protection from criticism, because they may be seen to fall under an "international umbrella," supported by foreign governments or NGOs. In other cases endorsement exacerbates tensions with national governments for precisely the same reasons.

There are strong transnational dimensions that at times can develop cyclical relationships with individuals moving between media and civil society groups, even regionally or internationally. This makes it difficult to speak about "local" input, as local civil society groups are often populated by individuals who have been at international organizations, sometimes abroad. These ostensibly "local" groups oftentimes adopt a stronger, more normative and less-localized view than international counterparts. In some cases, the less-localized view arises from a conditioning of language and discourse required to win donor funding or be seen as viable partners. It is increasingly difficult for media assistance organizations to seek innovative or locally rooted solutions to media development challenges when the prevailing discourse is solidly around international best practices and normative enabling environments. In the case of Somalia, for example, this is evident in the challenges of incorporating local customary law (*xeer* law) into national media law. Rather than examining what is working and asking why or how the current political and legal situation might be enabling innovation, there is a tendency to approach media development environments as a blank slate: a space upon which best practices and laws should be transplanted.

There is also increasingly activity by large technology corporations including Google and Facebook that are focused on "connecting the unconnected" and bringing the internet, along with some selected apps, to rural communities. While this is typically framed as a philanthropic initiative, there are clear business interests due to increasingly less growth in developed markets that are already near saturation points in terms of users. In Africa, for example, these technology companies are often behaving as media development organizations, supporting civil society groups, funding conferences and research, and seeking to shape policy as much as possible. Such companies recruit for dedicated "policy" posts that closely work with national governments, whose involvement stretches beyond lobbying and may involve providing expertise into the drafting of laws and policies.

Conclusion

Media development organizations have struggled to adapt to changing technologies and different political contexts beyond the democratizing narratives of the early 1990s that were so prevalent in Eastern and Central Europe. Given the emphasis in recent years on local partners and local context, particularly after the well-publicized struggles to reform (or rather reinvent) large media and information systems in Afghanistan and Iraq after the overthrow of earlier regimes, it is still surprising that this chapter concludes with an argument that greater sensitivity to local context is needed. Media assistance organizations must be reminded to avoid a "blank slate" approach, where it is assumed that nothing works or the media system needs to be constructed in its entirety, or near entirety. An example of this continued "blank slate" approach is Somalia where, despite a vibrant telecommunications sector and some local mechanisms for resolving conflicts that have enabled such a sector to grow, the role of *xeer* law, or customary law, in providing such an enabling environment is often overlooked. Organizations such as the World Bank have been putting tens of millions of dollars towards new communications legislations that often appear based more on what has been working in Nigeria rather than Somalia.[3] Despite criticisms against legal transplants (Legrand 1997; Twining 2004), in the media assistance sector it often quite alive, shrouded behind the discourse of "best practices" or "international norms."

As this chapter has argued, media assistance is highly political and is, in itself, a form of political engineering. Transparency about what projects and ideologies are being supported and why (including the implications for local power dynamics and the political marketplace) can strengthen and set forth a new contribution for media assistance. Traditional media assistance still has an important role to play when it comes to long-term elite interventions and coalition building through the mass media. Media assistance can strengthen networks, but actors need to be more realistic about how the interventions are shaping the political marketplaces. This includes critical analysis about how political markets are changing and what aspects of markets need to be supported will ensure greater relevance in governance interventions for media assistance groups.

Notes

1. "Policy Paper: Media development tools and political contexts," *International Media Support*, November 2012, Accessed 11 January 2018, https://www.mediasupport.org/wp-content/uploads/2012/11/media-dev-tools-ims.pdf.
2. https://irevolution.files.wordpress.com/2013/01/internewswpcrowdglobe_web-1.pdf.
3. http://projects.worldbank.org/P148588?lang=en.

Recommended for Further Reading

De Waal, Alex. 2015. *The Real Politics of the Horn of Africa: Money, War and the Business of Power*. Cambridge: Polity Press.

Snyder, Jack and Karen Ballentine. 1996. Nationalism and the Marketplace of Ideas. *International Security*, 21 (2): 5–40.
Stremlau, Nicole. 2018. *Media, Conflict and the State in Africa.* Cambridge: Cambridge University Press.

References

Allen, Tim, and Nicole Stremlau. 2005. "Media Policy, Peace and State Reconstruction." Crisis States Research Centre, London School of Economics, Discussion Paper No. 8.
Booth, David. 2009. "Elites, Governance and the Public Interest in Africa: Working with the Grain?" African Power and Politics Programme, Overseas Development Institute, Discussion Paper No. 6
Brancati, Dawn, and Jack L. Snyder. 2013. "Time to Kill: The Impact of Election Timing on Postconflict Stability." *Journal of Conflict Resolution*, 57 (5): 822–53.
Coase, Ronald H. 1974. "The Market for Goods and the Market for Ideas." *The American Economic Review*, 64 (2): 384–91.
Collier, Paul, Anke Hoeffler, and Mans Söderbom. 2008. "Post-conflict Risks." *Journal of Peace Research*, 45 (4): 46178.
De Waal, Alex. 2009. "Mission Without End? Peacekeeping in the African Political Marketplace." *International Affairs*, 85 (1): 99–113.
———. 2015. *The Real Politics of the Horn of Africa: Money, War and the Business of Power*. Cambridge, UK: Polity Press.
Gagliardone, Iginio, and Nicole Stremlau. 2012. *Digital Media, Conflict and Diasporas in the Horn of Africa*. Open Society Foundations.
Ingber, Stanley. 1984. "The Marketplace of Ideas: A legitimizing Myth." *Duke Law Journal*, 1–91.
Kagame, Paul. 2015, August 21. Welcome Remarks by President Paul Kagame. Retrieved from https://www.afdb.org/fileadmin/uploads/afdb/Documents/Generic-Documents/Remarks_by_President_Kagame_-_Meles_Zenawi_Symposium_-_21_08_2015.pdf.
Kelsall, Tim. 2012. "Neo-patrimonialism, Rent-seeking and Development: Going with the Grain?" *New Political Economy*, 17 (5): 677–82.
Legrand, Pierre. 1997. "The Impossibility of 'Legal Transplants.'" *Maastricht Journal of European and Comparative Law*, 4 (2): 111–24.
Lund, Christian. 2006. "Twilight Institutions: Public Authority and Local Politics in Africa." *Development and Change*, 37 (4): 685–705.
Paris, Roland. 2004. *At War's End: Building Peace after Civil Conflict*. Cambridge: Cambridge University Press.
Price, Monroe E. 1994. "The Market for Loyalties: Electronic Media and the Global Competition for Allegiances." *The Yale Law Journal*, 104 (3): 667–705.
———. 1997. "The Market for Loyalties and the Uses of Comparative Media Law." *Cardozo Journal International and Comparative Law*, 5, 445.

———. 2002. "Media and Sovereignty." *The Global Information Revolution and Its Challenge to State Power*. Cambridge, MA: MIT Press.

Ramseyer, John Mark, and Frances McCall Rosenbluth. 1993. *Japan's Political Marketplace.* Cambridge: Harvard University Press.

Snyder, Jack and Karen Ballentine. 1996. "Nationalism and the Marketplace of Ideas." *International Security*, 21 (2): 5–40.

Twining, William. 2004. "Diffusion of Law: A Global Perspective." *The Journal of Legal Pluralism and Unofficial Law*, 36 (49): 1–45.

CHAPTER EIGHT

Fake News and Disinformation

Promoting Facts with Press Freedoms

DOUGLAS GRIFFIN

Much has been written about the proliferation of undesirable and inappropriate content across a variety of societies, particularly that which is delivered over the internet and coming from abroad. Some of this content could be regarded as hate speech in those societies that regulate such speech. Some regulators of traditional media already try to address this through their licensing and regulatory frameworks. But, most existing frameworks cannot adequately enforce against content coming from outside the country via social media, cable, or satellite due to technological and jurisdictional limitations.

Another category of content (that sometimes also constitutes hate speech) is more akin to misinformation or disinformation—often labeled "fake news" in recent years.[1] Although this phenomenon is not new—the terms "fake news" goes back to the late 19th century[2]—the speed at which it can travel via the internet is, and many actors are finding ways to accelerate it. The use of algorithms, automation, and human curation to disseminate intentionally misleading information is now being described as "computational propaganda" (Woolley and Howard 2017).

The issues of fake news and computational propaganda received considerable attention in the context of the 2016 elections in the United States (Allcott and Gentzkow 2017; Dewey 2016), and in the United Kingdom's Brexit referendum (Booth, Weaver, Hern, Smith, and Walker 2017; Kollanyi, Howard, and Wooley 2016). This is not to say, however, that the phenomenon is limited to Europe and the United States, as the case of Kenya illustrates. Rumor and misinformation spread rapidly by SMS after Kenya's disputed 2007 elections, fueling the ensuing violence there (Ismail and Deane 2008); and in the run-up to elections ten years later, online fake news was highlighted as a growing problem in a national survey on the topic (GeoPoll and Portland Communications 2017).

While "fake news" and disinformation frequently emanate from domestic origins, it is the foreign influence on political discourse via social media networks, such as Facebook, that has become a prominent focus of politicians eager to guard against contemporary techniques of information warfare, many of which were first witnessed in the Russo-Ukrainian conflict that began in 2014 (Fox and Rossow 2017).

Amid growing concerns that social media platforms could be hijacked for the nefarious purposes of foreign agents, technological companies including Google, Facebook and Twitter have been called to testify before the U.S. Congress on the surprising reach of Russian content leading up to the U.S. elections, with at least one U.S. Senator proposing greater disclosure requirements for political ads, particularly those paid for or promoted by foreign resources.[3] A recent publication by the U.S. Advisory Commission on Public Diplomacy summarized the perceived dangers of foreign disinformation:

> While technological advances have enabled broader participation in public discussion, they have also fractured it into silos where dubious assertions and accusations can reverberate unchallenged. Fake news is disseminated for profit or political advantage. Extremists have new forums in which to spread hatred and lies with impunity. And foreign actors influence domestic policy undetected. Compounding the problems, individuals have little ability to discern the identity of interlocutors or basis for distinguishing fact from fiction. (Fukuyama 2017, 1)

Regulatory and Legal Approaches to Disinformation

In 2017, Germany took a legislative approach to attempt to rein in fake news, enacting a law that requires social media platforms to remove obviously illegal hate speech and other postings within 24 hours of receiving a notification. The law does not specify what content is "obviously illegal," but rather states that such content must be obviously illegal under other German laws. Although the law expressly targets hate speech, it has been reported that it was enacted to address concerns that hate speech in the form of "fake news" about migrants could sway the then upcoming German elections.

Under this German legislation, fines can be imposed where a platform systematically refuses to comply. Social media companies have, not surprisingly, come out against the law, estimating that they could face up to 50 million euros in fines. But, it is not only the potential fines that worry these platforms. Staff costs will escalate immediately as well. For example, Facebook purportedly plans to hire 3,500 to 4,500 employees for compliance with the law ("Germany approves plans to fine social media firms up to €50m," 2017). In 2018, France was considering similar legislation aimed at shielding the country from disinformation.

Such legislative mechanisms could go far to diminish the effects of hate speech and disinformation, particularly in jurisdictions with economic heft and a relatively well-developed and effective legal system. In both Germany and the United States, companies are relatively likely to comply because they value access to these large commercial markets. They also likely fear that the German and American legal systems could take action against their locally held assets.

Even in less developed environments, content created and hosted abroad could be addressed locally if local content hosts and internet Service Providers (ISPs) are ultimately held liable as the in-country actor that participated in the publication to the greatest degree—i.e., the entity that local authorities are best able to reach, even if not the one that was originally the publisher. It is important to note that efforts to establish such intermediary liability—or liability by an ISP or content host that did not actually publish the content—have been met with resistance, though they have survived legal scrutiny in a number of cases. One seminal decision on this issue was that of the European Court of Human Rights in 2015, in the case of Delfi AS v. Estonia, where the court upheld a fine against an Estonian news site for the posting of online comments by a user.

Notwithstanding any such legal precedent, the German law also continues to be subject to significant criticism from press freedom and other civil groups for its potential unintended negative consequences, such as encouraging self-censorship or putting greater pressure on tech companies to preemptively censor content. There are also concerns that this kind of heavy-handed legislation could be mimicked in countries with authoritarian-minded governments. In fact, a new Russian law, which closely resembles the German legislation, was slated to go into effect in 2018, prompting serious concerns among activists in that country (Efstathiou, Niko, and Bebe Santa-Wood 2017).

What these recent events make clear is that such regulatory or legal approaches to hate speech and disinformation in the digital age are not a universal prescription. In jurisdictions that are unwilling to establish such laws (because of a particularly strong tradition of protecting the freedom of expression) or that would be unable to enforce them if enacted (because of technological and jurisdictional limitations, coupled with relatively smaller economic market power or less developed legal systems), they are unlikely to succeed. And in countries with weak governmental accountability or a legacy of authoritarianism, they are likely to be abused.

Promoting Facts Without Legal Restrictions

There are, however, alternative approaches to legal restrictions that have been refined by practitioners of media development. The following is a brief summary of several projects where my organization, Albany Associates, has attempted to address the issue of hate speech and disinformation without the imposition of new legal restrictions.

Training Journalists and Editors in Fact-based Reporting

Training journalists to improve their reporting techniques is nothing new, and numerous organizations have done this for many years around the globe, with the goal of improving the accuracy and reliability of media. Albany has worked in Kazakhstan and Kyrgyzstan to improve reporting through a project funded by the U.K. Foreign and Commonwealth Office—with the specific goal of enhancing fact-checking skills.

In the Central Asian former-Soviet republics, as is the case in many parts of the world, a combination of self-censorship and low professional standards continues to prevent progress in the media sector. Many journalists in the region draw much of their reporting from press releases without verifying it against other sources. To make matters worse, coverage of international events is generally poor or one-sided. For example, information about the ongoing conflict in Ukraine is often based entirely on Russian-sympathizing sources. The effects of biased and inaccurate information are exacerbated by low levels of media literacy, with audiences having little awareness of the role or responsibilities of the media in a democratic society.

With this in mind, Albany developed a training program that builds upon traditional journalism training curricula—including basic instruction on proper news reporting, distinguishing fact from opinion, and seeking confirmation and alternative view points from reliable Russian language sources—and emphasizing fact-checking. In this training program, instructors discuss the information ecology in the context of the rise of the internet, citizen journalism, and social media. Participants, chosen from multiple media outlets in the region, play interactive games to discern fake from real news in order to demonstrate the effects of unreliable information. Debunking and fact-checking techniques are discussed in great depth, with trainers from well-known Russian language media teaching participants how to use certain web-based, readily available tools to verify the accuracy of photos, video, and text.

Additionally, a trainer from Bellingcat—an online investigative site (www.bellingcat.com)—was invited to discuss how to use online open-source information, crowd sourcing, and other digital tools to unearth the truth and create a more comprehensive picture of events. Participants were shown how to uncover facts where governments and armed groups provide little or no information about bombings, tortures, corruption, and other such activities that are in the public interest. Bellingcat highlighted examples of how it investigated incidents like the downing of the Malaysian Airlines flight over Ukraine, the failed coup attempt in Turkey, and airstrikes in the Middle East.

The program is designed to have impact well beyond the individuals who participate. A significant component (as is often the case in such training programs) is to train these participants as trainers so that they can impart these techniques to others within or outside their media organizations. Follow up work in media outlets' editorial offices is designed to ensure that the techniques are incorporated in their editorial practices. And, a training video in Russian and English, as well as in Kyrgyz and Kazakh, is being developed excerpting key learning points from the program and will be widely made available. The project will measure how well all of these techniques are accepted and sustained by the local organizations.

Albany's partner on the project, IREX Europe (http://irex-europe.fr/), is also working to improve the audience's ability to discern between unreliable and fact-based reporting in the region by, for example, assisting professors in including media literacy in their curricula and training local librarians in media literacy skills. The project thus has the comprehensive aims of making the information reported more accurate, as well as helping the public to digest it.

Advising on Guidelines for Media Reporting During Conflict

In Ukraine, I worked as part of a team of experts on an initiative led by Internews with the goal to develop a set of guidelines in consultation with media organizations and others representative of voices across the conflict. Specific issues that journalists there have raised include how to work in conflict zones (e.g., how to interact with the military and how to address military secrets) and, perhaps more importantly, how to define and confront propaganda from Russian sources.

Regarding the latter, the project acknowledges that there is no silver bullet, no single guideline that can or should be put in place to limit "propaganda." There is not agreement on a definition of the term in jurisprudence of the European Court of Human Rights or other relevant international law (Propaganda and Freedom of the Media, 2015). Rather, the subject is most commonly addressed through other international standards, namely those regarding accuracy, impartiality, hate speech and incitement to violence (which are longstanding and well-developed); and, the draft guidelines recognize this. The project is designed to arrive at self-regulatory standards, rather than heavy-handed statutory enforcement.

One major challenge of the project is that stakeholders on the ground expressly desire more concrete guidance for addressing Russian propaganda than European case law and other international law can currently provide. With that mind, the project aims to take the discussion beyond the norms set out in international law, and attempt to apply them to the Ukrainian context, by creating a consultative "living document" online where those who are interested can exchange ideas and provide comment. At a minimum the project will thus establish a platform for discussing some of the thorniest issues of media during conflict, with the open input of both local stakeholders working across the conflict and international observers.

Disseminating Fact-based Information to Diminish the Effects of Disinformation

In times where disinformation is widespread, the provision of accurate information, based on facts, must be supported. This is, of course, not a new idea; nor, can it combat disinformation on its own. As one expert has recognized:

> The traditional answer to the spread of bad information has been to inject good information into the mix, on the assumption that the truth would rise to the top. But in a world of trolls and bots, where simple facts are instantly countered by automated agents, this strategy may not be adequate. It is unclear how effectively democratic societies can continue to deliberate and function, and how hostile foreign actors can be identified and neutralized (Fukuyama, 2017).

Notwithstanding that caveat, disseminating facts in a trustworthy manner is still a valuable tool, and one that has the benefit of honesty. Publishing the truth is undoubtedly in the public interest, and a goal that donors and implementers can feel good about. As another expert has noted: "It is important to keep a focus on goals, objectives and our own values. Deception is often detrimental in the long term, and the costs to reputations can be severe. In one study asking people to rank traits, the one ranked lowest from a total of over 500 was "liar"" (Hancock 2017).

The value of such a fact-based approach was illustrated in Somalia where Albany assisted the African Union forces there (AMISOM) in media relations and communications strategy. The project required capacity building for spokespeople, assisting media outlets in coming to Somalia and providing photographic and video content for distribution globally. Perhaps most importantly, it also included strategic advice on messaging and narrative.

Taking control of the narrative was a key goal, and instrumental in changing how AMISOM was perceived in comparison with the terrorist group al-Shabaab that it was fighting. Initially, al-Shabaab was successful in presenting itself as a locally conceived rebellion against the international aggression that it alleged

AMISOM represented. Over time, through online campaigns and other stakeholder outreach, the project was able to (truthfully) frame al-Shabaab as a foreign force linked to the international terrorist network of al Qaeda. Once this was established in the media narrative, and al-Shabaab began to be consistently branded as "foreign fighters," it became more difficult for the group to discredit AMISOM.

In Albany's experience, a key issue in determining the efficacy of a public information campaign is timing. Unfortunately, public information projects are often established only after the damage has been done, and where a public information campaign is considered only as a way to make a regain. Instead, campaigns should be designed to present key factual information before disinformation starts to take a toll. One can think of this like a bank account: positive credit should be built from the beginning and over time, so that this credit will act as a foundation that mitigates the challenges as the debits come in, through disinformation or otherwise.

Disinformation is a pervasive problem. It is not something unique to the Central Asian, Ukrainian or Somali context, but rather is a topic with which the entire world is currently grappling, even obsessed. For the time being, no single legislative, regulatory, or capacity building solution will solve it. Instead, donors, media professionals and others interested in media development assistance will need to consider the broad range of tools available to them, including those mentioned here, and other fixes—perhaps technological—yet to be developed.

Notes

1. The term "fake news" here refers to both misinformation and disinformation. As discussed by University of Michigan Library Research Guides: "The universe of 'fake news' is much larger than simply false news stories. Some stories may have a nugget of truth, but lack any contextualizing details. They may not include any verifiable facts or sources. Some stories may include basic verifiable facts, but are written using language that is deliberately inflammatory, leaves out pertinent details or only presents one viewpoint. … 'Fake news' exists within a larger ecosystem of mis- and disinformation. Misinformation is false or inaccurate information that is mistakenly or inadvertently created or spread; the intent is not to deceive. Disinformation is false information that is deliberately created and spread 'in order to influence public opinion or obscure the truth'" (https://www.merriam-webster.com/dictionary/disinformation). *"Fake News," Lies and Propaganda: How to Sort Fact from Fiction*, University of Michigan Library Research Guides, http://guides.lib.umich.edu/fakenews.
2. See discussion of the history of the term "fake news" at https://www.merriam-webster.com/words-at-play/the-real-story-of-fake-news.

3. See "Key Senator Wants to See Social Media Companies Make 3 Changes to Election Ads." *CNBC,* 4 October 2017. Online: https://www.cnbc.com/2017/10/04/mark-warner-wants-to-see-facebook-change-election-ads.html

Recommended for Further Reading

Persily, Nathaniel. 2017. "Can Democracy Survive the Internet?" *Journal of Democracy* 28 (2): 63–75.

Wardle, Claire. February 16, 2017. "Fake News. It's Complicated," *First Draft.* https://firstdraftnews.com/fake- news-complicated/.

Woolley, Samuel, and Philip N. Howard. 2017. *Computational Propaganda Worldwide: Executive Summary.* Oxford: Computational Propaganda Research Project Working Paper.

References

Allcott, Hunt, and Matthew Gentzkow. 2017. "Social Media and Fake News in the 2016 Election." *Journal of Economic Perspectives* 31 (2): 211–36.

Booth, Robert, Matthew Weaver, Alex Hern, Stacee Smith, and Shaun Walker. November 14, 2017. "Russia Used Hundreds of Fake Accounts to Tweet about Brexit, Data Shows." *The Guardian,* accessed December 21, 2017. https://www.theguardian.com/world/2017/nov/14/how-400-russia-run-fake-accounts-posted-bogus-brexit-tweets.

Dewey, Caitlin. November 17, 2016. "Facebook Fake-News Writer: 'I Think Donald Trump Is in the White House Because of Me.'" *The Washington Post,* accessed Dec. 21. 2017. https://www.washingtonpost.com/news/the-intersect/wp/2016/11/17/facebook-fake-news-writer-i-think-donald-trump-is-in-the-white-house-because-of-me/?utm_term=.543764718c31.

Efstathiou, Niko, and Bebe Santa-Wood. August 30, 2017. "Germany's Fight Against Fake News: Can It Work?" CIMA Blog (web log), accessed December 19, 2017. https://www.cima.ned.org/blog/germanys-fight-fake-news-can-work/.

"Fake News," Lies and Propaganda: How to Sort Fact from Fiction. University of Michigan Library Research Guides. http://guides.lib.umich.edu/fakenews.

Fox, Amos, and Andrew Rossow. 2017. "Making Sense of Russian Hybrid Warfare: A Brief Assessment of the Russo-Ukrainian War." The Land Warfare Papers, No. 112 (The Institute of Land Warfare).

Fukuyama, Francis. May 2017. "Foreword: Public Diplomacy in a Post-Truth Society." In *Can Public Diplomacy Survive the Internet?, Bots, Echo Chambers, and Disinformation,* edited by Shawn Powers and Markos Kounalak is, 1. U.S. Advisory Commission on Public Diplomacy, Washington DC. https://www.state.gov/documents/organization/271028.pdf.

GeoPoll and Portland Communications. 2017. "The Reality of Fake News in Kenya," Nairobi.

Hancock, Jeffrey T. May 2017. "Psychological Principles for Public Diplomacy in an Evolving Information Ecosystem," *Can Public Diplomacy Survive the Internet?, Bots, Echo Chambers and Disinformation*, edited by Shawn Powers and Markos Kounalakis, 52. U.S. Advisory Commission on Public Diplomacy, Washington DC. https://www.state.gov/documents/organization/271028.pdf.

Ismail, Jamal Abdi and James Deane. 2008. "The Kenyan 2007 Elections and Their Aftermath: The Role of Media and Communication," *BBC World Service Trust Policy Briefing*, 1: 1–16.

Kollanyi, Bence, Philip N. Howard, and Samual C. Wooley. 2016. *Bots and Automation over Twitter during the U.S. Election*. Oxford, UK: Computational Propaganda Research Project Working Paper.

OSCE. November 26, 2015. "Propaganda and Freedom of the Media." Non-paper of the OSCE Office of the Representative on Freedom of the Media, Vienna, 31. http://www.osce.org/fom/203926.

Pramuk, Jacob. 4 October 2017. "Key Senator Wants to See Social Media Companies Make 3 Changes to Election Ads." *CNBC News*. https://www.cnbc.com/2017/10/04/mark-warner-wants-to-see-facebook-change-election-ads.html.

Staff and Agencies. 30 June 2017. "Germany Approves Plans to Fine Social Media Firms up to €50m," *The Guardian*. https://www.theguardian.com/media/2017/jun/30/germany-approves-plans-to-fine-social-media-firms-up-to-50m.

Woolley, Samuel, and Philip N. Howard. 2017. *Computational Propaganda Worldwide: Executive Summary*. Oxford: Computational Propaganda Research Project Working Paper

CHAPTER NINE

Gender, Research, and Media Development

A Feminist Perspective on Media Structures

CAROLYN M. BYERLY

To assure greater gender integration into the strategies and programs for national development, advocates have called for the media development sector to bring greater empirical rigor to their work (Aryal and LaMay 2013, 3). This call for closer alignment between media scholarship and media practice suggests the need for communication research in the service of women's empowerment. The questions, "What kind of information is needed?" and "How might media be used to integrate gender into local and national development?" move us closer to both scholarly and practical agendas to enlarge women's voice, visibility, and economic and political status through communication programs. We will try to attend to all of these issues in the following discussion, paying particular attention to why gender relations within the larger media landscape is a prerequisite to effective media development that incorporates principles of gender equality.

The arguments for this approach are many. Leaders for women's rights have long understood that women's access to the public sphere was a prerequisite for full social and political participation, and that news media form was an essential component of the public sphere. Increasing women's presence and authority within news organizations, thus, matter under the assumption that women would then be in a position to guide inclusion of women as news subjects, as well as encourage the hiring and advancement of additional women. For example, proponents of gender equality in Southern Africa's newsrooms have pointed out the critical need for equipping women with the skills, strategies and confidence to move to greater levels of decision making within their media companies. These skills could be acquired either in a variety of ways (e.g., through journalist unions or professional associations, through non-governmental-sponsored trainings, or by news organizations themselves). Such is surely needed, as research shows, in nations of Southern Africa women presently comprise only 23 percent of those in top management of news companies (Milosevic n.d., para. 7). This figure mirrors the situation of women in journalism in other regions of the world. *The Global Report on the Status of Women in News Media* (Byerly 2011), which surveyed 522 news companies in 59 nations, found that women occupied only a fourth of the positions in top management and governance roles across the world—positions of authority most able to determine pro-equality policies within news companies and the news they create. As Table 9.1 shows, the situation was particularly dire in some nations of Africa. Table 9.1, with selected data from the *Global Report*, indicates that in Egypt, Cameroon, Democratic Republic of Congo, and Jordan women have made minimal progress advancing to positions of authority within the news companies surveyed. This contrasts with Namibia and Uganda, where women have made more noticeable progress. The explanations for these differences in gender relations are both

Table 9.1. Women's representation in governance and top management of news companies in selected African nations.

Nation & Number of Companies Surveyed	Occupational Level	Number of Individuals	% Women
Egypt (6)	Governance	32	12.5
	Top Management	20	20.0
Cameroon (5)	Governance	6	16.7
	Top Management	8	0.0
Democratic Republic of Congo (12)	Governance	28	19.9
	Top Management	34	14.7
Jordan (10)	Governance	59	11.9
	Top Management	25	12.0
Namibia (9)	Governance	34.8	34.8
	Top Management	10	50.0
Uganda (8)	Governance	31	48.4
	Top Management	22	50.0

Source: Byerly, Carolyn M. (2011). *Global Report on the Status of Women in News Media*. Washington, D.C.: International Women's Media Foundation.

structural and historical, and the lessons emerge for those in media development to consider.

Factors Toward Women's Progress in Newsrooms

Explanations for women's greater advancement in news companies, even in developing nations where resources may be fewer and politics unstable, are offered by feminist journalists and scholars. Nghidinwa (2013), a former journalist turned development specialist, explains that before its independence from South Africa in 1990, Namibia "lacked a systematic agenda for gender development" (p. 304). However, a variety of economic and social factors, which included the active involvement of women in the struggle for Namibia's independence, created the conditions for opportunities for girls and women of all races. The author identifies the product of these conditions as the adoption of the Namibian Constitution containing gender-neutral language and the prohibition of sex discrimination; and the passage of gender-related laws and policies, including the Married Persons Equality Act of 1996, the Affirmative Action (Employment) Act of 1998, and laws against sexual and domestic violence, among others (Nghidinwa 2013, 304).

Kaija (2013), the editor of a progressive newspaper in Uganda, similarly looks to recently adopted laws to explain the progress of women in her nation's news companies. The media were liberalized in 1992, and freedom of expression in journalism was bolstered in 2010 through a court decision declaring the law on sedition unconstitutional. The author notes that women's parity with men in the eight companies she surveyed for the *Global Report* reflects women's similar equal status in other aspects of that society. For example, Uganda is among the top 10 ranking nations in wage equality, and the nation has strong laws prohibiting employment discrimination. However, Kaija also notes women's history of excelling in news reporting on beats typically thought of as men's, namely politics and war, is something that has contributed to their advancement. In addition, women are nearly half of the members in the nation's Journalists Association, which is influential in promoting gender equality. Even so, she notes, women are leaving the field in troubling numbers due to a range of practices, including corruption (between some reporters and their sources) and news company policies that are unsupportive of women, particularly in relation to maternity leave and child care (Kaija 2013, 316–326).

Researchers in industrialized nations with greater gender parity in governance and top management of news companies also point to the importance of laws and structural supports. Edstrom (2013) and Ovrebo (2013), for example, observe that there has been a national social consensus for gender equality in their respective nations of Sweden and Norway for many decades. This has resulted in national-level pro-equality labor laws, laws requiring both maternal and paternal leave, and nationally-mandated, locally funded child care—all factors that have enabled women in all professions, including journalism, to advance (Edstrom 2013, 78–79). In addition, Sweden passed legislation between 1980 and 2009 to ensure equal opportunity and non-discrimination, even establishing a special ombudsman to assure compliance (82). However, even with structural guarantees for gender equality at the macro-level, challenges for women remain in journalism. Edstrom laments that today, still only 32 percent of the news subjects are women in the Swedish news media, showing an entrenched preference for male norms in defining who and what becomes newsworthy (87–88).

These few examples illustrate the importance of national-level political and legal mechanisms that help to advance women professionally, but they also suggest the importance of addressing cultural norms and values around gender. The lessons from this research for media development, advocates to work for national-level laws that require and guide gender equality to facilitate the movement of women into the top posts of journalism organizations, while also addressing long-standing cultural biases toward women. The second of these lessons will differ markedly by nation and regional, since they tend to be imbedded in interpersonal and institutional practices.

A Structural Approach to Strategy-Making

The discussion thus far has emphasized the importance of having national-level laws and policies on gender equality and equal employment in place to enable women's advancement in news organizations. Feminist scholars like Gallagher (2014) have also made the case for understanding the socioeconomic and legal contexts of media structures and processes if activists are to effect change (25).

A useful way to enter women's structural relationship to media is by delineating dimensions, or levels, of the media landscape and situating women within them. At the macro level, concerns are with where and to what extent women fit into the bigger picture of national political policy, as well as organizational policy, finance, ownership and governance within media enterprises. At the meso level, the focus is on women's employment and working conditions in media. And, at the micro level, researchers examine gendered portrayals in media content. From an activist perspective—i.e., one concerned with developing and engaging strategies for change—the situation of women's persistent marginalization in content and employment can best be addressed by discerning what the gender dynamics are for women in the macro-level of the media landscape. The greatest amount of both economic and political power resides in the macro-level of the media landscape, but it is at this level where the safeguards for gender equality are put into place. The data have been eerily consistent over the years. While women have advanced slowly into reporting, they remain largely marginal in within news enterprises at the decision-making levels where policies are set and news is defined. The results are felt at the meso- and micro-levels of employment strata and news content.

Both the absence of women in serious news and programming as well as stereotypical portrayals have been the foci of popular feminist protests and academic critiques since the 1970s. Tuchman (1978) deemed the problem of women's absence one of symbolic annihilation in the early research, a characterization still relevant today. The companion problem of stereotypes has typically included the hyper-sexualization of women (often in product advertisements), depictions of women as inferior to men, and the pigeonholing of women in traditional roles of caretakers and servants even in years when they began to move more forcefully into the workforce and other social roles in nearly all nations. The Global Media Monitoring Project (GMMP), conducted every five years since 1995, has shown the persistence of women's marginalization in media content as well as in creative media roles producing that content (e.g., as writers and editors) in this two-decade span. In the latest round examining both traditional and digital media in 114 nations, the GMMP found women to be central to only 10 percent of news stories (across all genres) and to represent only 24 percent of all news subjects. These figures are up a mere 9 percent over two decades ago. Women are particularly absent in news about government and the economy—two sectors in which women's interests are substantial and their activism has been immense. Women serve as sources in only 20 percent of stories that the GMMP examined (Global Media Monitoring Project, 2015). The report states that this invisibility of women in conventional news formats (i.e., broadcast and print) has also crossed over into digital media, with only 25 percent of the news websites examined worldwide containing news about women. The report shows that neither are women reporters making much progress in being able to cover serious news, either about women or otherwise. The GMMP research found that political and crime news are the two topics least reported by women in most regions of the world, with the exception of Asia and Latin America, where they account for only 36 percent and 38 percent of the bylines, respectively. In most other regions, the figures fall between 27 percent and 30 percent (Global Media Monitoring Project 2015).

Feminists since the 1970s have argued that increasing the percentage of women in decision making positions of media organizations would provide the critical mass needed to shift these patterns in news toward both greater quantities and more favorable portrayals of women. However, the critical mass is still far from reality in both industrialized and developing nations. Surveying 28 European nations, Ross and Padovani (2017) found that women held only 35 percent of the senior-level operations positions and 31 percent of the top-level positions, but less than a fourth of those in higher decision-making ranks of the 100 mostly news media companies they studied. Byerly's (2011) *Global Report on the Status of Women in News*, which was sponsored by International Women's Media Foundation, found that women had generally been able to advance into the higher ranks of reporting, editing, and broadcast programming, but there they hit a glass ceiling.

Both studies showed more progress in the Nordic and Eastern European regions, where women in authority positions of news and other media were closer to parity with or even surpassed men. Two of the Nordic nations, Sweden and Norway, have already been discussed in relation to women's progress and remaining challenges. Interestingly, women's advance to parity in the news companies of some Eastern European nations, particularly Bulgaria and Russia, was not due to the long struggle for gender and worker rights as in the Nordic nations, but rather to a system of feminization in the profession under Soviet occupation. Then, news organizations were closely censored by the state and employees were paid very little—both making journalism less appealing places to work for men (Byerly, 2013). More women thus reached positions in governance and senior editorial ranks, even though they did not gain greater authority over news content under a governmental system that exercised state control and censorship.

In Eastern European nations' news industries, women were already in place to help redefine and democratize journalism after independence movements following the fall of the Berlin wall in 1989. While there were no individual nations' reports from the GMMP on either Bulgaria or Russia for 2015, we can gain some insights from Nastasia and Nastasia (2013), whose research on those nations observes that women make lower salaries in newsrooms than men in these feminized occupations, and that other vestiges of institutional gender prejudice, including stereotyping in news, continue in these Eastern European nations (37).

Findings in larger news-oriented studies are affirmed by several smaller regional studies on developing nations. For example, research in Asia-Pacific showed that companies in that area of the world are "largely led and governed by men," and that most owners are men. In this study, like others, the glass ceiling lets women in only to the mid-level occupations in reporting, editing and programming (Asian Journalism Network n.d., para. 10).

Women and Media Consolidation

One macro-level phenomenon affecting women in news is media consolidation, something occurring through a process of larger and wealthier companies buying out smaller ones, or two larger companies merging to form even a greater sized company. Conglomeration through consolidation, which has drastically increased since the 1980s in nearly all nations of the world, has been enabled by national-level communication policies shaped by neoliberalism, a pro-corporate, anti-labor, and free press philosophy that spread across the globe in the 1970s among those with the greatest power and influence within global capitalism (Byerly 2017). The films, television programs, advertisements, and news these companies produce extend into both developed and developing nations carrying messages and images that affirm the philosophy of the wealthy elites they represent. Nichols and McChesney (2013) have observed that a key feature of oligopolistic economic systems, i.e., those dominated by a few elitist corporations, is that they squeeze out newcomers and small owners, making it impossible for them to enter or stay in the market. Byerly (2011) has shown how these policies resulted in the systematic exclusion of women's ownership in broadcast radio and television stations within the United States. However, as Table 9.2 illustrates, the problems of media policies affecting women's ownership are also evident elsewhere in the world—Brazil, Australia, Canada, Mexico, and many other nations (Byerly 2013).

Table 9.2 reveals the power of the largest nations in terms of what they own, what they are worth, and how many women have been allowed into the ownership and policy ranks. The level of political and economic control that the corporate heads of these eight huge companies exercise in terms of their market value, and the number and reach of their subsidiaries' products is staggering, but so is the incredible gender imbalance at the top. Women on these parent company boards range from 8 percent (at Google) to 33 percent at both Verizon and Disney. But, even if all of the women in the boardrooms of these companies favored gender equality in employment practices and media content, would they be able to exercise their views in the behavior of these companies? Would companies hire and advance more women in the media professions, would their news and films and television programs demonstrate progressive gender values? Even if the answer might be yes, earlier portions of this discussion cite research that suggests this is not happening, either in employment or the production of media content, from the major media companies today.

Table 9.2. Women's representation at policy level in large global media conglomerates.

Media Conglomerate	Head-quarters	Owner-ship	Estimated Assets (USD)	Total on Board of Directors	Number of Women	Percentage Women
Disney	USA	Investors	$72.1 billion (2011)	10	4	40%
News Corp	USA	Investors	$61.9 billion (2011)	17	1	6%
Vivendi	France	Investors	$55.7 billion (2011)	12	4	33%
Time Warner	USA	Investors	$48.3 billion (2011)	11	2	18%
Bertelsmann AG	Germany	Family	$27.0 billion (2012)	21	5	24%
Viacom	USA	Investors	$14.9 billion (2011)	11	2	18%
Grupo Televisa	Mexico	Investors	$14.7 billion (2011)	20	2	10%
Times of India Group	India	Family	$1 billion (2009)	9	3	33%
Lagardère	France	Investors	$10.9 billion (2011)	6	1	17%
Naspers	South Africa	Investors	$8.5 million (2010)	14	3	21%

Source: Byerly, Carolyn M. "Women and Media Control: Feminist Interrogations at the Macro Level." In Cynthia Carter, Linda Steiner and Lisa McLaughlin (Eds.), *The Routledge Companion to Media and Gender*. London and New York: Routledge Taylor and Francism 2014 (108).

Joining Research, Activism and Media Development

Media activism has expanded in response to public policies that have enabled the rise of media oligopoly and its misogynistic tendencies. Bennett (2017) emphasizes that digital technologies (e.g., the internet, Twitter) provide an expanding public sphere for media activists to find each other, develop strategies, and mobilize ways of both circumventing and confronting the huge political-economy of media monopoly. Bennett refers to the media reform movement that has emerged since the early 2000s in varied nations, a movement that he, Castells and others have also tracked and theorized. However, women have found it particularly difficult to enter into media activism and intervene in the power structures associated with media policy and media ownership in order to increase their access to both traditional and new digital media at the employment, policy, and ownership levels.

Women's media activism has a varied and incomplete story, and there is insufficient space here for a full account. However, some few relevant points are warranted. Women's liberation movements have spawned multiple forms of feminist media activism since the 1970s—some aimed at creating alternative spaces for women-owned communication, other with making bigger spaces within existing male-owned media through both professional participation and external pressure (Byerly and Ross 2006). There have also been legal challenges, seen clearly in the 1970s in the United States when women journalists used newly passed federal equality laws to overcome employment discrimination in news companies (Byerly and Valentin 2017). However, creating effective groups and strategies to confront the policies that enable male-domination in the industries, either at employment or policy levels, in a sustained way has been difficult for women, both within developed and developing nations. Women in the United States have been unsuccessful in creating or sustaining pressure groups on media employment and ownership policies (Byerly and Valentin 2017; Byerly 2017). Women in European nations have able to exert pressure on the European Union regarding equality in employment practices since the 1990s, but the responsiveness on the part of some member nations has been less enthusiastic (Ross and Padovani 2017).

A bright sign of progress comes from a developing nation in the collaboration by Mexican feminist media researchers and activist journalists who have used academic studies about gender discrimination in ownership and content of Mexican media to secure new federal level policy in 2014. That year Mexican legislators approved an overhaul of telecommunications statutes that included nine provisions guaranteeing the eradication of sexist stereotypes, promoting access to resources so women and youth could develop their own programming, and assuring balanced perspectives in content along gender lines, among other things. What the impact of that law will be is yet to be tracked and measured (Chaher 2016, 138–142).

Conclusion

Women would benefit if there were clearer and stronger working relationships among key players concerned about gender equality in media. At present, there are few networks among or opportunities for media scholars, media reform activists and development specialists to sit down together and consider how to align their issues, questions, knowledge, agendas and work. The example from Mexico shows good synergy between feminist researchers and media reform activists. It suggests that feminist media research could be driven by the needs of those on the ground developing strategies for better national-level communication policies, as well as assuring that women in local communities receive the information and voice they seek and need through media.

Media activists could similarly help to guide researchers by indicating what kind of data they need to formulate legislative or policy strategies related to women's equality. At the same time, those seeking to use available research on women and media to integrate gender equality more squarely into media development strategies must confront the reality of corporate power. There is a sizable body of critical media scholarship, including feminist scholarship, which shows the extent to which wealthy male elites have been able to control news and other media industries, with harmful effects for women at macro-, meso-, and micro-levels, in nations with commercial media systems. The owners of media conglomerates who profit so greatly from their holdings also derive great political power in being able to influence those in elective office and appointed positions. How to confront these broader, macro-level issues of gender relations remains a conundrum but one that must be addressed if women are to gain fuller access to media through employment and if media content is to shift toward fuller coverage by and about women.

The task remains for academic researchers, activist organizations, and media development specialists to create strategies and mechanisms, nation-by-nation, to address the systemic political, economic, and legal structures that prevent women's right to communicate.

Recommended for Further Reading

Bielby, Denise D. 2014. "Gender Inequality in Culture Industries. In *The Routledge Companion to Media and Gender*, edited by Cynthia Carter, Linda Steiner and Lisa McLaughlin, pp. 137–46. London and New York: Routledge Taylor and Francis.

Byerly, Carolyn M. (Ed.). 2013. *The Palgrave International Handbook of Women and Media*. Abingdon, U.K.: Palgrave Macmillan,.

———. 2011. *Global Report on the Status of Women in News Media*. Washington, D.C.: International Women's Media Foundation.

References

Aryal, Manisha, and Craig LaMay. 2013. *From Counting Women to Making Women Count: Focusing on Women in Media Development Programs*. Washington, D.C.: Internews.

Asian Journalism Network. Media and Gender. n.d. Retrieved from http://www.asianjournalismnetwork.org/our-work/media-and-gender/.

Bennett, Lance. 2017. "Foreword: What is Media Activism?" In *Media Activism in the Digital Age*, edited by Victor Pickard and Guobin Yang, xiv-xviii. Abingdon, U.K.: Routledge, Taylor and Francis Group.

Bielby, Denise D. 2013. "Gender Inequality in Culture Industries. In *The Routledge Companion to Media and Gender*, edited by Cynthia Carter, Linda Steiner and Lisa McLaughlin, 137–46. London and New York: Routledge Taylor and Francis.

Byerly, Carolyn M. 2011. Behind the Scenes of Women's Broadcast Ownership. *Howard Journal of Communication, 29*(3), 24–42.

Byerly, Carolyn M. 2011. *Global Report on the Status of Women in News Media*. Washington, D.C.: International Women's Media Foundation.

———, ed. 2013. *The Palgrave International Handbook of Women and Journalism*. Abingdon, U.K.: Palgrave Macmillan.

———. 2013. "Women and Media Control: Feminist Interrogations at the Macro-level." In *The Routledge Companion to Media and Gender*, edited by Cynthia Carter, Linda Steiner and Lisa McLaughlin, 105–115. London and New York: Routledge, Taylor and Francis Group.

———. 2017. "Feminist Activism and U.S. Communication Policy." In *Media Activism in the Digital Age*, edited by Victor Pickard and Guobin Yang, 100–119. London and New York: Routledge Taylor and Francis Group.

Byerly, Carolyn M. and Karen Ross. 2006. *Women and Media: A Critical Introduction*. Malden, MA: Blackwell.

Byerly, Carolyn M. and Alisa Valentin. 2017. "Women's Access to Media: Legal Dimensions of Ownership and Employment in the United States." In *Race and Gender in Electronic Media: Content, Context, Culture*, edited by Rebecca A. Lind, 267–92. New York and London: Routledge, Taylor & Francis Group.

Chaher, Sandra. 2017. "Politicas de género y comunicación en México a partir de la apbrobación de la Ley Federal de Telecomunicaciones y Radio Difusión en materia de igualdad de género." In *Entre andares y retrocesos*, edited by Sandra Chacher, 138–142. Buenos Aires, Argentina: Asociación Civil Comunicación para la igualdad y la Defensoría del Público de Servicios de Comunicación Audiovisual de Argentina.

Edstrom, Maria. 2013. Sweden: Women Reach Parity but Gender Troubles Persist. In *The Palgrave International Handbook of Women and Journalism*, edited by Carolyn M. Byerly, 78–91. Abingdon, UK: Palgrave Macmillan.

Finland-GMMP. *Global Media Monitoring Project 2015, National Report.* http://cdn.agilitycms.com/who-makes-the-news/Imported/reports_2015/national/Finland.pdf.

Gallagher, Margaret. 2014. "Media and the Representation of Gender." In *The Routledge Companion to Media and Gender* edited by Cynthia Carter, Linda Steiner and Lisa McLaughlin, 21–31. London and New York: Routledge Taylor and Francis.

Global Media Monitoring Project. 2015. *Who Makes the News?* "Highlights of Findings." World Association of Christian Communication. http://cdn.agilitycms.com/who-makes-the-news/Imported/reports_2015/highlights/highlights_en.pdf.

Kaija, Barbara. 2013. "Uganda: Women Near Parity but Still Leaving Newsrooms. In *The Palgrave International Handbook of Women and Journalism,* edited by Carolyn M. Byerly, 315–32. Basingstoke, U.K.: Palgrave Macmillan.

Milosevic, Mira. n.d. "We Must Keep Women Media Professionals Within the Media Sector." Women in News (WAN-IFRA African Media Leadership Programme. http://www.wan-ifra.org/articles/2012/12/12/we-must-keep-women-media-professionals-within-the-media-sector.

Nastasia, Sorin, and Nastasia, Diana Iulia. 2013. "Bulgaria: Cinderella Went to Market, with Consequences for Women Journalists." In *The Palgrave International Handbook on Women and Journalism, edited by Carolyn M. Byerly,* 27–38. Basingstoke U.K.: Palgrave Macmillan.

National Public Radio. *Who Owns What Brands in Digital Media.* http://www.npr.org/sections/alltechconsidered/2016/10/28/499495517/big-media-companies-and-their-many-brands-in-one-chart, October 28, 2016.

Nghidinwa, Maria Mboono. 2013. "Namibia: Women Make Strides in Post-independence Newsrooms." In *The Palgrave International Handbook of Women and Journalism,* edited by Carolyn M. Byerly, 301–314. Basingstoke, U.K.: Palgrave Macmillan.

Ovrebo, Turid. 2013. Norway: The Uncomfortable Gender Gap in News Media. In *The Palgrave International Handbook of Women and Journalism,* edited by Carolyn M. Byerly, 137–150. Abingdon, UK: Palgrave Macmillan.

Ross, Karen and Claudia Padovani. 2017. *Gender Equality and the Media: A Challenge for Europe.* New York and London: Routledge.

Sweden-GMMP. 2015. *Global Media Monitoring Project 2015: Nationell Rapport Sverige.* http://cdn.agilitycms.com/who-makes-the-news/Imported/reports_2015/national/Sweden.pdf.

Tuchman, Gaye. 1978. "The Symbolic Annihilation of Women by the Mass Media." In *Hearth and Home: Images of Women in the Mass Media,* edited by Gaye Tuchman, Arlene Kaplan Daniels and Steven Benét. New York: Oxford University Press.

CHAPTER TEN

Media Capture

Media Ownership, Oligarchs, and the Challenge of Developing Independent Media

MARIUS DRAGOMIR

Kennedy Agyapong, a member of parliament (MP) of the New Patriotic Party (NPP) from the Assin Central region of Ghana, is notorious for his wacky, often disparaging comments. In March 2017, he said that he would drink poison if Ibrahim Mahama, the brother of Ghana's former president John Mahama, was not put behind bars for corruption. In a separate development, the head of a major company in Ghana sued Agyapong, accusing him of "defamatory" comments. Agyapong said, without providing evidence, that the businessman was stashing some $100 million in a bank account. In yet another development, Agyapong said that Charlotte Osei traded sex to gain the position of Electoral Commissioner of Ghana. Outraged, human rights activists and women organizations asked Agyapong to apologize. He refused to do so. Agyapong gets away with such libelous remarks mainly thanks to his wealth and political influence. He reportedly owns more than a dozen companies, including an air-conditioner distribution chain, farms, and retail facilities. However, arguably the most valuable asset in his portfolio is his media business, Kencity Media, a company that manages media outlets such as Oman FM radio channel and Net2 TV. The media investment gives the Ghanaian MP a platform not only to air his ravings, but also to attack his foes or wax lyrical about his friends and allies.

Agyapong is not a singular case. A third of the media outlets in Ghana are owned either by the state or by people with close political affiliations, especially with high ranking officials, according to a study from the Reporters Without Borders (known by its French initials RSF), a Paris-headquartered NGO. (RSF 2017c). For example, Frederick Blay, who heads the NPP, the party of Agyapong, holds a majority stake in Western Publications, the publisher of *Daily Guide* and *News One* newspapers.[1]

Ghana is not an isolated example either. Rather, it is the epitome of a global trend where political groups and industry players work together, more tightly than ever before, to capture as much of the local media sector as possible.

Media Capture: What Is It?

A new media capture model is emerging where private resources and political influence are coupled to empower an emerging elite consisting of politicians and oligarchs (sometimes indistinguishable actors) to defend their positions in the echelons of power and wealth. The term was broadly used after the 2008 financial crisis to describe the failure of regulatory authorities to properly watchdog the financial institutions that were to blame for the crisis.

The term "capture" was originally coined by economists to describe "what happens when regulators become overly empathetic or supportive of those they are meant to be regulating" (Schiffrin 2017, 4). The terms circulated in other fields as well. It was for the first time used in relation to media in 2006 by Timothy Besley of the London School of Economics (LSE) and Andrea Prat of the Columbia Business School (Besley and Prat 2006).

Arguably the clearest definition was given by Alina Mungiu-Pippidi, a political scientist at the Hertie School of Governance in Berlin. She saw media capture as

> […] a situation in which the media have not succeeded in becoming autonomous in manifesting a will of their own, nor able to exercise their main function, notably in informing people. Instead, they have persisted in an intermediate state, with vested interests, and not just the government, using them for other purposes. (Mungiu-Pippidi 2013, 41)

A Typology of Captures

The marriage of private interests with political clout in the media is not new. One of its most infamous progenitors was Silvio Berlusconi in the 1990s and 2000s, four times in power as prime minister of Italy and owner of the media conglomerate Mediaset, through which he controlled a sheaf of media outlets, including

Italy's most popular TV channels (Curran 2011). Eastern European countries, following their transition from communism, have all move toward similar models where oligarchs and politicians have hand-in-glove built media outlets purely to serve their varied interests. Many of these companies were loss-incurring; but that was totally acceptable by their owners as they valued political influence more than economic profitability. Media and communication scholars called that phenomenon "instrumentalization" of the media (Hallin and Papathanassopoulos 2002; Nielsen 2012).

The growing influence of media-owning oligarchs in politics and government coupled with the surging participation of political actors in the media industry is a continuation of an older trend. However, the profound crisis in the media sector, a result of both the economic downturn after 2007, coupled with the rapid technological advancement that disrupted old media business models, has accentuated the instrumentalization of the media to unprecedented levels.

Over the past two decades, efforts to analyze levels of media ownership concentration and to map media owners and their links with political parties and the government have intensified.[2] These datasets offer useful indications on the concentration of power in the media sector.

However, to better understand the actual scope of oligarch-politician-led media capture and how it manifests, more nuanced typologies are needed. One of them, which I propose in this paper, is an "intent-based" typology. It basically analyzes the key motivations that drive groups of oligarchs and politicians to capture a media market. Four paradigms emerge as follows:

(a) Media capture aimed at suppressing dissent/criticism;
(b) Media capture aimed at concealing corruption/theft;
(c) Media capture aimed at winning elections; and
(d) Media capture aimed at improving public relations.

The four intents usually appear in combination. Some of them are more prevalent at certain times (i.e., elections) but cases of oligarch-politician-led media capture driven by one single intent are rare. The four paradigms are briefly described below.

Capture to Suppress Dissent

Warding off criticism or dissent is the classic reason behind efforts aimed at capturing the media space. Governments and politicians are traditionally averse to critique, but in a captured environment, with the support of oligarchs, intolerant leaders have a spate of tools available to silence dissenting voices and critical journalism.

In Hungary, the opposition newspaper, *Nepszabadsag*, was suspended in October 2016 by its owners, the company Mediaworks, which is controlled by Vienna Capital Partners (VCP). The decision was allegedly endorsed by VCP's head, Heinrich Pecina, a controversial Austrian businessman (Dragomir 2017). Three weeks later, the *Nepszabadsag* brand was purchased by Opimus, a company that was reportedly under the influence of Lorinc Meszaros, a local oligarch known for his old friendship with the country's prime minister, Viktor Orban. The newspaper was the biggest opposition publication with a nationwide coverage in Hungary (Dragomir 2017).

The dissent-repellant paradigm is particularly relevant in countries with a long tradition of authoritarianism and dictatorship. In Zimbabwe, a country of 16 million that was under the iron-fist rule of Robert Mugabe for three decades, the media industry welcomed the launch in 2017 of new media products by Zimpapers and AB Communications, two of the country's largest media players.[3] However, some saw in the expansion an issue of concern. "It is those with resources that are not only spreading their wings across differing media platforms (newspaper to radio to television) but are also beginning to have uniform editorial policies that disable media diversity and in the final analysis determine what is 'news' in favor of their own political or economic interests," said media activist Takura Zhangazha (Ndlovu 2017).

Nonetheless, with the advent of online platforms and increased access to content, governments and oligarchs have to cope with growing criticism. Thus, they become more sophisticated and pragmatic and are increasingly shifting their attention to more specific goals when they embark on media capture projects.

Capture to Hide Corruption

One of the key drivers behind capture of media markets is the need to hide acts of corruption in which both governments and oligarchs are involved. The ever-tightening relations between oligarchs and governments are driven by common, mostly economic, interests. Oligarchs need the government not only to adopt policies and legislation protecting and promoting their business interests as much of their income is generated through public contracts, particularly in lucrative sectors such as infrastructure construction, mobile communications, or extractive industries. Public procurement is generally a corruption-laden process. Accusations of non-transparent awards of public orders abound. Because of media capture, few of these cases are documented or made public in the media. In Hungary, only investigative reporting outlets, *Atlatszo* and *Direkt36*, financed by foundations or through crowdfunding, publish such reports. However, their audience is small compared to the mainstream media in the country. Some 90 percent of the Hungarian media, following a string of shady deals, ended up in the hands of oligarchs close to the party in power, the conservative Fidesz. (Dragomir LSE Blog 2017)

In Mongolia, corruption is the main motivation for politicians to invest in the media. Most of the country's broadcast channels owned by members of the Democratic Party won their licenses during the party's time in power between 2004 and 2008, according to RSF (RSF 2017d). In spite of a few groundbreaking investigative reports that unveiled corruption, many of the shady deals politicians and oligarchs are involved in are out of the public eye. "Mongolian media tend to shy away from investigative reporting, from the difficult-to-prove stories," according to Mongolian journalist Lkhagva Erdene. "The truth stands no chance against voices silenced by owners, advertisers, and government" (RSF 2017d).

Capture to Sway Elections

Efforts to capture the media intensify mostly during electoral campaigns. Depending on the local context, this process starts one or two years before elections. Oligarchs, much reliant on funding from public coffers, have become a major player in this process.

Attacks on independent media before elections take numerous forms, including regulatory measures and legal provisions that hurt media companies critical of the government or lawsuits against editors and journalists. Nonetheless, media owners play an equally crucial role in the electoral game by buying, jointly with politicians and officials or on their behalf, wads of media assets.

In August 2017, *Cambodia Daily*, an English-language newspaper known for its critical stance towards government, was hit with a $6.3 million fine for back taxes. Failing to pay it, the newspaper ceased operations in September 2017. Hun Sen, a former Khmer Rouge commander who has been in power for over three decades called the newspaper's publishers "thieves." The move was widely believed to be politically motivated as elections are slated to take place in Cambodia in 2018 (Ponniah).

In Malaysia, mainstream media have been fully captured by the government. They include newspapers such as the *New Straits Times* and *Utusan Malaysia*, which have ownership links with the ruling coalition, and Media Prima, the largest owner of media assets including the popular TV3 channel, a slew of radio stations and three newspapers including the most popular paper, the Malay-language tabloid *Harian Metro*, which is also owned by people close to the political power. (Dragomir 2016).

Capture as a PR Machine

For decades, companies have been investing in media, not for economic reasons, but mainly to support other lines of business. Increasingly in the past decade, media investments ceased to be profit-driven, but are seen by companies as influence-gathering assets.

In Cambodia, a third of the 27 major media owners are involved in industries other than media. Four of the key media owners command through their channels more than three quarters of the country's nationwide TV viewership.[4] Many of these oligarchs use their media outlets "as channels for advertising their other business activities" (RSF 2017a).

In Colombia, Carlos Ardila Lulle owns more than 50 companies across an array of industries including communications and entertainment, finance and insurance, real estate, and automotive sectors. He also owns the country's largest radio chain by number of stations and the TV channel with the largest audience[5] (RSF 2017b).

This trend started to become more marked a decade or so ago. The links of media owners with other businesses "have a negative impact on editorial independence, because the owners use their outlets to advance their other business interests rather than to serve their viewers," according to a 2005 study from the Open Society Foundations (OSF 2005). That was the case back in mid-2000s in some transition countries in Eastern Europe, including Romania, Albania, Serbia, and the Republic of Macedonia as well as Turkey. Since then, the links between circles of oligarchs and political groups have strengthened significantly across Eastern Europe where, today, hardly any investments in media companies bring any returns at all.

Back to Policy?

The role of governments in the media has massively increased during the past decade. Governments today spend high record amounts of money in the media either in the form of public funding doled out to state-administered media outlets or in advertising dollars spent on friendly private media outlets. Such cash infusions, made through dysfunctional mechanisms and without clear criteria, badly distort media markets. The support from wealthy oligarchs further cements the control of the media by these elites leading to a state of capture where the entry of new journalistic outlets is nearly impossible and existing independent media can barely survive.[6]

Governments and representatives of the political class are increasingly involved in the private media through alliances with oligarchs and their companies, their control often exceeding three-quarters of the market, according to data gathered in 20 countries from all over the world by CEU Center for Media, Data and Society (CMDS).[7] This is becoming the most common media model across many nations in the world.

Over the course of the past five to ten years, the media capture process has been carried out in a more systematic manner than any time before. In countries ranging from Malaysia to Hungary to the Philippines to Cambodia to Ghana, oligarch-politician-controlled media groups have been created according to carefully designed plans. In Cambodia, out of 27 key media owners, at least 11 are on the government payroll or affiliated to the ruling party (RSF 2017a). Five of them own at least eight TV stations that together command two-thirds of the country's viewership. In Mongolia, a staggering 74 percent of media outlets have political affiliations.

In such environments, developing independent media is a major challenge. When it comes to funding, philanthropy is sometimes seen as a solution, but donors remain a minor player, unable to compete with governments or oligarchs. Other media organizations, funded through subscriptions or donations from individuals can hardly match the financial power of the groups behind mainstream media companies.

The solution should thus be sought through media policy reforms and efforts to raise public awareness and accountability. The growth of government-oligarchs-owned media was made possible by a system anchored in a set of rules that allow for indiscriminate spending of public money in the media, unfair licensing of media outlets, and non-transparent, often illegal media deals. Building a consensus for an effective plan of action to reform the media ecosystem in a country will require a broad movement to build support from civil society, the private sector, and lawmakers. The aim of such movements include strengthening oversight of government regulators, creating an informed and engaged civil society that pressures government and holds media owners accountable, and introducing incentives for a media industry that acts in the public interest.[8]

Revamping the rules on spending public money where civil society should have a say, should be the most urgent ask on media activists' agenda. This is going to be an arduous task as governments are not going to easily relinquish their control over allocation of public resources in the media and are traditionally opposed to mechanisms that would ensure transparency in decision-making on public money allocation. However, with civil society more connected than ever and groups increasingly calling for accountability in public funding management, pressure on governments is mounting.

The basis for developing new policies for fair and transparent public funding in the media should be a combination of the following:

- Criteria for disbursement of public funding that would not be politically biased (such as types of served audiences or types of content produced by media outlets)
- Guarantees that public funding would not hurt the independence and editorial freedom of media outlets (such as contractual terms that explicitly delink editorial policies of funded media outlets from the size or purpose of the public funding allocations)
- Transparent mechanisms for funding allocation (including registries and databases where all government's financial awards to the media would be publicly accessible)
- Rules that would ensure allocation of public funding to the media in an equitable and fair manner to avoid market distortion (such as caps on yearly allocations or contractual terms that would specify the causal link between the size of ad spending and the actual audience impact)
- Creation of governance structures around public media fund management that would be politically diverse and include also experts and civil society (such as supervisory committees that would include representatives of all key political parties as well as unaffiliated industry experts or professional associations).

These principles can be further developed and adapted, depending on the local context. They will lead to a variety of policy models as no one-fits-all solution can be designed to address the sheer specificities of local contexts, including economic development, societal values, technological development, and the state of journalism.

At a time when the funding crisis in journalism is becoming more and more profound, a progressive policy package that would spawn a fair and transparent use of taxpayer money in the media could turn out to an essential response to the crisis and offer a workable model of funding independent journalism; indirectly, it would make many news media less prone to capture.

Notes

1. The other politically affiliated media owners include: Dr. Kwabena Duffour who served as Minister of Finance in the National Democratic Congress government; Gabby

Otchere-Darko (The Statesman) who is a member of the New Patriotic Party (NPP) and a cousin of the President of the Republic of Ghana, Nana Akufo-Addo; Kwaku Baako Jnr. (*New Crusading Guide*) who is a member of the Conventions Peoples Party (CPP); Kwasi Sainti Baffoe-Bonnie (Gold TV, Radio Gold, MontieFM) who served in the government of the former president, President John Mahama; Dr. Kwesi Oteng (Angel FM, Angel TV) whose daughter, Franscisca Oteng Mensah, is the NPP Member of Parliament for Kwabre East; Kofi Coomson (*The Chronicle*) who is a friend of President Nana Akufo Addo.

2. Since the early 2000s, organizations such as Open Society Foundations (OSF), Reporters Without Borders (RSF), Center for International Media Assistance (CIMA) at the National Endowment for Democracy (NED), World Association of Newspapers (WAN-IFRA), have led multi-year projects monitoring media ownership.
3. Zimpapers publishes nine newspaper titles, two magazines and one regional newspaper. Its newspapers include The Herald, The Chronicle and H-Metro. The company also owns broadcaster Star FM. AB Communications is a company invested mainly in broadcasting, owner among other assets of the ZiFM Stereo and the TV production company Mighty Movies.
4. The Royal Group alone has nearly half of the television audience in Cambodia through its media vehicle Cambodia Broadcasting Service (CBS).
5. The broadcasters owned by Lulle include the TV channels Canal RCN, NTN24, Nuestra Tele and MundoMax. He also owns the radio station RCN Radio, among a dozen of other radio channels. Through his media groups, Lulle owns nearly 20 digital media.
6. In 2016, for example, the government of Hungary increased its advertising spending by 80 percent year on year, a staggering increase that according to local experts bolstered the government's leading position among the largest ad spenders in the country. (See MTI-Econews, "Advertising spending in Hungary continues to rise, says MRSZ," accessed 20 October 2017, https://bbj.hu/economy/advertising-spending-in-hungary-continues-to-rise-says-mrsz_129487). On television alone, the government spent HUF 6.3bn (EUR 5.1m) in advertising, which was roughly 12 percent of the total TV ad spend in the country. On top of ad spending, Hungarian government allocates from the state budget over EUR 250m a year to MTVA, the public broadcaster. The exact figure for 2016 was not made public. For 2017, the government approved a total budget for MTVA of EUR 258.5m. (See "Hungarian state media to have daily budget of over EUR 700,000 in 2017," accessed 20 October 2017, http://hungarytoday.hu/news/hungarian-state-media-daily-budget-e700000-2017). An independent news outlet in Hungary, like Atlatszo, spends in one year half the amount the country's public TV spends in one day.
7. At the time of writing, the Center for Media, Data and Society (CMDS) at CEU, a university in Budapest, is running a research project collecting data on government (public) spending in the media aimed at mapping the key trends in state financing of media companies.
8. For a discussion of media policy reform processes to address media capture see Mark M. Nelson, "What is to be done? Options for combating the menace of media capture," in

Anya Schiffrin, ed., *In the Service of Power: Media Capture and the Threat to Democracy, 2017, pp. 143162.*

Recommended for Further Reading

Besley, Timothy, and Andrea Prat. 2006. "Handcuffs for the Grabbing Hand? Media Capture and Government Accountability." *American Economic Review* 96 (3): 720–36.

Mungiu-Pippidi, Alina. 2013. "Freedom without Impartiality: The Vicious Circle of Media Capture." In *Media Transformations in the Post-Communist World*, edited by Peter Gross and Karol Jakubowicz, 33–48. Plymouth, UK: Lexington Books.

Nelson, Mark N. 2017. "What Is to Be Done? Options for Combating the Menace of Media Capture." In *In the Service of Power: Media Capture and the Threat to Democracy,* edited by Anya Schiffrin, 143-62. Washington, DC: Center for International Media Assistance.

References

Besley, Timothy, and Andrea Prat. 2006. "Handcuffs for the Grabbing Hand? Media Capture and Government Accountability." *American Economic Review* 96 (3): 720–36.

Curran, James. 2011. *Media and Democracy*. New York, NY: Routledge. 18–21.

Dragomir, Marius. 2016. "Malaysiakini Under Fire" *Media Power Monitor*. Accessed 20 August 2017. http://mediapowermonitor.com/content/malaysiakini-under-fire.

———. 2017. "The State of Hungarian media; Endgame" Media Policy Project blog, London School of Economics and Political Science. Accessed 25 August 2017. http://blogs.lse.ac.uk/mediapolicyproject/2017/08/29/the-state-of-hungarian-media-endgame/.

Hallin, Daniel C. & Stylianos Papathanassopoulos. 2002. "Political Clientelism and the Media: Southern Europe and Latin America in Comparative Perspective." *Media, Culture & Society* 24 (2): 175–95.

Mungiu-Pippidi, Alina. 2013. "Freedom without Impartiality: The Vicious Circle of Media Capture." In *Media Transformations in the Post-Communist World*, edited by Peter Gross and Karol Jakubowicz, 3348. Plymouth, UK: Lexington Books.

Ndlovu, Faith. 2017. "Zimbabwe media capture" *Bulawayo24*. Accessed 1 August 2017. http://bulawayo24.com/opinion/columnist/114970.

Nielsen, Rasmus Klein. February 17, 2012. "The Rendell Inquirer? The Specter of the Instrumentalization of American News Media." *Nieman Lab*. Accessed 4 August 2017. http://www.niemanlab.org/2012/02/the-rendell-inquirer-the-specter-of-the-instrumentalization-of-american-news-media/.

Ponniah, Kevin. August 24, 2017. "Cambodia Leader Tells Critics to Pay Up, or Pack Up." *BBC News*. Accessed 2 August 2017. http://www.bbc.com/news/world-asia-41025255.

Reporters Without Borders (RSF). 2017a. Media Ownership Monitor Cambodia. Accessed 10 July 2017. http://mom-kh.com/.

———. 2017b. Media Ownership Monitor, Colombia, 2017, available online at https://www.mom-rsf.org/en/countries/colombia/.

———. 2017c. Media Ownership Monitor Ghana. Accessed 15 August 2017. http://ghana.mom-rsf.org/en/.

———. 2017d. Media Ownership Monitor Mongolia. Accessed 10 July 2017. https://rsf.org/en/mongolia.

Schiffrin, Anya. 2017. "Introduction." In *In the Service of Power: Media Capture and the Threat to Democracy,* edited by Anya Schiffrin, 1–9. Washington, D.C.: National Endowment for Democracy.

CHAPTER ELEVEN

The New Normal

Transnational Authoritarian Threats to Independent Media

SHANTHI KALATHIL

For years, the international media development community has supported independent media in authoritarian, semi-authoritarian, backsliding and weak democratic environments. The fundamental premise underpinning these types of programs—that a country's media system is primarily conditioned by its national political and economic system—is informed by political science and communications scholarship, as well as the country-based template typically employed by donors and program implementers. Hence, the overarching framework for support to independent media has concentrated on understanding factors that relate primarily to the domestic environment. For instance, supporting the "enabling environment" has traditionally emphasized the role of national laws, regulations, informal norms, and so on within a specific country's purview (Kalathil 2011a).

In addition, the key measures by which civil society actors, analysts, program implementers and donors tend to gauge change and/or make programmatic decisions are also primarily country-based. Traditional major indicators of the media environment and press freedom have included Freedom House's Freedom of the Press, which ranks countries, Reporters Without Borders' World Press Freedom Index, and the Committee to Protect Journalists' reports on attacks on the press (highlighting which countries are the worst offenders) and most censored countries. IREX's Media Sustainability Index tracks analysis of the conditions for independent media in 80 countries around the world. Qualitative donor evaluations of media development programs (and thus the follow-on learning and programmatic implications that emerge from them), due to the country-based framework for funding, also tend to be performed on a discrete country-by-country system (Kalathil 2011b).

National Roles

Certainly, it is true that national governments have traditionally been the key actors shaping the environment for the media in a country context, particularly where censorship is concerned. National laws governing speech, broadcasting regulators, media licensing boards, domestic advertising markets, and the formal/informal networks between editorial departments and those holding political power dramatically shape how the media evolves within national borders. Government attitudes toward "national sovereignty" in the media space also affect how foreign investment affects a country's media sector. Even in the supposedly borderless online space, national government legislation plays a key role in determining internet access and usage patterns, in addition to regulating speech, surveillance, user privacy, and other aspects of emerging digital rights.

Yet in recent years, as "the internet" has broadly converged with the dominant social media platforms through which much of the world now communicates, some of the key threats to the global information space—and the independent media ecosystems within that—have come from sources other than national governments seeking to censor or shape speech within their borders. While authoritarian states have always sought to exert outside influence, the emergence of easily accessible—and in some cases, manipulated—global platforms in a hyperconnected world has enabled these states to play a much more active role in weakening independent media outside their borders.

They have done so by co-opting dominant global media platforms to serve their purposes, and flooding the information ecosystem with disinformation and propaganda, which contributes to distrust in local media, weakened media literacy, and an inhospitable financial and editorial environment for independent media broadly. Moreover, they have also sought to control or influence the key physical and normative infrastructure that is likely to shape global communication in the years to come (Walker 2016).

The Global Media Space

This is part of a broader trend with respect to authoritarian influence in an era of near-ubiquitous (if not equally distributed) interconnection. Authoritarian governments have increasingly sought to use the networks and institutions of globalization—traditionally thought to empower democracy and weaken authoritarianism—for their own purposes. The global media space is a crucial arena of contestation for those authoritarian governments who seek to shield themselves from scrutiny, protect their assets, exert influence and achieve strategic objectives on a global scale. Moreover, the increasing concentration of power in several key platforms has afforded more opportunities for authoritarians to affect networked communication, especially in the context of weakened local media markets. Increasingly, the battle to control media systems is engaged on a global level.

Not all authoritarian states seek to shape communication on such a large scale. Some smaller authoritarian governments, such as those in central Asia, have influenced the media space beyond their borders primarily in an effort to protect stolen assets or to shield key political figures from scrutiny (Cooley and Heathershaw 2017). Yet some, such as Russia and China, possess broader ambitions and exert stronger influence on the global media ecosystem. Their efforts have weakened independent media not only in semi-authoritarian or backsliding democracies, but in major industrialized democracies as well. They have done so in different ways.

The Russian government has taken advantage of aspects of the modern information space, dominated by the ecology of "sharing" (particularly among like-minded groups) and propelled by the proprietary and non-transparent algorithms of major social media companies, to deliberately and strategically spread disinformation (Paul and Matthews 2016). Disinformation here should be understood to be distinct from propaganda, which may use false information to burnish a particular country's image or achieve a strategic aim. Rather, disinformation may combine true information with untrue information, and seeks to sow confusion, chaos, and division. The recent proliferation of often highly targeted, at-times automated disinformation, particularly around elections, has been highlighted by many observers as one of the chief challenges to democracy in the modern age (Persily 2017).

The Kremlin has tested techniques and narratives in former Soviet republics for several years, exploiting weak local media markets to heavily influence the public sphere with propaganda and disinformation (Satter 2014). Local media outlets can potentially play a strong role in combatting disinformation and ensuring the accuracy of widely circulating stories. Yet studies are showing that some fact-checking and "fake news" identification exercises aimed at the general public may prove ineffective as currently conceived (Pennycook and Rand 2017), and anecdotal evidence suggests that long-form, explanatory and/or narrative journalism may be more effective in combatting disinformation (Antelava 2017). It seems likely beyond the capacity of local media outlets (many of whom are struggling with financial sustainability) to act as effectively as they might. The inability of local media outlets to provide vigorous independent journalism in a sea of disinformation further widens the gap between media and the public, which in turns puts even greater pressure on already weak business models. Even in developed, mature democracies with highly robust independent media systems, disinformation is wreaking havoc by exploiting erosion of editorial capacity, citizens' growing distrust of media, and shifting norms on protection of speech.

The Chinese government, on the other hand, has focused less on disinformation than on developing, controlling and co-opting the major platforms for communication, as well as the arenas in which those issues are decided (Brady 2016). Beijing's long-term strategy is to shape international news media and guide the evolution of the global internet, using its economic clout to influence norms and practices in local media markets. In major regions ranging from southeast Asia to sub-Saharan Africa to central and eastern Europe, China has exerted influence over journalism training and exchanges, often through formalized mechanisms (such as, for instance, the Forum on China-Africa Cooperation). Such influence often encourages non-critical reporting of issues sensitive to China, and at times emphasizes "constructive" journalism over a traditional accountability-based approach. Moreover, in its actions to shape internet governance, China (and Russia) seek to uphold a sovereignty-based model of the internet that would allow for greater censorship of speech and wider surveillance (Kalathil 2017).

The Future of Independent Media Ecosystems

Over the course of the past year or so, the international community has increasingly recognized the growing influence of authoritarian governments on the health of independent media ecosystems worldwide. Certainly, this recognition does not mean that scrutinizing the role of national governments in shaping their countries' media ecosystems should be discarded or minimized. Indeed, the sovereignty-based model of the internet extolled by Russia and China would further empower national governments to control internet speech and surveillance within their borders as they see fit (Segal 2016). Nor should the field of media development wholly discard a body of practice honed through years of experience in a variety of political and economic environments.

In light of pressing current challenges, though, the media development community should actively look to broaden its frame of reference. Specifically, it should consider examining the role of powerful new actors, including authoritarian governments looking beyond their borders; the communities and networks powering the disinformation phenomenon; the concentration of power in a select handful of global platforms, on which independent media systems now increasingly depend; the regulatory and norm-based frameworks governing speech, privacy and data collection/utilization on those platforms; and the formal and informal arenas in which decisions that shape the future of independent media get made.

It is no surprise that the media development community has struggled with the emerging transnational threats to independent media. As noted earlier, the entire framework for media development has essentially been predicated on a country-by-country format. Understanding, analyzing, educating around and eventually programming to address these new challenges will require a reframing of the traditional, state-focused approach, as well as some of the "categories" that have dominated media development. While the core concepts of media development remain relevant, they require rethinking and expansion for a global environment in which speech, surveillance, disinformation, propaganda, data-mining and data-enabled objects are all intermingling seamlessly.

At the very least, this will require stronger networks of democratic actors in spaces of global information governance (as in, for instance, the Internet Governance Forum or the Internet Engineering Task Force); greater cross-border civil society cooperation, particularly around interdisciplinary and emerging disruptions in the global information space; and the seeding of more global knowledge hubs focused on new threats to the global information space. At a more granular level, for instance, this may also require that "training" go beyond the fundamentals of good journalism to encompass a holistic, sophisticated and long-term approach to media literacy. The IREX project "Learn to Discern," which initially focused on helping citizens recognize and resist highly sophisticated disinformation in Ukraine, and has since been broadened to other areas, might contain valuable lessons for future efforts. Similarly, training on the implications of "big data" might focus not only on data journalists, but all who function in the media ecosystem. The media development community should also consider a transnational emphasis that analyzes authoritarian influence at the international level, not just the national level, and in areas beyond censorship, including business models, media capture, disinformation, surveillance, and so on. Promising projects in these areas include the Journalism Trust Initiative and Trust Project, which combine a media self regulatory approach with an emphasis on working within current advertising models to find paths toward financial sustainability and the privileging of trustworthy content. Finally, in an era in which surveillance, hacking, disinformation and manipulation are blended seamlessly at a global level by authoritarian governments and others, the media development community should consider that "censorship/free speech" may no longer be the right or primary lens through which to view threats to independent media or the prerogatives of the media development community.

Recommended for Further Reading

Kalathil, Shanthi. 2017. *Beyond the Great Firewall: How China Became a Global Information Power.* Washington, D.C.: Center for International Media Assistance.

Persily, Nathan. 2017. "Can Democracy Survive the Internet?" *Journal of Democracy* 28 (2): 63–76.

Walker, Christopher. 2016. "Dealing with the Authoritarian Resurgence." In *Authoritarianism Goes Global: The Challenge to Democracy*, edited by Larry Diamond, Marc Plattner and Christopher Walker, 216–34. Baltimore: Johns Hopkins University Press.

References

Antelava, Natalia. 2017. "How (Not to) Cover Lies." Coda, March 28, 2017. https://codastory.com/disinformation-crisis/information-war/how-not-to-cover-lies.

Brady, Anne-Marie. 2016. "China's Foreign Propaganda Machine." In *Authoritarianism Goes Global: The Challenge to Democracy*, edited by Larry Diamond, Marc Plattner, and Christopher Walker, 187–97. Baltimore, MD: Johns Hopkins University Press.

Cooley, Alexander and John Heathershaw. 2017. *Dictators Without Borders: Power and Money in Central Asia.* New Haven, CT: Yale University Press.

Kalathil, Shanthi. 2011a. *Developing Independent Media as an Institution of Accountable Governance.* Washington, D.C.: The World Bank.

———. 2011b. "Measuring the Media: Examining the Interdisciplinary Approach." In *Measures of Press Freedom and Media Contributions to Development: Evaluating the Evaluators*, edited by Monroe E. Price, Susan Abbott and Libby Morgan, 271–80. New York, NY: Peter Lang.

———. 2017. *Beyond the Great Firewall: How China Became a Global Information Power.* Washington, D.C.: Center for International Media Assistance.

Paul, Christopher and Miriam Matthews. 2016. "The Russian 'Firehouse of Falsehood' Propaganda Model: Why It Might Work and Options to Counter It." Arlington: *The RAND Corporation.* https://www.rand.org/content/dam/rand/pubs/perspectives/PE100/PE198/RAND_PE198.pdf

Pennycook, Gordon and David G. Rand. 2017. "Assessing the Effect of 'Disputed' Warnings and Source Salience on Perceptions of Fake News Accuracy." Abstract, *Working paper.* (September 15, 2017) https://ssrn.com/abstract=3035384.

Persily, Nathan. 2017. "Can Democracy Survive the Internet?" *Journal of Democracy* 28 (2): 63–76.

Satter, David. 2014. *The Last Gasp of Empire: Russia's Attempt to Control the Media in the Former Soviet Republics*. Washington, D.C.: Center for International Media Assistance.

Segal, Adam. 2016. *Hacked World Order: How Nations Fight, Trade, Maneuver, and Manipulate in the Digital Age*. New York: PublicAffairs.

Walker, Christopher. 2016. "Dealing with the Authoritarian Resurgence." In *Authoritarianism Goes Global: Challenge to Democracy*, edited by Larry Diamond, Marc Plattner, and Christopher Walker, 216–34. Baltimore, MD: Johns Hopkins University Press.

PART THREE

Regional Perspectives

CHAPTER TWELVE

Refocusing Media Development in Africa

WINSTON MANO

Media Development as Agency, Technological Innovation, and Social Change

Real needs drive the communicative agency and innovation of Africans. Take for example the creative way in which Alfred Sirleaf, founder of a roadside chalkboard newspaper in Monrovia, Liberia, *The Daily Talk,* used symbols so that those with little education are "able to follow along with those who have education know-how."[1] He has been successful in developing a daily "newspaper" that communicates news in a more accessible way to Liberians. Sirleaf was previously arrested and imprisoned for criticizing the government, but has continued to publish and even has a presence on Facebook.[2]

Many media producers in Mozambique have followed a similarly unconventional path. "In other countries, printed newspapers often produce online offshoots. But in Mozambique the reverse is true. Local publications often start off distributing by fax or email. They only develop a printed version once they have really got going."[3] *Mediafax* was founded in 1991 by Carlos Cardoso, an investigative journalist who was murdered for his work in 2000. It operated out of a garage and was distributed by fax and email to cut costs. With limited financial support from the Norwegian Development Agency (NORAD), *Mediafax's* high-quality journalism quickly attracted subscribers, including the Presidential Office (though perhaps for different reasons). The fax newspapers become online newspapers, often initiated and run on the "side-line" by journalists employed by legacy media. Such innovation allows for the development of a news style which is more critical of the authorities.

These examples, and many more besides, attest to how actors shape their communicative environment to suit their needs and the needs of their fellow citizens. Yet, in spite of the innovations and agency found on the continent, African media remains strongly influenced by colonial legacies ranging from colonial media infrastructure and operational logic. What's more, models of journalism, especially those from Britain, Germany and France, are taught and practiced in independent African countries; meanwhile African talk shows, soap operas, and newscasts follow formats developed in the colonial era; and the very messages transmitted by African broadcasts and in African newspapers can frequently be traced back to news sources in Britain, France and Germany. Amid this contradiction, those pursuing media development must remain uniquely focused on ensuring that the media being developed is relevant. This chapter gives some indication of where more relevant forms of media development are likely to emerge in Africa.

What is needed are new ways of thinking to overcome the colonial models. The guiding principle of such an orientation is not just decolonization, but the alleviation of the suffering of Africans and the furtherance of societal emancipation. It should arise from a recognition that institutional practices have for centuries been dominated by application of Arabic and Western-centric modes, Old Thought, and are no longer fully responsive to continental situations and clearly can no longer sustain the "dynamics of an awakening youth population of Africa" (Asante 2016, 2). "New Thought" deliberately privileges "African ideals and values, interrogates indigenous languages and cultures" (Asante 2016, 2). "More, decolonization is not about ignoring Western and Eastern contributions to the world pool of information; these are considerable achievements and must be appreciated and examined in context of a more energetic Afrocentric school of thought that seeks African agency, while seeking other ways of seeing, viewing reality and knowing" (Asante 2016: 4). This chapter discusses African agency in media development so that media practices and output are more suited to African conditions and needs.

A refocused media development approach in Africa will need to grasp the observation made years ago by Lucian Pye (1963) that "innovation and tidiness rarely go together." The media developer will need to engage with communication and media as part of social change, incorporating emerging, formal, and informal aspects of social and mediated processes that have an impact on communications. Pye (1963, 3) also points out that "in the future it will be the creation of new channels of communication and the ready acceptance of new content of communications which will be decisive" in building new societies. It is important that media developers reconnect with the notion that communication is "one way of studying social life" (4).

If the theory is to be trusted, then media development in Africa is most likely to be driven by initiatives and efforts that feature African agency, focus on social change, and are embedded in technological innovation. These characteristics, I will argue in the rest of the chapter, are most frequently found in the sphere of alternative, digital media.

Old Thought and Media Development in Africa

Media development in postcolonial Africa has so far been driven by both national and international organizations intervening in country-level or regional media sectors to produce outcomes associated with notions of media pluralism, independence, freedom and the like. After gaining independence in 1980, Zimbabwe set up the Zimbabwe Mass Media Trust to promote media in the public interest covering newspapers, a national news agency, and bookstores. South Africa's Media Development and Diversity Agency (MDDA) is another example of a statutory development agency set up to promote and ensure media development and diversity. These national efforts at media development have been especially driven by governments and have targeted formal media institutions. Shortage of resources has meant that international organizations, however, play a more prominent media development role in Africa.

The organizations most commonly found working to support media development in Africa include UNESCO, Article 19, BBC Media Action, Thompson Foundation, Internews, IREX, Friedrich Ebert Stiftung and International Media Support. It should be mentioned that China and other countries in the Global South are now also undertaking their own form of "media development" as soft power within their broader development projects (Zhang, Wasserman and Mano 2016). International media developers have championed various strategies to influence media in specific African countries and have to some extent formalized and set global standards in media development, though much debate remains about what kinds of approaches are most effective. Nelson and Susman-Peña (2012) have, for example, pointed out that existing approaches to media development have been "poorly coordinated" and without much input from recipient countries.

Though frequently involving both local and international actors, the dominant approach has been to promote media development from the perspective of Western democratic thinking, which often does not take into account particular issues in the context where they are applied (Nelson and Susman-Peña 2012). For

Relly and Zanger, media development has become a "Wild West atmosphere" ... a "free-for-all" with all manner of media actors and training agencies whose stated objective is to create a "new media landscape" (Relly and Zanger 2017, 1234).

Worse, interventionist media development projects are thought to be driven by "ulterior purpose" and an "instrumentalist understanding of the media" which emphasizes "externally originating steps to develop the media, and usually between North-South developers and 'developees'" (Berger 2010, 550). The idea of "media missionaries" from the Global North who come to "develop," "assist," "support," or "strengthen" media in the Global South inevitably generates skepticism across Africa as it carries the intention of "media manipulation" or "media meddling" (550).

This is not to say, however, that genuine media development has not occurred in Africa, or that the efforts of international donors or organizations have not, at times, been supportive for this development, but that challenges remain within the field of international media assistance that are an obstacle to more effective support. Refocusing media development efforts could avoid mistakes of the Old Thought and can instead adhere to New Thought that promotes African agency, innovation, and social change.

Legacy Media's Limitations in Africa

While it is an undeniable fact that radio, newspapers, and television remain significant media in Africa, which should continue to receive support from media development, many of the so-called legacy media outlets in Africa do not meet the communication needs of the majority, and their capacity to be reformed to meet public needs remains in question.

In South Africa, Kenya, Nigeria and Zimbabwe, to name but a few countries, legacy media have been "captured" by narrow interests. The notion of "media capture" is being put forward by journalists and scholars in Africa to describe the manner in which political and business elites have ganged up to own and control what comes out of the media (Schiffrin 2017).[4]

For instance, in Kenya during the 2017 elections, media owners, editors and journalists failed to perform the information, education and watchdog roles due to capture. The coverage was polarized as media sided with political parties or candidates. According to the *Media monitoring Report on the coverage of the Kenya General Elections 2017*[5] Kenyan "media platforms such as *The Star Newspapers* and community radio stations such as Namlolwe, Kameme FM and KASS FM were notorious for airing or printing sensational, unbalanced, hate speech, inflammatory, ethnic profiling and generally unethical content that goes against media ethics in Kenya. There was a meltdown of gate-keeping roles in mainstream media houses such as Nation Media Group and Standard Group. The Editors, either by design or just negligence, passed stories for either broadcast or publications that were sensational, biased, or slanted to suite political interests of either Jubilee Party or NASA" (6). Kenyan media were afflicted by "apparent ineptitude, wrangles, state capture" (15). Biased coverage extended to the social media space as fake news became more pronounced. The failure of journalism in Kenya resulted in lawlessness which endangered the lives of journalists and judges, among other groups. There was next to no public outcry because citizens were misinformed.

Similarly, in South Africa there are serious concerns about how media houses such as Media 24, Independent Media, Caxton and the Times Media Group (with Media24/Naspers controlling 40% alone) constitute a white monopoly that that has unhealthy effect on South African democracy. What has come to be described as white monopoly capital owned and controlled mainstream media is thought to be in support of white economic hegemony in South Africa. The ruling politicians are also implicated in scandals to control both the state and private media. Collusions between politicians and businesspersons have undermined the role of media with a tendency of focusing on middle class issues squabbles at the expense of issues affecting marginalized groups who are in the majority.

In Zimbabwe, the November 2017 political crisis, which forced the resignation of Zimbabwe's 93-year old President Robert Mugabe after 37 years of continuous rule, highlighted problems with the selective coverage of traditional media and lack of professionalism in the Zimbabwe Broadcasting Corporation (ZBC). The ZBC has since 1980 received media support and resources from Britain, Germany and China, to name but a few countries. The resources failed to sustain professionalism at a critical moment, with the ZBC transmitting the ruling party's statements, while ignoring the messages conveyed by the army. Starved with information about the military involvement in party politics, citizens had to rely on online sources.

As Reimer (2007, 317) noted: "The problem with traditional news journalism is that it has said 'No!' to the role of the interpreter. Rather, it is a transmitter of what has happened; a transmitter without a voice of its own. News journalists are invisible. They have forgotten that meaningful journalism must be creative; work in which you interpret and assign meaning through your manner of interpretation." Due to censorship, the invisibility of journalists is worse. Added to economic controls, deregulation, fierce competition, audience segmentation, and rapid technological transformation, the African traditional journalism has failed to deliver journalism that moves people. Ownership of both state and commercial media has favored a few economic and political elites.

The Case for Development of Alternative Citizen News Websites in Africa

The chapter has so far highlighted the need for media developers to recognize the agency and innovation of Africans, and it has argued that legacy media remains too "captured" to offer space for such agency and innovation. But Africa has also witnessed the rise of many digitally-enabled alternatives to traditional journalism.

Since the 1990s continent has seen the growth of independent and pluralistic media characterized by "move from top-down, state-driven propaganda to message-driven and participatory forms of dialogue and expressions" (Esipisu and Kariithi 2007, 21). They add that "organic community media networks and associations across Africa emerged to give voice to marginalized and isolated communities in the wave of democratic reform that was sweeping the continent" (21).

In defining the emerging alternative news spaces, the chapter finds useful the concept of "third sector" which defines "media companies representing a sector of media production understood to be relatively autonomous of state and commercial interests, and operating in the interest of community and public life" (Mutibwa 2015, 278). The operations of third sector media companies are bounded by socio-political imperatives such as providing news tailored to the readers. The problem is that such companies are often controlled by sponsors and donors, unless they have good training and support from democratic media development actors.

The emergence of third sector media companies in Africa and on Africa "is in large part due to the space created by the shift from dictatorial regimes to multiparty democracies and elections as well as the end of the Cold War and internal calls for democratic reforms" (Esipisu and Kariithi 2007, 2). The so-called mainstream journalism in Africa has also created spaces that compete with citizen journalism on the internet. The problem, as Mutsvairo (2016, 4) rightly observes, is that citizen journalists lack basic training, are not obliged to observe principles of accuracy or fact-checking and "do not have specific ethical standards guiding their conduct." If mainstream media is not trusted because they do not present "facts," why on earth would citizen journalism be trusted when they proudly eschew facts? As Reimer (2007, 305) puts it, "another kind of journalism is required; a more interpretive journalism and a journalism capable of dealing with both rationality and emotions." This is a move towards "expressivist politics" that moves people, "an output that makes them talk and act" (312).

Mutsvairo (2016) observes that it does not matter whether it is called "community journalism," "networked journalism," "open-source journalism," what is at stake is "citizen journalism," whereby "citizens have, regardless of their location, benefited through the use of hashtags, retweets and image shares in a powerful citizenry collaboration and engagement that intriguingly rivals reports provided by mainstream media outlets" (3).

Citizen journalism provides faster, interactive, and accessible forms of content sharing and customization that can strengthen democratization in Africa. Kperogi (2016, 19) similarly observes that emergent "genres of web-based journalism are supervening upon the traditional media as sites for the push and pull of democratic discourses," serving as alternative sources of news. Given the widespread and deep-seated democratic problems in Sub-Saharan Africa, Mutsvairo (2016, 4) states that it is "no understatement to conclude that the very manifestation of citizen journalism is potentially a revolution itself … that technology will have a role to play in the way the continent will be governed."

As is in other regions of the world, and although it is still limited, factors such as digital interactivity have resulted in blogs, weblogs, meta-sites commenting on news in Africa. These are becoming increasingly influential as news and cultural information websites run by locals and the African diaspora get more effective as alternatives. The ongoing rapid social changes in Africa is resulting in new information needs and giving force to alternative voices that are located in the New Thought which media developers need to take into account. Media developers will need to shift and rethink their approach to help develop more relevant journalism that connects with citizens. Even though access and download speeds are slow, the African media sector is experiencing a significant disruption due to the introduction of digital options, given how the internet and smartphones are enabling an increased audience to access new content.

The websites below offer two contrasting dimensions of the emerging citizen journalism organisations in Africa. While both can be described as responses to represessive political environments in Nigeria and Zimbabwe, SaharaReporters is donor supported while Sokwanele is a grassroot initiative that combines a journalistic function with offline activism. They both show the nature of the variety of journalism in these emerging spaces.

SaharaReporters

Most of the evolving online news practices that should be factored in media development have been instigated by African diasporas, most of whom have access to better training and resources. As Kperogi (2016, 23) observes that "The negligence of the mainstream institutional media in Nigeria in calling to corruption, misgovernance and abuse of power—in addition to their ability to stay up to speed with the dizzying pace of multimediality and interactivity of twenty-first century news—inspired the advent and explosion of citizen media sites by Nigerians resident in the

United States." These include SaharaReporters.com (published from New York) and the NigeriaVillageSquare.com (published from Houston, Texas), amongst many others whose journalism has become key to Nigeria. SaharaReporters has emerged as the "standard-bearer of Nigerian diasporan citizen journalism, in time became the go-to-news site for breaking news and news about corruption in government." Media development should promote the concept of community in the discursive preoccupation of the new sites. These emerging sites for news "provide a model for the future of journalism in transitional societies." Such sites do not fall within the remit of traditional media development organizations that come to Africa as they are deemed to be based in the West. The SaharaReporters online sites, including its Twitter and Facebook pages register more hits than any of the traditional media in Nigeria, clearly showing how its news is reaching Nigerians. "Typically, news now starts from social media chatter, percolates into online news networks, and then into mainstream media, from where it is further shared by social media users to create social stories" (30). Media developers can focus on these new sites as they are performing an important role in the public sphere.

Zvakwana-Sokwanele

In the case of Zimbabwe, Moyo (2016, 35) warns against making a strict comparison of the traditional and citizen journalism as these are often different. He instead points out that citizen journalism must be seen as responsive to unique needs in restrictive, politically volatile and authoritarian media environments and must be analyzed in terms of how it is underpinned by "a humanist moral obligation that seeks to wrestle journalism from the publishing monopolies" (35). Like Nigeria, Zimbabwe has many citizen journalism websites, with NewZimbabwe.com, ZimDaily.com and NehandaRadio.com published from the diaspora. Some of these were founded and run by professional journalists, in self-imposed exiled from Zimbabwe. Moyo identifies Zvakwana-Sokwanele as a leading example of how citizen journalism has developed within Zimbabwe. "Zvakwana-Sokwanele is a civic organization that uses cyber activism to highlight democracy and human rights issues in the country. It is an underground social movement that uses innovative multimedia strategies online and offline. Apart from its media, it also uses graffiti, leaflets, CDs, videos and condoms inscribed with messages of resistance that aim to wake up the masses through conscientization." The citizen journalism practice is "fluid" as it involves unrestrictive flow of witness accounts, news and information flow with professional journalists, amateurs, academics and people previously outside news. The problem is that some of the stories published on the site are published with no sources or bylines and "have no pretensions towards objectivity and balance" (Moyo, 2016, 15). In the events leading to the fall of Robert Mugabe in November

2017, this civic group mobilized people to demonstrate and push him to resign. The point here is that media development think carefully about how to extent help to citizen journalism sites even though they come across as mere "social media chatterers." To attract donor support the news function of such websites might need to first show a commitment towards being more of a professional journalistic outfit. I'm raising this as an important question where there is need to think through how this can be done. Popularity only should not be the criteria, rather a carefully tool needs to be developed to measure the role and impact of these emerging sites for democratization. Such a tool can especially examine how these emerging sites perform within and outside key democratic events, such as elections. The test should include matters of access and their ability to set and shift the news agenda among all categories of citizens, including youths, workers, rural and elderly citizens.

Towards a Model of Media Development for Citizen Journalism

This chapter has discussed the problems facing media development and identified alternative citizen journalism as an important area that needs supporting. However, citizen news media has a complex character as shown by the variety review above. What media developers might need is to put the emphasis on defining the practice and actors involved. For example, this could mean a focus on what Willems (2015, 90) calls "alternative mediation" and "mediated civic agency" rather than alternative media institutions or civil society organisations, which could enable us to "gain a fuller understanding of the multiple ways in which different forms of media are involved in resisting different forms of power." "The concept of mediated agency," according to Willems (2015, 92), "points to a wider spectrum of actions in which citizens engage power through a range of media forms, whether formal or informal." It is one way in which media developers can foster new media modes that are non-Eurocentric, decolonized, and more effectively informing of African citizens. The notion of alternative mediation and its link to mediated civic agency could be productive across Africa. In reality, independence for the alternative news sites is difficult to achieve and would require careful strategies and support. Media development organizations will need to find ways to make these sites viable by offering them training and strategies to raise independent funding. The example of Zvakwana-Sokwanele discussed above shows that definitions of alternative journalism need to be loosened. A typology for supporting progressive alternative citizen journalism, some of which may be linked to social movements, is needed. Citizen alternative media is important because it facilitates democratic communication through providing relevant content and encouraging broader links with popular culture. The refocusing can help include actors and content that plays a key part in social change. Wasserman and Benequista's (2017) call for a shift in focus and solidarity among media development organizations in Africa needs to be taken seriously. This chapter has called for a shift in the focus in media development in Africa in the digital age towards alternative mediation and mediated civic agency which include formal and informal spaces.

Notes

1. Lydia Polgreen, "All the News That Fits: Liberia's Blackboard Headlines," in *New York Times*, 4 August, 2006, available at: https://nyti.ms/2GJD865 (accessed 20 November, 2017).
2. The Facebook is however not updated regularly. It is available here: https://www.facebook.com/Daily-Talk-News-Liberia-397868653696599/ (accessed 20 November, 2017).
3. CDAC Network "Electronic newspapers thrive in Mozambique", available at: http://www.cdacnetwork.org/i/20140624154838-uephl (accessed 25 November 2018).
4. see *South Africa Media Capture—Gupta versus White Capital*, blackopinion.co.za/2016/04/15/our-captured-media, *Is there media capture in Zimbabwe?—openparly.co.zw;* openparly.co.zw/2017/09/08/is-there-media... and *Media capture in the Digital Age | The Star, Kenya*, www.the-star.co.ke/news/2017/08/25/media-capture.
5. Peace Pen Communications (2017) "Media Besieged." http://www.peacepencommunications.org/wp-content/uploads/2017/12/Media_Besieged.pdf.

Recommended for Further Reading

Mano, Winston, and Lynete Mukhongo. 2016. Towards Alternative Media as Critical Media in Africa *Journal of Alternative and Community Media*. 1 (1): 27–29.

Nyamnjoh, Francis B. 2011. "De-Westernizing Media Theory to Make Room for African Experience." In *Popular Media, Democracy and Development in Africa*, edited by Herman Wasserman, 19–31. New York, NY: Routledge.

Willems, Wendy, and Winston Mano, eds. 2017. *Everyday Media Culture in Africa: Audiences and Users*. Abingdon, Oxon: Routledge.

References

Asante, Molefi Kete. 2016. "Decolonizing the Universities in Africa: An Approach to Transformation." In *Contemporary Critical Thought in Africology and Africana Studies, edited by* Molefi Kete Asante and Clyde E. Ledbetter Jr., 1–14. Lanham, MD: Lexington Books.

Berger, Guy. 2010. "Problematizing 'Media Development' as a Bandwagon Gets Rolling." *International Communication Gazette* 72 (7): 547–65.

Esipisu, Isaac, and Nixon Kariithi. 2007. "New Media Development in Africa." *Global Media Journal: African Edition* 1 (1): 21–63.

Kperogi, Farooq A. 2016. "Networked Social Journalism: Media, Citizen Participation and Democracy in Nigeria." In *Participatory Politics and Citizen Journalism in Networked Africa: A Connected Continent*, edited by Bruce Mutsvairo, 19–33. London: Palgrave Mcmcmillan

Mano, 2010. "Communication: An African Perspective." In *Rethinking communication: Keywords in Communication Research*, edited by Stuart Allan, 11–13. New Jersey: Hampton Press.

Moyo, Last. 2016. "Crossing Taboo Lines: Citizen Journalism Ethics in Political Crisis Settings." In *Participatory Politics and Citizen Journalism in Networked Africa: A Connected Continent,* edited by Bruce Mutsvairo, 34–58. London: Palgrave Mcmcmillan.

Mutsvairo, Bruce. 2016. "Recapturing Citizen Journalism: Processes and Patterns." In *Participatory Politics and Citizen Journalism in Networked Africa: A Connected Continent,* edited by Bruce Mutsvairo, 1–15. London: Palgrave Mcmcmillan.

Mutibwa, Daniel H. 2015. "Between Aspiration and Reality: A Study of Contemporary Third Sector Media Production." In *The Routledge Companion to Alternative and Community Media*, edited by Chris Atton, 278–88. London and New York: Routledge.

Nelson, Mark, and Tara Susman-Peña. 2012. "Rethinking Media Development: A Report on the Media Map Project," *Media Map Project*, Internews, World Bank Institute.

———. 2011. "De-Westernizing Media Theory to Make Room for African Experience." In *Popular media, Democracy and Development in Africa*, edited by Herman Wasserman, 19–31. New York, NY: Routledge.

Pye, Lucian W. 1963. "Preface and Acknowledgements." In *Communications and Political Development,* edited by Lucian W. Pye, ix–xi. Princeton, NJ: Princeton University Press.

Reimer, Bo. 2007. "Journalism, Politics and the Public Sphere: On Emotions and Objectivity." In *New Publics with/out Democracy,* edited by Henrik Bang and Anders Esmark, 305–23. Frederiksberg: Samfundslitteratur Press/NORDICOM.

Relly, Jeannine and Margaret Zanger. 2017. "The Enigma of News Media Development with Multi-pronged 'Capture': The Afghanistan Case." *Journalism: Theory, Practice and Criticism* 18(10): 1233–55.

Schiffrin, Anya. 2017. "Introduction." In *In the Service of Power: Media Capture and the Threat to Democracy,* edited by Anya Schiffrin, 1–8. CIMA: National Endowment for Democracy/ Columbia University.

Wasserman, Herman, and Nicholas Benequista. 2017. *Pathways to Media Reform in Sub-Saharan Africa Reflections from a Regional Consultation.* Washington: National Endowment for Democracy (NED)/CIMA. Willems, Wendy. 2015. "Alternative Mediation, Power and Civic Agency in Africa." In *The Routledge Companion to Alternative and Community Media,* edited by Chris Atton, 88–95. London and New York: Routledge.

Willems, Wendy. 2015. "Alternative mediation, power and civic agency in Africa." In *The Routledge Companion to Alternative and Community Media,* Chris Atton, 88–95. London and New York: Routledge.

Zhang, Xiaoling, Herman Wasserman, and Winston Mano, eds. 2016. *China's Media and Soft Power in Africa: Promotion and Perceptions.* New York, NY: Palgrave Macmillan.

CHAPTER THIRTEEN

The Impact of Foreign Aid on the Development of Media and Communication in Latin America[1]

MARÍA SOLEDAD SEGURA

This chapter examines the influence and impact of international assistance on communication and media practice, research, education, and policies in Latin America since the 1970s. It addresses a gap within regional communication studies: The historical and material foundations of the Latin American communication field. Despite the relevance of foreign aid in this sector, there are extremely few researchers studying this issue.

For the purpose of this article I will define media development as the set of strategies, actions, resources, actors, and organizations promoting freedom of speech, media pluralism, and diversity, with a view of media as a key institution of democracy (UNESCO 2008). Foreign aid agencies are among many actors who support strategies to bolster media development.

The analysis, grounded in a critical perspective, recognizes that donors and implementers occupy unequal positions of power. International aid can only exist in a world where historical patterns of economic exploitation have given some countries or regions the ability to appear charitable towards others. Foreign assistance, in other words, is characterized by relationships of dominance and dependence and can be viewed as a palliative to an unjust system. (Eikenberry & Nickel 2006)

Nonetheless, the analysis also considers how disempowered actors can negotiate, resist, re-signify, and use foreign assistance for different purposes and in distinct ways. Not every aid program promotes the same ideology, nor do donors fully control how local organizations use the money. At the same time, the nonprofit sector is not purely altruistic, independent, or nonpartisan. The civil society recipients of aid must be seen as heterogeneous and conflictive, and examined with consideration of their institutional links to governments, political parties, churches, commercial enterprises, and philanthropists, among others (Roelofs 1995).

Conceptualizing and measuring the impact of international assistance is challenging. As with other forms of social action, the consequences of foreign aid depend on a complex set of factors. These results are not only linked to the explicit, rational goals and frameworks of funding institutions and practitioners. The influence is also related to opportunities and junctures during project formulation and implementation; relations between donors and grantees; and actors' strategies, competencies, and trajectories (Segura & Waisbord 2016).

This chapter discusses the following questions: What has been the role of foreign aid in shaping communication and media practices, research, education, and policies in Latin America? Has it supported participatory or modernization models of communication? My argument is that international media assistance in Latin America has achieved several goals. The aid has bolstered some actors, experiences, policies, and values associated with more participatory models of communication, while promoting others firmly rooted in modernization theory. And it has also had other unexpected impacts. Overall, the aid flows to the region in support of media have been crucial to (1) developing the main institutions of the regional communication sector; (2) promoting intellectuals, activists, and politicians in both the communication and political fields; and (3) supporting the groups that have had an impact on media policy reform over the last 15 years.

The analysis is based on interviews with former and current officials from the three regional networks of community media, the two Latin American academic associations, and different types of donors. In these interviews, I sought access to the historical memory of actors and institutions from the 1970s to the 2010s to understand their perceptions about the processes and impact of international aid.

In this chapter, I will first analyze the context, interests, organizations, and consequences of foreign aid on media and communication during the Cold War Era. Then, I will examine the continuities and discontinuities of international assistance during the post-Cold War Era. Finally, I will offer conclusions.

Community Media and Education

Context and Interests

Why did public and private organizations based in Northern countries finance programs in support of communication practices, education, and research in Latin America during the Cold War? To answer this question, it is necessary to look historically at the political and media conditions at the time, and to the democratic problems and challenges then encountered in the region and in Northern countries.

During the 1960s and 1970s, most Latin American countries were ruled by military dictatorships or facing civil wars. Political turmoil was evident in the political and social movements and organizations practicing guerrilla warfare. In the following decade, countries experienced a transition to democracy with precarious economies tethered to huge debts to foreign creditors. In those years, community media were banned in all countries. Under the dictatorships, they were persecuted, and their members were kidnapped, tortured, murdered, or forced into exile. Left-wing academics, researchers, and journalists suffered the same fate.

In this context, during the Cold War, Northern countries were interested in stopping the advance of communist and other left-wing parties, unions, guerrilla groups, and popular social movements in the Latin American region. In many European countries of the time, democratic and center-left governments that were in power were very active in development cooperation (Cortés 2017). Meanwhile, the Movement of Non-Aligned Countries drove the New World Information and Communication Order (NWICO) in international debates. The demand for a free and balanced flow of communication was expressed in the UNESCO debates that led to the MacBride Commission and its 1980 report (International Commission for the Study of Communication Problems 1980).[2]

Christian churches, especially the Catholic Church but also those from Protestant denominations, that had a strong presence in the region increasingly adopted a Liberation Theology framework following the Second Vatican Council (1965) and the Medellín Episcopal Conference (1968). Driven by the principles of Liberation Theology, these churches provided support to grassroots groups in communities and contributed to the international debates about NWICO (Uranga, Valle, and Vandenbulcke 2017).

Donors

In this context, the main international cooperation agencies of the period were:

1. Christian Churches: The Catholic Media Council (CAMECO), headquartered in Germany, was founded in 1969 by international Catholic media associations to provide consultative services related to media and communication in developing countries. Among the agencies using CAMECO were the German donors, Misereor (a development agency founded in 1958) and Adveniat (a pastoral agency founded in 1961). In addition, the CIDSE network functioned as a leading coordinating body

and lobby network of 18 Catholic development agencies from Europe and North America, including Cordaid[3] (Netherlands), Broederlijk Delen (Belgium), CAFOD (United Kingdom), Manos Unidas (Spain), and Fastenopfer (Switzerland), among others. The Protestant World Association of Christian Communication (WACC) also worked in Latin America, funded by various agencies like Christian Aid (United Kingdom), Comité catholique contre la faim et pour le développement (France), Brot für die Welt (Germany), and the Lutheran World Federation (Dietz, Uranga, Cortés, Vandenbulcke, Valle, Lee 2017).

2. Public media: The German international broadcaster, Deutsche Welle, and the Dutch radio network for international audiences, Radio Netherland Worldwide, also supported communication initiatives in the region. Radio Netherland's Latin American Training Center provided services from 1968 to 2008 (Prieto Castillo 2008; Uranga, Cortés 2017).
3. Political foundations: Friedrich Ebert Stiftung (FES) aligned with the Social Democrats (SPD), and the Konrad Adenauer Stiftung (KAS), aligned with the Christian Democrats (CDU), have been active in media assistance and media policy for decades.
4. Governments: The United States Agency for International Development (USAID) provided substantial support to projects using radio and television to promote agricultural, educational, and health reforms in El Salvador, Nicaragua, Dominican Republic, Honduras, Costa Rica, Colombia, and Brazil (Beltrán 1993).
5. Multilateral organizations: During those years, UNESCO promoted several communication initiatives aimed at fostering national communication policies (Uranga, Cortés, Lamas 2017). UNESCO urged Latin American countries to formulate integrated, explicit, durable, and coherent guidelines to "orient the conduct of specialized institutions in the management of the overall communication process of a country" (Beltrán 1976, 4). Communication was considered an economic, socio-political, and a cultural process, so it could not be left to market competition, individual interests, or the decisions of state officials. FAO, UNICEF, UNDP, the Pan-American Health Organization, and the Organization of American States (OAS) also supported communication initiatives (Beltrán 2005; Dragon 2017).

Frameworks

These foreign aid agencies not only had different institutional and financial origins, but also diverse political and theoretical frameworks, goals, and strategies. In this period, they largely promoted two opposite models of communication, each one linked to a different interpretation of development.

In the 1940s and 1950s, some governmental agencies—especially those linked to the United States, Germany, and the Netherlands governments—and international organizations such as United Nations and OAS supported "communication for development" projects in Latin America that were characterized by the diffusion model of communication and the modernization paradigm of development, both of which were in line with the developmental theories promoted in the region at the time by CEPAL and the diffusionist theories imported from the United States (Segura 2008).

According to this perspective, the advancement of prosperity and well-being is organized rationally through active state interventions and with the support of technological innovations. As the theory goes, the process of development requires that countries leave traditional society behind to achieve the benefits of modernization, and media is expected to play an important role in facilitating this. Media were seen as a tool of persuasion and influence that should be used to create "a public atmosphere favorable to change" of behavior and customs (Beltrán 2005).

In the 1960s, other international assistance agencies linked to Christian churches, political foundations, and international organizations began to support initiatives with a participatory and critical model.[4] During this time, Latin American researchers undertook a radical critique of the modernization theories, and produced initiatives that broke with "the vertical mode of transmission of development ideals" (Mattelart & Mattelart 1997). They challenged diffusionist theories, analyzed media economics, made theoretical contributions to popular and alternative communication, and studied the link between communication and grassroots movements. Researchers believed that communication should contribute to the "awareness" of the subaltern classes to promote social change that would lead to their "emancipation" and to independent development processes. Therefore, it was considered essential that peasants, indigenous people, miners and other workers have their own media and produce their own messages (Segura 2008).

Local Organizations

What are the consequences of foreign aid on Latin American communication practices and theories over the years? During the Cold War Era, international assistance agencies financed local NGOs and groups focusing on:

1. Community communication: Community radios, popular videos, etc.
2. Education on communication and development: Publications, trainings, meetings, and research.

They also supported many institutions specialized in popular communication, research, and education. These institutions later shaped the regional communication field and served as training grounds in communication for future political leaders and intellectuals. The institutions created in that period were:

1. Popular communication associations: ALER (Latin American Association of Radio Education), the regional association of community radios, was founded in 1972 and financed by various Christian agencies. These agencies supported specific projects, but ALER received consistent global funding from the 80s to the mid-90s, which it used to support educational radio. The national community and educational radio stations networks, such as ERBOL (Bolivia), UCBC and UNDA (Brasil), CNR (Peru), Arpas (El Salvador), IGER (Guatemala), CORAPE (Ecuador), and UDECA (Dominican Republic) also received international support in this period (Vandenbulcke, Uranga, Dietz 2017).
2. Academic institutions for research, education and the production of media content: These were mainly funded by German political foundations, churches, governments and UNESCO. CIESPAL (Centro Internacional de Estudios Superiores de Comunicación para América Latina) was founded in 1959 in Ecuador by the X General Conference of UNESCO and was the first academic research center for communication in the region. CIESPAL was founded to spread the modernization model of communication for development (Segura 2008), but in 1973 it organized a seminar to issue "the first broad call for Latin American critical thinking on communication" (Bolaño, Crovi Druetta & Cimadevilla 2015). During the dictatorships of the 70s and 80s, communication research moved from universities to non-governmental organizations (NGOs) with international support. Some of these 35 national academic institutes were ILET (Mexico), CENECA (Chile) and IPAL (Peru). These NGOs built and spread Latin American critical communication theories, and their contributions to regional communication field are internationally recognized by academics (García Canclini 1994; Uranga 2017).
3. Academic networks: They were mainly funded by German political foundations and UNESCO. FELAFACS, the regional association of communication faculties, was created in 1979. It promoted the creation of national associations for university communication careers, established an important regional journal, and encouraged and funded postgraduate studies, libraries, researches, seminars, conferences all over the sub-continent (Puebla 2017). ALAIC, the regional communication researchers network, was created in 1978 in Caracas, Venezuela, by a group of intellectuals from different

countries and diverse institutions and was engaged with the movement that championed the NWICO. In the early phases, it had UNESCO support for research projects, although this did not extend throughout the lifespan of ALAIC (Cimadevilla 2017).

From Media to Media Policy Reform

A Shift in Context and Priorities

Beginning in the 1990s, the situation in the Latin American region and in Northern countries drastically changed due to political, economic and media developments.

The geopolitical interests of Northern countries were transformed in this period, and with these changes, funding flows. European countries reduced foreign aid to Latin America, shifting the funds to Eastern Europe, Africa, and the Middle East due to a confluence of factors, not least of which was the end of the Cold War, which diverted a great deal of international assistance to former Soviet bloc countries. Also influential over aid flows in this period were the end of the debates about the NWICO following strong opposition from the United Kingdom and the United States in UNESCO; the advance of right-wing, nationalist governments in Europe; and the economic crisis of 2008 (Uranga, Lamas, Cortés, Valle 2017).

Meanwhile, in Latin America during the 1990s, most right-wing governments implemented anti-inflationary policies to inspire economic growth. In addition, most democracies stabilized as civil societies strengthened. In the 2000s many leftist governments focused on poverty alleviation with social, health, and educational programs. Moreover, most of them pushed media policy reforms to limit market interests in media systems and legalize and promote community media (Vandenbulcke, Cortés, Lamas 2017).

The Latin American mass media offering has since expanded, while digitization has simultaneously enabled the flourishing of media producers targeting specific audiences on a small budget. In these conditions, NGOs are discovering that they can promote their agendas directly, without having to fund media as intermediaries. Communication strategies by NGOs now typically combine engagement with traditional media with more direct forms of communication through social media (Dietz 2017).

Since the 1990s, the technological development of computer networks and the digitization of information have allowed for the expansion of a techno-utopian, modernizing, and neo-diffusionist view that sees technology as the solution to the economic crisis and the democracy problems. From this perspective, technology serves as the "new economy" and a "democracy in real time" (Segura 2008).

New Agencies

In this contemporary context, donors' priorities have changed in the following ways:

1. Since the 1980s, when the United States and the United Kingdom left UNESCO, funding for media and communication in Latin America has declined (Uranga, Cortés 2017). Nonetheless, financing continued for some Latin American communication programs, including from other United Nations institutions such as UNICEF, UNDP, FAO, and WHO (Dietz, Dragon 2017).
2. Agencies linked to European governments, public media, and political foundations started to prioritize national initiatives. For example, KAS has closed its Latin American media program (first based in Lima, then in Buenos Aires), though FES continues its operations from its regional media office in Bogotá. Funds from European Christian agencies also declined (Uranga, Valle, Dietz 2017).
3. U.S. support to media and communication in the region, however, has remained strong, particularly through the National Endowment for Democracy (NED) and USAID.
4. Since the late 1990s, one of the most significant changes is the growing presence of private philanthropic foundations such as the Open Society Foundation (George Soros), the Ford Foundation (Edsel and Henry Ford) and the Avina Foundation (Stephan Schmidheiny). These foundations are linked to big corporations and/or owners from the United States, United Kingdom, Germany, Sweden, the Netherlands, Canada and other contemporary donor countries (Mochkosvsky 2011; Segura & Waisbord 2016).

Geopolitical Shifts, Grassroots Changes

What are the continuities and discontinuities of the impact of development assistance on the Latin American communication field in the post-Cold War era?

1. Academic institutes and networks: Without international support, ALAIC in the 1980s and FELAFACS in the late 1990s weakened, but they continued to function and remained a point of reference in the field. Presently, they are supported by membership fees and occasionally receive foreign funding for specific projects (Cimadevilla 2017). Most national academic NGOs closed down, and their researchers and teachers returned to universities, where many of them are leading scholars in the region,

including Rafael Roncagliolo, Regina Festa, Héctor Schmucler, Alcira Argumedo, Juan Somavía and Fernando Reyes Matta.

2. Community media and networks: Some radio stations were weakened or forced to close after struggling to survive on local funds, but most of them continued to function and, in some cases, still receive foreign funding for specific activities. ALER, meanwhile, continues to be an important institution in the region. Since the 1980s, ALER adopted a new framework and began to work with the participatory and critical model of "popular communication." Another community media network, the World Association of Community Radio Broadcasters-Latin America and Caribbean (AMARC-ALC), was created in 1990 and received financing that afforded it institutional stability until at least 2010. AMARC-ALC not only worked as a media network, but also conducted research and lobbied to improve the broadcasting regulations in many countries; it had particular success in legalizing and promoting community media, as well as in limiting private media concentration (Lamas Dietz 2017).
3. New digital media: Since the 2000s, new digital media outlets aimed for quality and independence, contributing to the growth of investigative journalism in Latin America. Many of these new outlets are non-profit media that have benefitted from foreign aid (Palau 2017).
4. New advocacy coalitions: Most of the academic and community media networks have also expanded their aims to include advocacy for communication policy reform. They frequently form part of national, regional, and international coalitions that receive foreign funding for specific activities. Their focus has been on restricting private media concentration, legalizing and promoting community and indigenous media, and fostering national, local and independent production. These efforts have had varying levels of impact on the eleven new broadcasting and telecommunication laws passed from 2000 to 2015 in Latin American countries (Segura & Waisbord 2016).
5. New advocacy NGOs: Since the 1980s and 1990s, new NGOs have emerged with a focus on limiting the discretionary power of governments on public communication. They do this by promoting independent and investigative journalism, the elimination of libel laws, the regulation of official advertising, and increasing public access to information. They have taken advantage of certain national opportunities to promote the passage of access to information laws in seventeen countries, and to encourage the repeal of libel laws as well as the removal of criminal penalties for defamation in nine countries from 2000 to 2015 (Segura & Waisbord 2016).

6. New digital rights organizations: These organizations emerged in 2000 in the region to advocate for internet policies protecting civil rights, especially rights related to privacy, security, net neutrality, the freedom of expression, and access to information. Some long-standing human rights NGOs also started to include digital rights in their agendas.
7. Academic, social and political leaders: The academic and community media networks and associations were training grounds for intellectuals, activists and politicians in both the communication and political fields. They played key roles in coalitions and NGOs, bolstering communication policy reforms in the 2000s. Some of them even became important state officials like Augusto Dos Santos, Minister of Communications during the presidency of Fernando Lugo in Paraguay, or Rafael Roncagliolo, Minister of Foreign Affairs during the government of Ollanta Humala in Peru. "Community radio had a service function, but also served as fertile ground for committed people who afterwards made a political career" (Dietz 2017).

Conclusions

It is difficult to imagine the emergence, growth, and continuity of popular media, networks of community radio stations, or even academic associations and institutes, without foreign assistance. These media and institutions were created with international support, and when this financial aid was reduced or interrupted, local networks faced serious threats to their survival.

As result of local, national and regional organizations' initiatives with international aid, there are "thousands of people trained in communication, education and development" (Cortes 2017), and new community radios networks "that provide an important service function to their communities" (Dietz 2017).

These achievements, along with other factors, also contributed to some expected impacts at the macro level. In general, "the media offer grew" in the region (Dietz 2017). Between 1960 and 1990, "radio stations had the goal of strengthening democracies after dictatorships, and that effectively happened" (Vandenbulcke 2017). Since the 2000s, "international cooperation has helped community media to fight for state recognition" and they succeeded in many countries (Lamas 2017), with people who have been educated and mobilized with regard communication rights promoting media policy reforms in specific local contexts.

The cases reviewed confirm the complex relations and the inequalities of power between funders and recipients, but also highlight the relevant, unexpected, and long-term impacts. Despite many community media and academic NGOs weakening or disappearing over the years when international aid declined, regional institutions created in the 1970s are still the most important ones in the current regional communication field. Intellectuals, activists, and politicians educated decades ago still play key roles in media and politics today. Internationally-funded media organizations and civil society groups have had a significant influence over the past 15 years on media policy reforms grounded in critical, rights-based framework. Most of these institutions, media outlets, civil society organizations and activists developed a critical understanding of communication and development, even when some of them were initially supported by donors motivated by the modernization paradigm.

The evidence thus suggests that international aid has an influence, but that it does not unilaterally determine the impact. Instead, national governments, domestic politics, local opportunities, and other specific contexts are crucial, especially organizations and coalitions on the ground that are engaged in social mobilization and advocacy (Segura & Waisbord 2016). "The impact depends on both the project and the environment. In media, this is even more evident as they are also political actors. That's why media development projects are relatively fragile" (Dietz 2017). Indeed, the impact can be seen as the result of international support, but in interaction with the strategies of local organizations and activists, national opportunities, and states policies.

So what does this tell us about how to do media development better? Adapting to local situations and the work of domestic organizations is essential to increase the chances of success. International organizations need to cultivate linkages with local movements to support forms of media development that truly meet local needs and ambitions.

Notes

1. This chapter is based on a paper presented at IAMCR 2017 preconference "Reflections on Foreign Aid, Philanthropy and Change in Media Systems" organized by Aid and Journalism Network, CIMA, CAMRI and Global Forum for Media Development, in Cartagena, July 15th and 16th.
2. For more on the role of the MacBride Report on global communication debates, see Marc Raboy, "Global media: New Issues, Old Story chapter" (this volume).
3. Formerly CEBEMO.
4. For more on the difference between diffusion and participatory models of communication, see Morris, Nancy, "The Diffusion and Participatory Models: A Comparative Analysis," In *Media and Glocal Change: Rethinking Communication for Development*, edited by Oscar Hemer and Thomas Tufte, 123–44, Göteborg: Nordicom, 2005.

Recommended for Further Reading

Mochkofsky, Graciela. 2011. "What's New in Latin American Journalism. An Overview." *Harvard Review of Latin America*, vol. X (2): 15–17.

Roelofs, Joan. 1995. "The Third Sector as a Protective Layer for Capitalism." *Monthly Review*, 47 (4).

Segura, María Soledad, and Silvio Waisbord. 2016. *Media Movements: Civil Society and Media Policy Reform in Latin America*. London: Zed Books.

References

Beltrán, Luis Ramiro. 1976. "Políticas nacionales de comunicación en América Latina: Los primeros pasos." *Nueva Sociedad*, 25.

———. 1993. Opening speech. *IV Round Table on Communication and Development*, Lima: IPAL, February 23–26.

———. 2005. "La comunicación para el desarrollo en Latinoamérica: un recuento de medio siglo." In Participación y democracia en la Sociedad de la Información, edited by D. Loreti, G. Mastrini, and M. Baranchuk, 149–88. Buenos Aires: Prometeo.

Bolaño, César, Delia Crovi Druetta, and Gustavo Cimadevilla. (coords.). 2015. La contribución de América Latina al campo de la comunicación, Buenos Aires: Prometeo.

Eikenberry, Angela M., and Patricia Mooney Nickel. 2006. *Towards a Critical Social Theory of Philanthropy in an Era of Governance*. (Unpublished manuscript).

García Canclini, Nestor. 1994. "Los estudios culturales de los 80 a los 90: perspectivas antropólogicas y sociológicas en América Latina." In *Posmodernidad en la periferia: Enfoques latinoamericanos de la nueva teoría cultural*, edited by Hermann Herlinghauss and Monika Walter, 111–33. Berlin: Langer Verlag.

International Commission for the Study of Communication Problems (UNESCO). 1980. *Many Voices One World*. London: Kogan Page.

Mattelart, Armand and Michéle Mattelart. 1997. *Historia de las teorías de la comunicación*. Barcelona: Paidós.

Mochkofsky, Graciela. 2011. "What's New in Latin American Journalism. An Overview." *Harvard Review of Latin America*, vol. X (2).

Palau, D. 2017. "Media and philanthropy: Latin America as a Field of Interest." *Symposium on foreign aid and journalism in Latin America and Africa*, University of Leeds.

Prieto Castillo, Daniel. 2008. Radio Nederland Training Center en América Latina: Memoria pedagógica de tres décadas, San José: RNTC.

Roelofs, Joan. 1995. "The Third Sector as a Protective Layer for Capitalism." *Monthly Review*, 47 (4).

Segura, María Soledad. 2008. Procesos políticos y comunicacionales en Latinoamérica en los últimos 50 años. *Perspectivas de la Comunicación*, 1 (1): 81–96, Temuco: Universidad de la Frontera, July.

Segura, María Soledad, and Silvio Waisbord. 2016. *Media Movements: Civil Society and Media Policy Reform in Latin America*, London: Zed Books.
UNESCO. 2008. *Media Development Indicators. A framework for Assessing Media Development.* Paris: UNESCO.

Interviewees

Cimadevilla, G. (2017) ALAIC.
Cortés, C. E. (2017) Radio Nederland Training Center-AL.
Dietz, C. (2017) CAMECO.
Dragon, G. (2017) UNESCO/FAO.
Lamas, E. (2017) AMARC-AL.
Lee, P. (2017) WACC, Personal communication.
Puebla, A. C. (2017) FADECCOS/FELAFACS.
Uranga, W. (2017) La Crujía.
Valle, C. (2017) WACC-AL.
Vandenbulcke, H. (2017) ALER.

CHAPTER FOURTEEN

India's Media Development Seesaw

Advancement and Vulnerability in the World's Largest Democracy

SAVYASAACHI JAIN

It is perhaps impossible to provide a simple answer to the question of whether the Indian media system is a "developed" media system or not. By some yardsticks, it outpaces most others. At the same time, it demonstrably does not perform well along many other measures associated with the term "media development." This is perhaps to be expected, for it is difficult to unambiguously map the elements of media development to the realities of Indian media.

The Indian media system is a loose conglomerate of about two dozen linguistic sub-systems, distinguished by language, political and historical contexts, but linked by overlapping ownership, structures, and audiences, as well as common legal and regulatory frameworks. Within each sub-system there is a full range of practices and scales of operation. Its internal structures and processes are byzantine and often opaque, making it more difficult to characterize than any other national media system. On the other side of the equation, the term media development is also a multipart concept that encompasses a range of indicators, assumptions, and values. And of course the term is used in different ways at different times and places. Answering the basic question about the state of development of the Indian media system requires the complexity on either side to be unpacked. This essay draws upon my earlier research into the Indian media system and the phenomenon known within it as "paid news" (Jain 2016b) to reveal a more nuanced picture, showing that media development is not always a cohesive process whose constituent elements march to the same drummer. In fact, as the case of Indian media demonstrates, some aspects considered as development of the media can be linked to a regression in other aspects—in effect, a seesaw.

Media Development

The term media development is used in at least two major ways—as an activity and as a normative concept or set of outcomes. Media development as an activity refers to the targeting and delivery of international assistance to develop the capacity of media practitioners in specific countries, accompanied by encouragement for the creation of supportive institutional structures (see, for instance, Peters 2010). This is not the subject of this analysis. Media development as a normative concept, which is the broad meaning adopted here, loosely defines the elements of what is meant by the state of being developed. There are different formulations, but they all draw upon normative conceptions of the media's role in democratic politics, governance, society and the economy. The media's communicative power is credited with the ability to effect political accountability, social cohesion, stability and economic reform. In this essay, the term media development is understood to indicate this broad normative concept and its constituent elements.

Taken in this sense, the state of development of a media system is sought to be assessed by a range of indicators, which variously include independence from government ownership, editorial independence, pluralism and diversity, business viability, the quality of the legal environment, institutional support, and the professional performance of journalism (UNESCO 2008, among others).

The Indian case shows that the influence exerted by these variables can be at odds with each other—the media can develop along some of these measures but simultaneously slide back along others. Specifically, when systemic developments in Indian media are analysed, it becomes evident that they have developed in terms of size, reach, levels of private ownership, pluralism and diversity, editorial independence, and have also shrugged off oppressive regulation. However, they have simultaneously taken a step backwards in one important indicator—the professional performance of journalism. These two movements in opposite directions have been contemporaneous; while one developed, the other withered, and there is evidence to support a tangible linkage between the two.

My contention is that the vulnerability of journalism is significant, perhaps more significant than advances in other aspects of media development. The performance of high quality journalism must necessarily be accorded pole position within the concept of media development—after all, in this framework, it is clear that the term media refers to journalism rather than to films, game shows, or music videos. It is journalism and its truth-telling and deliberative functions that support the normative values of freedom and democracy. If some aspects of development impair journalism's fulfilment of its "first obligation" to truth and its "first loyalty" to citizens (Kovach and Rosenstiel 2014), then, in any analysis, this must be set off against the positive movement along other indicators while making an overall evaluation of the state of media development. This essay establishes the contours of this internal contradiction with a study of how development and vulnerability go hand in hand in the case of the Indian media.

The Indian Media System

While researching the phenomenon known as paid news, I asked one of India's best known journalists, Rajdeep Sardesai, how Indian journalism today is better than it used to be. He paused for nearly 10 seconds before coming up with: "Energy, passion and aggression" (research interview). It is likely that the question stumped the normally articulate Sardesai because for at least a decade the discourse on the ethics of Indian journalism has been fiercely critical. Stepping into modernity through an idealistic nationalism as it did, Indian journalism has long taken pride in performing a public service role. It continues to adhere to this self-image, and not without justification. However, journalism's many achievements have been overshadowed by frequent high profile incidents of influence-peddling, corruption, and egregious ethical breaches. Even accounting for an overblown nostalgia for a more ethical and responsible past, there is widespread recognition within the profession that all is not well in Indian journalism.

This contrasts with the equally important reality that in many aspects, the Indian media system, which serves the largest democratically governed population on the planet, has developed very rapidly indeed since the 1990s in the case of newspapers and the early 2000s in the case of television. Economic reforms in the 1990s ushered in what is perhaps best described as an age of explosive growth in the media (Jain 2015). At a time when traditional media have been in rapid decline in the advanced economies of the West, Indian newspapers and television have witnessed double-digit growth rates over more than a decade. *The Times of India*, now the widest circulated English-language daily in the world, expanded operations from 12 editions to 33 between 2010 and 2014. Private television channels offering news and factual content were unknown till the mid-1990s but today they are more than 400. The media has reaped the benefits of increases in population, literacy and buying power, but penetration rates are still low by international standards, which mean that there is a lot of headroom and the trajectory of rapid growth is expected to be maintained in the near future.

India is now arguably the most vibrant of all media systems. It is the largest newspaper market in the world, having overtaken China in 2010; has more than 105,000 registered publications, of which nearly 15,000 are daily newspapers; and hosts more than 800 television channels. The rapid multiplication of media outlets represents a substantive disjuncture from its historical past (Jain 2016a), which can broadly be divided into phases that were formative (extending from early beginnings in 1780 to 1919); characterized by nationalism (1919 to independence in 1947); nation-building (1947 to the end of the Emergency in 1977); and aggressive journalism (1977 to the early 1990s).

The Vulnerabilities of Journalism

This rapid growth ticks several of the boxes of media development, including private ownership; independence from government control; independence from oppressive regulation; and pluralism and diversity within the media. But there is an important downside as well, and that is sustainability. Indian media organizations are struggling to survive in what can only be described as an overcrowded and hyper-competitive market. Large numbers of new entrants exert pressure on existing players, forcing everybody into strategies of aggressive expansion, rampant price wars and undercutting, which place revenue models under further strain. In addition, the media are growing far faster than the economy as a whole—twice as fast in many years over the past decade—which means that the advertising pie is not keeping pace, apart from being sliced up ever thinner among more outlets. Only a handful of players in each segment of the market, typically the top two or three, are profitable, but even they remain under constant pressure to stay ahead of the pack. This unrelieved struggle for survival has strongly affected ways of conducting business in the media and, inevitably, the pressures on journalism to play a role in generating revenue.

The phenomenon of paid news provides an excellent illustration of the processes through which these developments have influenced the quality of journalism. Paid news, which refers to political advertising being surreptitiously passed off as news by media organizations in exchange for unaccounted cash, came to attention during the 2009 national general elections when Palgummi Sainath, recipient of more than 40 Indian and international awards for his journalism, reported that candidates were being subject to "media extortion" and being asked to buy "coverage packages" if they wanted any media coverage at all (Sainath 2009). Soon after, *The Wall Street Journal* reported a remarkably similar story from a different part of India about 1,300 km away, a region dominated by entirely different media organizations:

> Ajay Goyal is a serious, independent candidate contesting for a Lok Sabha [the directly elected lower house of the bicameral Indian Parliament] seat in Chandigarh. [...] So far, he says, he's been approached by about 10 people—some brokers and public relations managers acting on behalf of newspaper owners, some reporters and editors—with the message that he'll only get written about in the news pages for a fee. We're not talking advertising; we're talking news. (Beckett 2009)

It became clear that these were not isolated incidents, neither were they stealthy acts of corruption undertaken by opportunistic individuals. Marketing departments of news organizations initiated and developed the practice, and it was fuelled by a desperate desire to boost revenues by grabbing what they could of politicians' election spending. Not only was the practice institutionalized, it witnessed virulent adoption across the full breadth of the media system, across linguistic sub-systems and ownership patterns (Jain 2016b). By all accounts, only a handful of media organizations resisted the temptation. Apart from being illegal, paid news is widely recognized as a serious breach of the values central to journalism by observers, regulators and institutions of state. There is not a single voice defending the practice from within the Indian journalistic community, but at the same time active disapproval and steps to combat it have not been as forthcoming as might have been expected from a professional media. Inquiries have been instituted and reports commissioned, all the way from the Press Council of India to Parliament, but corrective action from within or outside the media has been largely ineffective. The practice persevered in subsequent elections.

Many of the trends and influences significant in the emergence of paid news are counted among the indicators of media development. One is freedom from government and regulatory control. In the Indian case, it has at times become freedom so extreme it is expressed as impunity, undermining of the law, and snubbing institutions of state. The practice of paid news represents the media refusing to subject itself to the influence of politics, pushing back against the political establishment, setting the terms of engagement and indulging in what has been termed as extortion. A second positive indicator is independence from government ownership. Today Indian media is overwhelmingly privately owned—the only major government-controlled media outlets are the bouquet of television channels and radio stations of the state broadcaster, Prasar Bharati (Broadcasting Corporation of India), but they command a small and diminishing fraction of the audience. The real problem here seems to be the unfettered entry of private owners. On the face of it, they tick the boxes of diversity and pluralism. However the reality is that there are far too many new entrants in this rapidly expanding market, which has led to an overcrowded, hyper-competitive and hyper-commercialized media sphere. Even more disturbing is the nature of the private ownership—it includes many who have apparently entered the media with the specific intention of instrumentalizing journalism for profit or political gain.

This environment is directly implicated in the pressures exerted on journalism and the embarrassing inability of journalists to prevent the collapse of professional values. The reaction to paid news from within the journalistic fraternity is perhaps best characterized as a slightly guilty but helpless wringing of hands. Those who should have exercised control over the channels through which paid news was published—indeed, whose *raison d'etre* it is—appear to have ceded authority to owners and managements with barely a murmur. The outcome: a system-wide and institutionalized ethical fault-line so outrageous that it can only be classified as a huge step backwards, even as it is linked intricately to several indicators that count as media development.

Conclusion

This essay uses a prominent phenomenon in the Indian media to argue that media development is not a unitary, synchronized concept that indicates an unambiguous direction of movement. The movement from government to pluralistic private control that is central to the concept of media development can cut both ways. Paid news shows that the deregulatory impulse that is implicit in the concept, and which has undoubted relevance to controlled and undemocratic media systems, can wreak havoc on the core functions of democratic media if taken too far. This seesaw pairing of advancements in some areas with vulnerabilities in others necessitates a more nuanced approach to the broad conception of media development if it is to reflect the complexities of reality.

Paid news is but one of many phenomena that have bedeviled Indian media, chosen as a case for this essay because it represents the confluence of multiple structural, institutional and organizational factors. The problem in most countries in need of media development is a lack of media independence, but the problem in India seems to be that the media have gravitated to the other end of the spectrum. As media output has increased many fold, it has become increasingly central to determining the direction of public discourse, and media organizations have become powerful enough to display impunity in the face of widespread disquiet. The effective locus of civil society—and even journalistic—concern about media standards has been relegated to the arena of blogs, online forums and social media, but with little meaningful impact on standards within the mainstream media.

Many of the pressures on journalism arise from the political economy of media organizations—the demands of politically aligned or profit-seeking owners, the struggle for survival, an intense focus on revenue, and the political, social and religious polarization in contemporary India. The forces driving the fall in standards are strong, stronger than mere civil society concern can counteract. Journalism education has not been effective either—students who emerge from journalism schools report that the first thing they have to unlearn is their classroom learning about media ethics. The culture of professionalism in journalism has buckled under the pressure of owners and managements and it is ironical that in an increasingly powerful media, journalists at its heart have lost the power to uphold the norms they claim to espouse. Perhaps the route to promoting media development lies in the hands of the audience. Few initiatives have targeted media literacy and this may well be a viable but long term route to inducing cultural change within the media.

Recommended for Further Reading

Rao, Shakuntala, and Herman Wasserman, eds. 2015. *Media Ethics and Justice in the Age of Globalization*. Basingstoke: Palgrave Macmillan, 2015.

UNESCO. 2008. *Media Development Indicators: A Framework for Assessing Media Development.* Paris: UNESCO International Programme for the Development of Communication.

References

Beckett, Paul. 2009. "Want Press Coverage? Give Me Some Money". *The Wall Street Journal*, 6 May 2009. http://online.wsj.com/article/SB124158152250690795.html.

Jain, Savyasaachi. 2015. "India: Multiple Media Explosions". In *Mapping BRICS Media*, edited by Kaarle Nordenstreng and Daya Kishan Thussu, 145–65. Abingdon: Routledge.

———. 2016a. "India: You Ain't Seen Nothing Yet". In *Last words? How Can Journalism Survive the Death of Print?*, edited by. John Mair, Tor Clark, Neil Fowler, Raymond Snoddy, and Richard Tait, 260–68. Bury St. Edmunds: Abramis..

———. 2016b. *Rethinking Media Systems: Insights from a Case Study of Paid News in India.* Unpublished thesis, London: University of Westminster.

Kovach, Bill, and Tom Rosenstiel. 2014. *The Elements of Journalism*, 3rd edition. New York, NY: Three Rivers Press.

Peters, Bettina. 2010. "The Future of Journalism and Challenges for Media Development." *Journalism Practice*, 4 (3): 268–73.

Sainath, Palgummi. 2009. "Package Deals—With Credibility Discounts." *The Hindu*, 7 April. http://www.thehindu.com/todays-paper/tp-national/package-deals-with-credibility-discounts/article299513.ece.

CHAPTER FIFTEEN

The State of Media Development in Eastern Europe and the Former Soviet Republics

GILLIAN MCCORMACK

At the very end of the Soviet period, one year before the failed coup in Moscow that signaled the Communist Party's collapse, a new U.S.S.R. Law was passed on the Press and Other Mass Media (August 1, 1990) that banned censorship and allowed private individuals to found their own media companies. In the ensuing period of transition that occurred in the former Soviet republics and Eastern Bloc countries, one of the most profound and immediately noticeable changes was the exponential growth of new, commercial broadcasters and newspapers, bringing alternative sources of information to the public for the first time in 70 years. At the same time, the Soviet notion that the media represent a tool with which to manipulate, control, and influence the minds of the masses retained its appeal for emerging political and economic elites and made private media companies vulnerable to capture by these new (and sometimes same old) special interests. International media development assistance interventions had been made prior to this time, chiefly in Latin American countries, but there is a general consensus (Price, De Luce, and Davis Noll 2002) that the big test for this field came with the opening of opportunities to foster the growth of independent media in Eastern Europe and the former Soviet republics in the 1990s.

Efforts to Support Media Development in the 1990s

This was a period where any enthusiast with an engineering degree could build a transmitter and start broadcasting out of the basement. Commercial broadcasting and publishing was in its infancy, amateur TV, amateur radio, amateur newspapers, amateur porn, amateur everything flourished. In Russia, *Internews* began working with small regional companies that went on to become major regional players. Assistance was simple and effective: provide equipment and teach people how to use it. Practical schools of journalism created a new cadre of young people who knew how to do a "stand-up" to camera and had learned something about professional ethics. This generation grew up to become the managers and leaders of their industry (Kumar 2004). On the other hand, training in this period could be ad hoc, "parachuting" in experts who worked on the basis of donor priorities (i.e., investigative reporting or how to cover EU-related issues) that did not necessarily reflect media needs (Marko 2013).

The 1990 law set up some ground rules for the media sphere but in general the now ex-Communist bloc needed to elaborate a totally new and different set of regulations for how media should operate in the newly independent republics. There were no laws pertaining to broadcasting or advertising, for example, and new legislatures were busy creating constitutions and laws that placed strict restrictions on media freedom. Assistance focused on bringing European and U.S. experience to bear, which turned out to be problematic: the approach of trying to transplant Western models of institutional reforms onto developing countries with very different local contexts was not a success. Media law reform was difficult to achieve in environments described by Zielonka and Mancini (2011) as having common characteristics which included "floating laws" that were frequently changed and inconsistent, creating legal insecurity across the region (Jusić and Ahmetašević, 2013). Media law advocacy often focused on combatting the criminal prosecution of criticism of the president and defamation more generally, because of the debilitating nature of these cases. A decade later these efforts started to pay off (e.g., the death penalty for criticizing Turkmenistan's president was lifted in 1999; Tajikistan decriminalized insult in 2012).

At first, civil society organizations and dynamic individuals took up the interests of the new private media industry as a matter of public interest, lobbying for better laws and access to licenses and printing houses. During the 1990s, advocacy and support organizations began to spring up, like the South East Europe Media Organisation (SEEMO), the Independent Association of Broadcasters (IAB) in

Ukraine, the Association of Independent Electronic Media (ANEM) in Serbia, the Association of Electronic Press in Moldova, the Yerevan Press Club, the Baku Press Club, the Association of Private Broadcasters in Czechia, among many others. Not all press clubs, journalists' unions and industry associations survived long-term, but they played an extremely important role and helped the sector define for itself its priorities and needs throughout this nascent period of development.

In the early days of banking in these new independent republics that were transitioning from total state control to private ownership of companies, loans and credits for new businesses were difficult, if not impossible, to come by. The launch of the Media Development Loan Fund—now the Media Development Investment Fund—in 1996 was a pivotal moment for new media companies that had a plan, but no financing. Since its inception, the MDIF offered capital investments and loans to around 90 independent media in over 30 countries grow and flourish.

Transition from one-party rule and the competition of regional elites over resources and power led to violence, border conflicts, and outright war in some places. Armenia and Azerbaijan went to war over the disputed territory of Nagorno-Karabakh (Russia intervened on Armenia's side), Georgia experienced conflict with two breakaway republics (Russia supported the breakaway republics), Moldova had a conflict over the breakaway Transnistria region (Russia supported Transnistria), civil war erupted in Tajikistan (Russia intervened on the side of government forces), Chechnya tried unsuccessfully to break away from the Russian Federation, and the Balkans descended into a horrific series of wars that cost the lives of approximately 100,000 people. The role of the media in conflict suddenly became an alarming problem facing the region and a number of organizations and programs designed approaches to address it; for example, the work of *Conciliation Resources* on civil society and media in the Caucasus, and the USAID-funded "Children's Crossroads" program that brought young people together to work on a television program that was broadcast by TV partners in all three countries.

Diverging Needs in the 2000s

By the end of the 1990s, the divergence of the former Eastern Bloc countries and the former Soviet Republics was more or less complete. Countries like Czechia, Slovakia, Hungary, Poland, Romania, and Bulgaria were on their way towards EU membership. Their needs lay in reforming their regulatory environment to be in line with European legal standards and provisions. The major recipient of media development assistance in the region was the Balkans, which went towards strengthening media capacity, content production grants, and media law reform. The former Soviet bloc diverged still further, with the Baltics preparing to enter the EU, and Moldova, Armenia, Georgia and Ukraine also keen to look to the EU for partnership agreements. Meanwhile Russia, Belarus, Azerbaijan, and the Central Asian countries all saw democratic downturns, with growing state intolerance of civic, political, and media rights. The outlier in Central Asia was Kyrgyzstan, which like Ukraine witnessed a series of popular uprisings against corrupt regimes, with mixed results—some progress towards greater protections for transparency and media rights, but also occasional reversals.

Programs began to focus on strengthening the capacity of local media serving the needs of regional audiences (that is, those residing outside of capital cities). The national media in most countries were either controlled by the state or by oligarchs. National broadcasters were used by elites to throw mud at each other and the word "kompromat" (short for "compromising material" in Russian) came into general use. Many people lost trust in national media, and local media began to fill this gap by providing reliable, locally relevant information on topics that people cared about (i.e., local education and health services, the state of roads, local tax issues etc.). By the mid-2000s, the Russian government had captured all the national TV broadcasters and turned its attention to exerting control over independent regional broadcasters. Independent and critical local media came under attack and the leading national NGO providing media assistance—the Educated Media Foundation (formerly Internews Russia)—was forced to close. In 2012, the Russian government expelled USAID from the country. Belarus, Azerbaijan and Uzbekistan also became increasingly closed during this period. In Central and Eastern Europe, by contrast, and in countries looking towards European partnership, the operating environment and growth of investigative reporting began to strengthen popular perception of the media as playing a key role in promoting progress.

By the end of the 1990s the number of media training opportunities led to complaints of "training fatigue" in some countries (like Serbia). Donors worried about "per diem-itis"—the notion that participants only attended training events to collect the daily stipend given to cover their expenses. However, the ensuing drop in training opportunities exposed the lack of alternatives, with the absence of effective journalism education at universities or any other training opportunities for new media personnel. Individual media companies could not afford to provide in-house education, media technology was advancing, and the industry began to perceive the lack of trained professional cadre as a serious problem.

Media assistance began to make progress in rebalancing the media's legal operating environment. A major achievement of these years was the decriminalization in many European and Eurasian countries of defamation. This freed media from the burden of fighting frequent and debilitating law suits. Additionally, there was some success in introducing and improving the implementation of access to information laws, backed by useful global initiatives such as the Open Government Partnership initiative, which encouraged even fairly authoritarian countries (like Kazakhstan and Azerbaijan) to become part of the club. This helped. Even in Russia, the law on access to information seems to result in a 50 percent success rate for information requests to officials.

Challenges for Media Development in 2017

Back in 1999, a report by USAID's Center for Democracy and Governance identified the biggest challenges for the media (globally) to overcome as being: "media oligarchs, hostile political regimes, and restrictive economic environments," (The Role of Media in Democracy, 1999, 35). While this remains true, the efforts of the Russian government to maintain influence in its neighborhood represent the preeminent challenge for many countries in the region today. Russia's influence is persistent, through aggressive exportation of its most anti-Western laws (e.g., labelling civil society organizations receiving funding from abroad as "foreign agents" and banning "propaganda" of "non-traditional sexual orientation"), exhortation to join the Eurasian Economic Union, the annexation of Crimea, and the continued territorial destabilization of Ukraine, Moldova, Georgia, Armenia, and Azerbaijan by supporting frozen, as well as live, conflicts with breakaway regions. These efforts are accompanied by the still privileged access of Russian government-controlled TV channels and online news agencies throughout the former Soviet space, as well as efforts to influence public opinion through highly targeted media disinformation campaigns in Europe and the United States.

In the past few years, the region has been presenting critical challenges related to the use of media that exert an influence far beyond its borders. The abuse of social media to spread misinformation, the "fake news" phenomenon, troll factories, distributed denial of service attacks, and mass distribution of malware are all emanating from here. At the same time, the old challenges of dealing with media capture, economic instability, and political repression remain.

If you ask many people running media companies in Europe and Eurasia what their main problem is, they usually refer to "the economic crisis" and a downturn in advertising revenue. In Europe the last major economic upheaval was the sovereign debt crisis in 2009, but the effects of that contraction are still felt today. The former Soviet republics remain disproportionately affected by the state of the Russian Federation's economy, which suffered a hit in 2014 when the international financial sanctions against it for its illegal annexation of Crimea coincided with a dramatic downturn in the value of oil, on which its economy still heavily depends. Ukraine's economy suffered a double blow, in that trade with its biggest trading partner (Russia) was adversely affected by being in an undeclared conflict with that country, and the necessity of militarily defending its borders added an extra burden to the budget. Ukrainian media companies described a 30 percent drop in advertising revenue. In Central Asia too, advertising revenue fell by between 30–60 percent, according to media industry estimates, and has been slow to recover.

Has There Been Any Progress?

Two of the major indices of progress on media freedom and sustainability—Freedom House's *Freedom of the Press* and *IREX's Media Sustainability Index*—show a mixed picture in terms of progress in Europe and Eurasia. In Freedom House's index, high scores indicate a low level of freedom. By that standard (see the graph below comparing 2001 and 2017) Uzbekistan has not improved at all, and things have become objectively worse in Turkmenistan, Tajikistan, Russia, Poland, Romania, Macedonia, Lithuania, Latvia, Kazakhstan, Hungary, Croatia, Bulgaria, Belarus, Azerbaijan, Armenia, and Albania. Sixty-five percent of countries in the region show a decline in media freedom between 2001 to now. Freedom House's global average shows only 35 percent of countries in the world as "free." In that sense, Europe and Eurasia are well within the global average, which is poor. However, this does represent an improvement on the 1986 global average, which was 76 percent "not free" or "partly free." So, it would be fair to say that in the last 30 years, some progress has been made.

If we look at the Media Sustainability Index, where a score of less than two indicates an unsustainable system and higher than two indicates a movement towards sustainability, sustainable models seem to be appearing in Ukraine, Romania, Montenegro, Moldova, Macedonia, Georgia, Croatia, Bulgaria, Armenia and Albania. While Tajikistan, Kazakhstan, Belarus, and Bosnia-Herzegovina have made some progress, their media landscapes continue to suffer a multitude of problems connected to media capture, state interference, and legal impediments to the creation of truly independent and free media. Serbia, Macedonia, Croatia, and Bulgaria show several areas of decline and failure to thrive. Uzbekistan continues to languish with one of the lowest scores, although hopes remain that the situation may improve following the death of Islam Karimov in 2016. Turkmenistan is not included in the graph below because it was not measured in 2001 but its score in 2017 was 0.24. It remains almost completely closed and independent media do not exist there. The 2006 replacement of the eccentric Soviet-era leader Saparmurat Niyazov upon his demise, best known for commissioning a magnificent rotating golden statue of himself and renaming the months of the year after members of his family, did not result in any notable reform (The Personality Cult of Turkmenbashi, 2016).

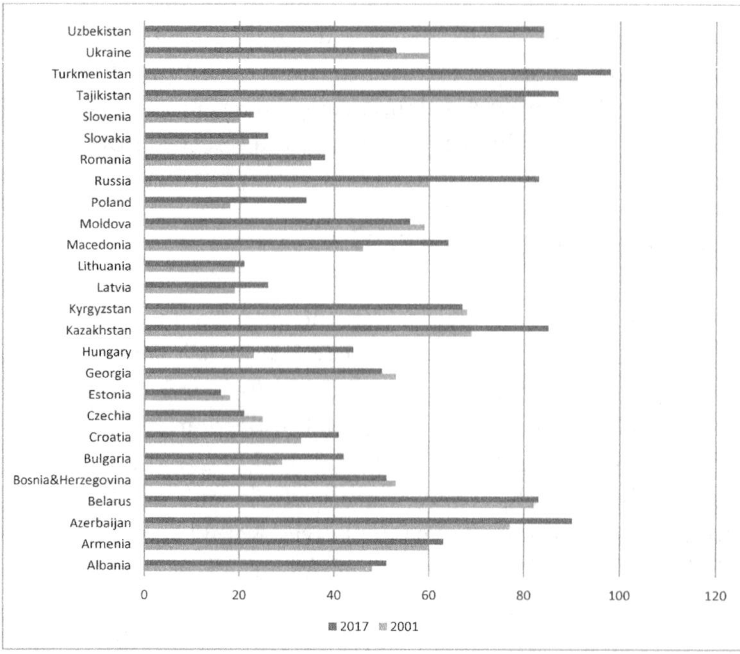

Figure 15.1. Freedom House's Freedom of the Press Index for Eastern European countries, 2001 and 2017.

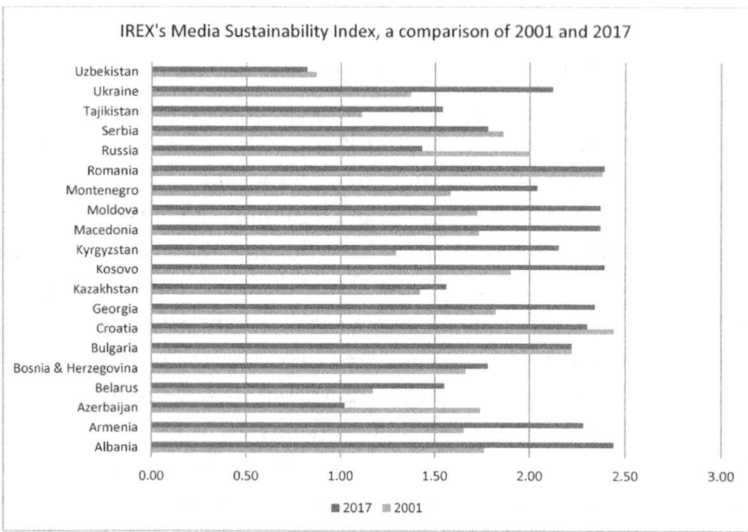

Figure 15.2. IREX's Media Sustainability Index, a comparison of 2001 and 2017.

Looked at from this perspective, the region's results for media sustainability are even worse than those for media freedom, with the majority of countries in the region struggling to create a healthy economic and legal environment for media to flourish. Nevertheless, relatively few of the countries included in this overview have seen major declines in media sustainability overall—only Uzbekistan, Serbia, Russia, Croatia and Azerbaijan have had setbacks. Around 75 percent of countries in the region have seen improvements in the conditions for media sustainability.

Is Media Development Making a Difference?

Nearly a decade ago Krishna Kumar (2009) wrote that donors had focused too much on media development as part of democracy work, failing to consider the wider role of the media in supporting all kinds of economic, social, and cultural development. Donors and implementers concentrated for too long on the narrow performance period of media around specific periods of political flux—elections, and post-conflict transition. Countries that appeared to be doing well enough on democratic progress were often deprioritized for media assistance. However, the financial investment of international donors into the survival of independent media in Europe and Eurasia has been impressive. Consider that between 2007 and 2012 the U.S. government spent $126m on media development and freedom of expression in this region alone (Cary & D'Amour, 2013).

The success of media development is hard to measure (although not impossible),[1] but analysis is complicated by the fact that the media do not exist in a vacuum. Where there are political and economic declines, the media obviously cannot thrive. However, it is perhaps at these times that media development assistance can make the most difference to the lives of citizens in closed or closing societies. Historically, revolutions and transitions provided a fertile environment for the overhaul of legal systems regulating and protecting media. Efforts at self-regulation in the region tended to fail, as agreement on shared professional standards and ethics faltered at the hurdles of fierce economic competition and resistance to controls that felt to many like additional forms of self-censorship. The reluctance of governments to release control of publicly-funded media meant that transition to fully-fledged public service broadcasting has stalled in many places. At the same time, oligarchs across the region hold on to media companies like vanity projects, making these media incapable of legitimately serving the interests of audiences.

In the best-case scenarios, media development assistance has helped achieve fairer laws, challenge monopolies of ownership of media distribution networks, and promote peaceful dialogue between populations riven by war and unrest. And journalists are at the forefront of exposing corruption and crime in high office.

In Ukraine, journalists work with transparency activists to verify public officials' income and asset declarations, and in Moldova and Russia drone journalism has been used effectively to expose the fabulous properties of the elite to wider public scrutiny than those elites would prefer. In Kyrgyzstan, the public service broadcaster Yntymak—which serves populations in the south with multilingual reporting in Kyrgyz, Uzbek and Russian—has become the most popular and trusted source of information in that part of the country. Stories produced by Yntymak and other media across the region have inspired local communities to organize urban regeneration projects for their towns, encouraged local authorities to fix roads and rebuild schools, uncovered the obscene wealth of state officials and oligarchs, and made use of publicly available data to show levels of environmental pollution that succeeded in shaming some industrial polluters into improving their behavior.

What Does the Region Need Now?

With advertising revenue moving to larger players that provide high-production value entertainment (as is the trend globally) (Foster, 2017), local, independent media are more vulnerable to capture by special interests and more likely to fail as businesses. On the other hand, smaller local media have the advantage of being better positioned to provide relevant information and content to their audiences, in the language they prefer to consume it in. To help media navigate the switch to mobile, while continuing to serve audiences that want access to information across whatever platform they are most comfortable using, media across Europe and Eurasia—regardless of membership of the European Union (which is by no means an indicator that all is well with the media)—need a combination of new skills, as well as the old professional basics which should not be forgotten in the rush towards innovation. New generations of reporters and influencers are appearing from all spheres. Media development needs to support the potential of people reporting not just from the traditional media, but from civil society, industry, science and the arts. Creative collaborations are the future. For media in this region, survival will depend on their ability to adapt to new technology, move quickly toward convergence, localize entertainment models, produce transmedia storytelling, and maintain digital security. They must also analyze their audiences beyond demographics, not only to strengthen sales, but to strengthen engagement, ensuring that content and services provided by media are responsive to what audiences need in their daily lives.

Finally, citizens in Europe and Eurasia are fielding a greater number of challenges than ever before in terms of finding trustworthy information, with education lagging behind new trends in spreading disinformation. Helping independent media survive is not enough in these times. Media literacy initiatives need to become a priority too—to enhance the ability of media audiences to critically consume messages, exercise reasonable doubt without becoming skeptical of all sources, and verify information effectively themselves.

Note

1. See Susan Abbott's chapter in this volume for more on measurement issues in the field of media development.

Recommended for Further Reading

Abbott, Susan. 2016. "Rethinking Public Service Broadcasting's Place in International Media Development." The Center for International Media Assistance.

Foster, Michelle. 2014. "Measuring the Audience: Why It Matters to Independent Media and How It Can Contribute to Media Development." The Center for International Media Assistance.

Gross, Peter, and Jakubowicz, Karol, eds. 2012. *Media Transformations in the Post-Communist World: Eastern Europe's Tortured Path to Change*. Lanham, MD: Lexington Books.

Kumar, Krishna. 2009. "One Size Does Not Fit All: Objectives and Priority Areas for Media Assistance in Different Societies." The Center for International Media Assistance ...

References

Cary, Peter, and Rosemary D'Amour. 2013. *U.S. Government Funding for Media: Trends and Strategies*. Washington, D.C.: Center for International Media Assistance

Foster, Michelle J. 2017. *Media Feast, News Famine: Ten Global Advertising Trends That Threaten Independent Journalism*. Washington, D.C.: Center for International Media Assistance.

Jusić Tarik and Nidžara Ahmetašević. 2013. *Media Reforms through Intervention: International Media Assistance in Bosnia and Herzegovina*. Analitika Center for Social Research.

Kumar, Krishna. 2004. *USAID's Media Assistance: Policy and Programmatic Lessons*. PPC Evaluation Working Paper No. 16. Bureau for Policy and Program Coordination USAID, Washington D.C.

Marko, Davor. 2013. *Media Reforms in Turbulent Times: The Role of Media Assistance in the Establishment of Independent Media Institutions in Serbia*. Analitika Center for Social Research.

Price, Monroe, Daniel De Luce and Bethany Davis Noll. 2002. *Mapping Media Assistance*. University of Pennsylvania.

Staff and Agencies. 2006. "The Personality Cult of Turkmenbashi" *The Guardian*. December 21. https://www.theguardian.com/world/2006/dec/21/1

USAID. 1999. *The Role of Media in Democracy: A Strategic Approach, Center for Democracy and Governance, Bureau for GlobalPrograms, Field Support, and Research.* Washington D.C: U.S. Agency for International Development.

Zielonka, Jan, and Paolo Mancini. 2011. *Executive Summary: A Media Map of Central and Eastern Europe, Media and Democracy in Central and Eastern Europe.* Department of Politics and International Relations of the University of Oxford and Department of Media and Communications, The London School of Economics and Political Science.

PART FOUR

Models, Strategies, and Practices

CHAPTER SIXTEEN

How the Fault-Lines in Media Development Assistance Make Us Ill-Prepared for the Future

A Densely Potted Historical Analysis

JAMES DEANE

What is the purpose of supporting independent media? What are the motivations and expectations of those who do so? How have they changed and how can they be expected to do so in the future?

These questions matter more now perhaps than they ever have. The reasons that independent media around the world are under such intense threat are complex—encompassing national politics, international power rivalries, money, technology, and economics. The response to these threats needs to both make sense of this complexity and be clear in its purpose if it is to have impact. While the efforts of those who seek to undermine the independence of the media and democratic public debate are often well organized and strategic in their intent and operation, the efforts of those who exist to defend it are relatively inchoate, inconsistent, and fragmented. It matters what this field consists of, how it is organized, and what it exists to achieve.

Media Development: What Is It Good For?

There is a reasonable consensus on what media development is. The National Endowment for Democracy's Center for International Media Assistance defines it as the:

> evolution and change in the fields of news media and communications. Such change relates to a range of institutions, practices, and behaviours including the rule of law, freedoms of expression and press, education systems for journalists, business environments, capacities of journalists and managers, as well as support for a diversity of views in society. This evolution can be stimulated by donor support, private investment, or local processes of change led by media owners, managers, journalists, media industry associations, and other collective efforts. (Center for International Media Assistance, n.d.)

The purpose of this chapter is to interrogate whether there is a similarly clear consensus of what media development is *for*, especially from the perspective of those who financially support it. Understanding issues of incentive and motivation and the expectation of what media development will actually result in can help illuminate the urgent challenges that are confronting the field in the future and, perhaps, better prepare it for how to meet those challenges.

For many, the motivation of supporting media development is or at least should be clear: to support freedom of expression and an independent fourth estate as a critical component underpinning a free and open society and a functioning democratic system. The principal focus of such support in this view is to build the capacities and help shape environments most capable of supporting and defending independent public-interest journalism characterized by a set of professional standards (in this sense, it is distinct from the pure advocacy objectives of many excellent media freedom organizations).

This was the conception of media development which powered its greatest phase of expansion in the 1990s as part of the democratic pressure blast that swept around the world following the "big bang" of the fall of the Berlin Wall. Success from that support was defined in intrinsic terms. As country after country liberalized its media laws, could the media that flourished become genuinely independent of government? Could it develop strong professional journalistic standards? Could it become sufficiently sustainable both to survive and to fend off undue political or other influence? It was an apparent consensus that appeared to bind highly disparate donors and organizations, one that was rooted as much in an African vision articulated in Windhoek Declaration of 1991 as that of the U.S. constitution or Article 19 of the Universal Declaration of Human Rights.

In reality, the philosophies and objectives of different donors and media support organizations were often quite distinct and have become more so as time has worn on. The interests and expectations of the Open Society Foundation in supporting independent media were not necessarily the same as those of the Ford Foundation; those of the British Department for International Development not the same as those of the Swedish International Development Cooperation

Agency; those of USAID not the same as the European Union; those of the World Bank not the same as those of UNESCO. And yet all of these have in different ways sought to support independent media. Some were focused on advancing freedom, others on fostering greater state citizen accountability or reducing corruption, others still on reducing conflict or improving social cohesion, or supporting more inclusive elections.

The diversity of objectives became more acute as political and development realities changed. By the 2000s, the focus of much media support had shifted from supporting media in the context of home grown democratic transitions (commonly termed democracy assistance) to being a component of building democracy in the context of "nation building" in the wake of military invasion, especially in Afghanistan, Iraq and Somalia (commonly termed *democracy promotion*). The expectations of those financially supporting media in such contexts were often closely allied to larger efforts designed to foster a Western model of democratic governance and, at least sometimes, support the objectives of the invasion.

By this time too, a growing skepticism was emerging against international media support, especially when it was focused on fragile, conflict affected or "crisis" states. Criticism centred on concerns that support appeared to be rolling out a preconceived, mostly Western, notion or "template" of what a free and independent media looked like. It argued that, in the words of one London School of Economics report, "in situations where the state is fragile, and where the political process is unstable and de-legitimated, the primary objective of donor assistance should be supporting the formation of a functioning state" (Putzel and Van Der Zwan 2005, 22). The same report argued that media development approaches were often naïve and lacked understanding of the complexity of political and developmental contexts, particularly in fragile settings where political tension could easily spill out into violence.

Such concerns meshed with a growing trend at least in the development sector in the 2000s to focus more intently on building state capacity as well as with efforts to improve aid effectiveness. The Paris Declaration on Aid Effectiveness in 2005 heralded a fresh phase of development cooperation rooted in ensuring aid responded to developing country agendas, not the donor ones. Principles of "country ownership" and "mutual accountability" underpinned such agreements and bilateral aid in particular, increasingly took the form of budget support provided directly to governments by groups of donors working cooperatively. The role of the media became increasingly invisible and deprioritized in many bilateral development strategies mainly because developing country governments were highly unlikely to prioritize media support (Paris Declaration on Aid Effectiveness 2005).

Shifting Toward a Governance Approach

To the extent that media support was prioritized, it was increasingly within a governance agenda focused on making the state perform better for its citizens. A U.K. Department for International Development paper (which this author contributed to drafting) placed support for media clearly within its overall governance approach of making the state more capable, responsive, and accountable. The conception that support to a free and plural media should be a development priority in and of itself had given way to one where support for media was legitimate and potentially important, but was expected to deliver clear, measurable governance outcomes (UK Department for International Development 2008).

By the beginning of the 2010s disillusionment with budget support was beginning to set in as mismanagement and corruption in their spending increased (something, ironically, that might have been better prevented had there been a more strategic approach to investing in independent media capable of holding government to account). A new wave of accountability and transparency initiatives[1] gained traction in donor support strategies in response but while many of these focused on improving access to information (through opening up budgets, providing citizens with a right to information or ensuring government data was more widely accessible), the focus on support to independent media was a relatively peripheral component of these efforts.

Other trends have run parallel to or increasingly characterized media development support. The growing focus on digital and technology-first initiatives provide an example of the latter. The developing field of communication for development focused on supporting media and other communication initiatives to improve public health or other development priorities in the context of the Millennium Development Goals (and now the Sustainable Development Goals) is an example of the former.

The oscillation between the intrinsic and instrumental motivations underpinning donor support to media have continued through this current decade. The turn of the decade heralded the arrival of the "Arab Spring," enabled substantially by the increased access in authoritarian regimes of mobile telephony and the internet, as well as by independent sources of information such as the BBC and Al Jazeera. An immediate resurgence of interest in media support as a vital component of a democratic transition took only two or three years to transmute into a more confused, dislocated and sometimes disillusioned perspective as those same countries (with a small number of exceptions) descended into chaos or reverted back to authoritarianism. A darker, more pessimistic approach to media development has emerged in recent years as attempts have focused on defending, not advancing, independent media and civic space in the face of multiple attempts to co-opt (Deane 2013) and erode it (Schiffrin 2017).

The use of online media by terrorist groups to advance their agendas has prompted an apparent further and more recent shift of some donor strategies away from support to independent public interest media towards attempts to countering extremist narratives. This has continued even when the evidence that counter narrative approaches has been highlighted as being thin or non-existence (and indeed in the face of arguments that it is public interest media that may present the most effective response to addressing the drivers of extremism) (Ferguson 2016).

The purpose of this chapter has not been to provide a comprehensive history of media development over the last three decades. Missing from the above is any meaningful analysis of how different philanthropic foundations have responded, a proper examination of how the largest governmental supporter to independent media, the United States, has prioritized and approached this issue under different administrations, how multilateral agencies such as UNESCO have evolved in their approaches or indeed multiple other actors and events.

But missing too is a sense of a coherent agenda or any serious attempt to learn lessons between different donor agencies and media support organizations of what works and does not work. It is rather to provide an argument drawn from just some examples that over the last 30 years, the motivations of support to media development have shifted and oscillated and waxed and waned markedly. Organizations that depend on this support have inevitably had to shift strategies at least in part to reflect the priorities of those who fund them (though they have also sought to shape funding priorities based on their own experience and have, through organizations like the Global Forum for Media Development, sought to create greater coherence within the field itself).

The net result is an immense difficulty in determining a sense of a long-term strategy, clear mechanisms of coordination or lesson learning, or even an effective space for a conversation between donors who have so often supported the media for very different reasons with very different objectives. This is not an argument against a diversity of approaches—such diversity is both necessary and desirable given the complexity of the challenge. It is an argument against the often siloed, poorly connected strategies that characterize the field.

The situation is exacerbated by a research and academic community that is similarly siloed. Academic research relevant to media development derives from a range of disciplines from media and communication, cultural studies, technology, political science, governance, economics, and anthropology among others. It is rare that academic study from one discipline focused on the role of the media commands respect or real credibility in another: the degree of interdisciplinary academic enquiry remains very limited. Academics who have spent years studying the dynamics of Habermasian notions of the public sphere struggle to be cited by economists who see the role of the media as crucial to fostering state-citizen accountability but who may have missed entirely the fundamental transformation of governance arrangements caused by shifts in how publics understand and debate with each other. Political scientists who have spent years understanding how weak states characterized by violence and strife in part caused by the co-option of media by religious, ethnic or factional forces struggle to be cited by media and communication scholars. With exceptions—such as the National Endowment for Democracy's Center for International Media Assistance—mechanisms to draw disciplines and insights together are sparse.

All of which leaves both donors and the media development field poorly prepared for perhaps the greatest challenge, and greatest need, it has yet faced. Democracy has suffered years of recession (Diamond 2015), civic spaces are shrinking (Carothers 2016), and independent public interest media around the world, including in the West, are under pressure economically and under attack politically.

And yet the importance of independent media to a functioning democracy is becoming recognized as being unprecedentedly vital in a communicative age characterized by misinformation and disinformation. Media development is making a comeback. Many foundations have reprioritized their support for journalism and there is a significant increase in donor funding of public interest media (this is most marked in the United States, but it may spread internationally).

The international donor community—or at least that section of the community that is rooted in democratic values—has arguably spent the last 30 years deploying a series of relatively inchoate, sometimes successive sometimes siloed and parallel strategies characterized by different motivations, expectations, theories of change and results. That is not necessarily a bad thing given the diversity, fluidity and complexity of shifting challenges, but it has shown little sign of collective lesson learning of what works and does not, coordination or even a clear semblance of a long term strategic ambition.

International actors who are not rooted in democratic values, on the other hand, appear to have had far clearer strategic approaches and much more consistent approaches to advancing them. While these have little in common with each other (they might include Russian investments in strategies designed to support misinformation and disinformation, major Chinese investments in advancing a soft power narrative, middle eastern and other investments in exporting political or religious ideologies, and even the efforts of so called Islamic State and other terrorist groups to advance extremist narratives), they are characterized by a high degree of organization, coherence and (to differing degrees) effectiveness in disrupting or undermining democracy.

There is a potentially vital future for media development as a critical component of supporting sustainable and functioning democracies. For that future to actually translate into media that serves and is credible to publics increasingly distrusting of the information they receive, that can adapt to shifting technological and especially political tremors and retains its independence will depend on a far more organized and evidence based set of support strategies than those that have characterized the field in the last three decades.

Note

1. See, for example, Transparency and Accountability Initiative: http://www.transparency-initiative.org/archive/about.

Recommended for Further Reading

Diamond, Larry. 2015. "Facing Up to the Democratic Recession." *Journal of Democracy* 26 (1): 141–55.

Myers, Mary, and Juma, Linet. 2018. *Defending Independent Media: A Comprehensive Analysis of Aid Flows.* Washington, D.C.: Center for International Media Assistance.

U.K. Department for International Development. 2008. *Media and Good Governance: A DFID Practice Paper*. London.

References

Carothers, Thomas. 2016. "Closing Space and Fragility." *Fragility Study Group* (Oct): Carnegie Endowment for International Peace.

CIMA. "About Center for International Media Assistance." https://www.cima.ned.org/about/

Deane, James. 2013. "Fragile States: The Role of Media and Communication." *BBC Media Action Policy Briefing* No. 10, London.

Diamond, Larry. 2015. "Facing Up to the Democratic Recession." *Journal of Democracy* 26 (1): 141–55.

Ferguson, Kate. 2016. "Countering Violent Extremism through Media and Communication Strategies: A review of the evidence." Research Partnership for Conflict, Crime and Security Research (PaCCS): Cambridge.

OECD Development Assistance Committee. 2005. *Paris Declaration on Aid Effectiveness.*

Putzel, James, and Joost Van Der Zwan. 2005. *Why Templates for Media Development do not Work in Crisis States: Defining and Understanding Media Development Strategies in Post-War and Crisis States*. London: London School of Economics and Political Science, Crisis States Research Centre. http://www.lse.ac.uk/international-development/Assets/Documents/PDFs/csrc-background-papers/Why-Templates-for-Media-Development-do-not-work-in-Crisis-States.pdf.

Schiffrin, Anya, ed. 2017. *In the Service of Power: Media Capture and the Threat to Democracy*. Washington, D.C.: Center for International Media Assistance/School of International and Public Affairs Columbia.

U.K. Department for International Development. 2008. *Media and Good Governance: A DFID Practice Paper*. London.

CHAPTER SEVENTEEN

Media Literacy in the Context of Media Development

Framework, Interventions, and Assessment

TATJANA LJUBIC

Introduction

Think about this for a moment:

> 90% of all of the data today was created in the last two years; every minute, 3.7 billion internet users worldwide send almost half a million tweets, conduct over 3.5 million Google searches, watch over 4 million YouTube videos. (Domo 2017)

There is so much data and information constantly flowing around us that it is almost impossible to grasp and understand the scope of it. Fast technological changes are continuously impacting and changing the media and information landscape and, consequently, our lives. As Buckingham and Domaille (2009) rightly asserted—it is hard to overstate the economic, social, and cultural importance of the media in the modern world. The media "provide us with most of our information about political process; and they offer us ideas, images and representations (both factual and fictional) that inevitably play a part in shaping our views of reality" (Buckingham and Domaille, in Cheung 2009, 19).

In the current media ecosystem, characterized by growth in media exposure, content consumption, and sharing of news, the public is becoming increasingly polarized. This is referred to as a post-fact or post-truth era[1], with issues of disinformation[2], alternative facts, propaganda, hate speech, radicalization, violent extremism, and harvesting of personal data under the spotlight. The public is also influenced by the immense amount of information—sometimes deliberately misleading—that they are exposed to through social media. The 2016 U.S. presidential election and Brexit have brought social media's ability to sway public opinion to the forefront of global discussions. This is further implicated by recent revelation of major Facebook data breach by a data analytic company and allegations of deliberate influence on voter's choices (*The Guardian* 2018). It remains to be seen what will be the consequences of this case, but it will certainly be an issue that will be a cornerstone of future discussions about social media, privacy and security online.

Other issues include deteriorating truth and trust in the media, social media filter bubbles (Pariser 2011) that expose us only to like-minded content, and the tension between facts and emotions in reporting. According to Polizzi (2017), this is the "post truth era where facts and objectivity are overshadowed by personal beliefs and emotions; while the internet is not the ultimate cause of post-truth, it multiplies the possibilities of producing and consuming misinformation." Finally, there is the need to balance the fears and threats of digital communications with the unprecedented opportunities and benefits they present. In this context, strong support for media literacy—the capability to access, critically evaluate, and create a wide range of media—as a strategy to help tackle the above-mentioned threats is urgently needed.

Responses to this changing media and information environment, and issues of disinformation in particular, have been multi-dimensional. The EU High level Group on fake news and online disinformation assembles the good practice of responses as initiatives promoting transparency, trust enhancement and media and information literacy (European Commission 2018, 14). Development of digital media enabled wide and unprecedented spreading of disinformation, in ways that have not been seen before and consequently some initiatives looked at the functioning of social media, as well as interaction of algorithms and human behavior in the spread of misleading information. Numerous fact-checking and verification initiatives around the world emerged. Regulators and self-regulators are approaching these issues, and direct support for independent and ethical news also remains an important part of the equation. As the EU report by Fake news group asserted, not all news media maintain the same standards of professionalism and editorial independence; "while news media can play an important role in combating disinformation and increasing societal resilience, some news media contribute to disinformation problems" (European Commission 2018, 11).

This, consequently, decreases the trust in the media. However, the initiatives mentioned are all on the production-side, and while they are important, they can be inadequate without the equal support to the reception side—the citizens as users. Content in this digital ecosystem is distributed by many new actors—citizens producing content for social media, as journalists, bloggers, etc. In this context, media literacy initiatives among the general population are going to be an essential component to an ethical and healthy public sphere; only with collaboration of all stakeholders, those from the production side with others at the recipient side, can media literacy initiatives be essentially effective. With this approach, the preventive strength of media literacy is most effective.

Media literacy is an emerging and evolving concept. It is also a dynamic field that crosscuts many disciplines, including media education, information sciences, social sciences, economics, and other fields, and covers the wide spectrum of media types, including digital, news, film, games, visuals, and others. However, media development organizations face challenges to developing effective interventions to improve media literacy and employing efficient mechanisms for measuring their impact.

It is against this backdrop that this chapter explores the various definitions of media literacy, how this concept is approached, possible ways of developing media literacy programs, and key challenges that lie ahead.

Understanding Media Literacy

There is no single agreed-upon definition for media literacy. A highly interdisciplinary field of study, media literacy incorporates methodologies and tools from sociology, psychology, political theory, and gender and race studies as well as cultural studies, art, and aesthetics (Koltay, 2011, 212). As Burn and Durran (2007, 2) stress, "any attempt to clarify and simplify such a complex set of practices must also recognize how contested all definitions are, and how different interests and perspectives of teachers, researchers and policymakers can pull in different directions."

One of the first comprehensive media literacy definitions was introduced at an Aspen Institute meeting, and reported by Patricia Aufderheide in 1992, stating that anyone is entitled to become a media literate person, while "the fundamental objective of media literacy is critical autonomy in relationship to all media" (Koltay 2011, 212). This description emphases the creation of an informed citizenship, aesthetic appreciation and expression, social advocacy, self-esteem, and consumer competence (Koltay 2011, 212). Many in the field continue to use this definition.

With this in mind, the three most prevailing concepts—media literacy, information literacy, and digital literacy—focus on empowering citizens to read media messages critically (Koltay 2011, 211). Most often, media literacy, as un umbrella term, applies to both traditional and digital media, while digital literacy refers to just the latter (Polizzi 2017).

UNESCO, one of the first organizations to work in this field, widened the concept of media literacy to include information intermediaries, such as libraries, museums, and archives. From the Grünwald Declaration (UNESCO 1982) it has evolved into the globally accepted composite concept of Media and Information Literacy (MIL). MIL, in this context, relates to the knowledge, skills, and attitudes of individual citizens and underscores the importance of lifelong learning and the ethical use of information. UNESCO explains:

> On the one hand, Information Literacy emphasizes the importance of access to information and the evaluation and ethical use of that information. On the other hand, Media Literacy emphasizes the ability to understand media functions, evaluate how those functions are performed and to rationally engage with media for self-expression. (UNESCO 2011, 18)

The European Commission has an important and active role in the progression of media literacy in Europe; European Audiovisual Media Services Directive highlights that the media-literate person is not a simply a passive media consumer but rather someone who selects what he/she wishes to consume by means of an informed choice. (Tornero and Pi, 2013, 332)

The U.S. National Association for Media Literacy Education describes media literacy as an expansion of traditional literacy that empowers people to be critical, effective communicators and active citizens, with the "ability to access, analyze, evaluate, create, and act using all forms of communication" (NAMLE). Renee Hobbs has also underscored the importance of reflection and action as media literacy competencies (Hobbs 2010, 18). She framed the "seven great debates in the media literacy movement" in 1998, which are still relevant today:

1. Should media literacy education aim to protect children and young people from negative media influences?
2. Should media production be an essential feature of media literacy education?
3. Should media literacy focus on popular culture texts?
4. Should media literacy have a more explicit political and/or ideological agenda?
5. Should media literacy be focused on school-based K-12 educational environments?
6. Should media literacy be taught as a specialist subject or integrated within the context of existing subjects?

7. Should media literacy initiatives be supported financially by media organizations?

Hobbs also asserted that

> when people have digital and media literacy competencies, they recognize personal, corporate and political agendas and are empowered to speak out on behalf of the missing voices and omitted perspectives in our communities. By identifying and attempting to solve problems, people use their powerful voices and their rights under the law to improve the world around them. (Hobbs 2010, 17)

The U.S.-based Center for Media Literacy articulated an approach that provides a process for inquiry and analysis based on Five Core Concepts of media literacy (Center for Media Literacy 2005), which include the following statements:

1. All media messages are "constructed."
2. Media messages are constructed using a creative language with their own rules.
3. Different people experience the same media message differently.
4. Media have embedded values and points of view.
5. Most media messages are organized to gain profit and/or power.

In Latin America, the concept of *edu-communication* emerged as a combination of the academic fields of education and communication; it calls for global citizenship and "has a civic purpose, that is, it must be endowed with an ethical, social and democratic base that empowers citizens in their dealings with the media" (Yildiz and Keengwe 2016, 22).

There is also the concept of *transliteracy*, as described by Divina Frau-Meigs and it's analysis involves exchanges between the research communities that do not always work together—computer scientists, media researchers, information and library scientists, and education scientists (Frau-Meigs 2012, 21). Transliteracy is thus defined as:

"1. the ability to embrace the full layout of multimedia which encompasses skills for reading, writing and calculating with all the available tools (from paper to image, from book to wiki);
2. the capacity to navigate through multiple domains, which entails the ability to search, evaluate, test, validate and modify information according to its relevant contexts of use (as code, news and document)." (Frau-Meigs 2012,16).

News literacy, a subcategory of media literacy, is currently very prominent and deserves a brief explanation. News literacy focuses exclusively on analyzing the reliability and credibility of the news. As described by Stony Brook University's Center for News Literacy (2016), it is a form of literacy that empowers news consumers to determine whether information is reliable and then to be able to make informed decisions based on it.

From this analysis of how media and information literacy is described and understood it is clear that there are approaches that highlight certain elements. Some researchers, like Mihailidis and Viotty, are calling for media literacy to be adapted to the current political environment and repositioned to respond to the current era of partisanship and distrust (Mihailidis and Viotty 2017). There is no one-size-fits-all definition or description. Media literacy needs to be understood within the context of a particular medium, culture, political and social environment. This is why different authors and organizations have aimed to expand and apply the concept in different contexts.

Designing Interventions

In spite of the now frequent lip service paid to the importance of media literacy, as a programmatic area of governments and international organizations, it remains "under-funded, ill-understood, yet desperately needed" (Burgess 2013). In 2013 The Center for International Media Assistance (CIMA) has reported that media development organizations "uniformly say that it is a vital part of their work" (Burgess 2013). However, programming and spending patterns suggest that media literacy programs still represent a small, though growing, focus of overall media development work.[3] A 2017 CIMA report shows that instead of constituting a main objective of media development efforts, media literacy training tends to be included as a skillset within a larger initiative (Kalathil 2017).

Still, media literacy has gained a lot of attention in the last 20 years both academically (in terms of developing the field) and in practice (in terms of the number of projects). For example, there is a *Journal of Media Literacy Education*, published by the U.S.-based National Association for Media Literacy Education, UNESCO's *Media and Information Literacy and Intercultural Dialogue (MILID) Yearbook*, and media literacy clearinghouses. Interventions are growing and increasingly widespread. The European Audiovisual Observatory's 2016 publication *Mapping of Media Literacy Practices and Actions in EU-28* highlighted 547 media literacy–related projects across the European Union (EU).[4] The European Commission also recognizes the importance of media literacy through its pilot initiative Media Literacy for All, which issued a call for proposals in 2016 and 2017.

Thus, there is a vibrant and developing field, involving an array of different stakeholders, and multiple opportunities for new kinds of programming. This section will discuss the possibilities for building media literacy through programmatic interventions.

Civil society organizations (CSOs) play a crucial role in delivering media literacy programs. "Most media literacy or education training is provided as part of informal networks or a feature of non-governmentally funded projects" (Frau-Meigs, Velez, and Michel 2017, 132). State authorities, the public sector, academic research institutions, the media industry, and the private sector also play key roles, but "CSOs in most of the European countries remain the most cohesive societal actor in media literacy (ML) and media and information literacy (MIL)" (Kanizaj 2017, 70).

Moreover, the *development of MIL competencies* can occur through formal and non-formal initiatives, including by using social media as the platform for learning.

Formal Education

Structured approaches towards media literacy interventions take place in formal learning environments at all school levels through media education.[5] Some countries have well-developed media education programs. For example, "in many parts of the Anglophone world, ideas of media literacy are often well-established in school curricula, and typically located in English, literacy or language arts sections of the curriculum" (Burn, Durran, 2007, 6). However, though such programs are the best way to achieve long-term media literacy, the topic often remains at the periphery of schools' curricula. Formalizing media literacy into school curricula is not an easy process, and is one that takes several steps and requires a lot of political will: endorsement and adoption of specific regulations by governmental institutions, formalization in school curricula, and continuous and strategic training of teachers. This is an area where civil society and government cooperation can work well, as piloted by the EU and UNESCO–supported project Building Trust in Media in South East Europe and Turkey.

It should also be noted that merely including technology in schools without adequate teacher training and curriculum adaptations is not sufficient. The Portuguese program *e-escolinha*, for example, "was presented as revolutionary at the pedagogical level [distribution of personal computers to children], but the assessment results showed a completely different scenario: it had no significant effect on the classroom pedagogical practice, mainly due to the lack of previous teacher training" (Yildiz, Funk, and De Abreu 2018, 1).

Thus, investment in teacher training is a crucial prerequisite for media literacy training's successful establishment in the formal education system. Even though dominant media education models come from English-speaking Western countries, models of intervention should also be tailored for different societies; as

Buckingham and Domaille assert, it might be a mistake for educators in Asian countries, for example, to simply look to the West and import a model of education, as it might not be relevant to their political, social, and economic circumstances (Buckingham and Domaille, in Cheung 2009, 20).

Publishing media literacy training materials in multiple languages would also be beneficial. While media literacy has the potential to grow in Arab states, for example, what is mostly hindering the expansion is the deficiency of qualified and trained teachers and instructors, jointly with insufficient amount of curricular material in languages other than English (Singh, Kerr and Hamburger 2016, 294). Education initiatives must train and equip a generation of academics, teachers, and CSOs around the world who can take this field forward.

Resources such as UNESCO's Media and Information Literacy Curriculum for Teachers, which provides detailed descriptions of MIL-focused content through different modules and pedagogy, can be used as a model. The curriculum is offered in multiple languages.

The CSO Sector and Media Support

The importance of civil society in the development of media literacy cannot be overstated. As stressed by Kanižaj (2017), "CSOs in most of the European countries remain the most cohesive societal actor in media literacy (ML) and media and information literacy (MIL)." This is reiterated by Frau-Meigs and Torrent (Kanižaj 2017), who underline that civil society organizations are among the most important media literacy stakeholders in many societies, especially given how positively correlated civic engagement is with media literacy. There are a wide variety of ways the CSO sector can intervene to improve media literacy, as illustrated by the over 500 interventions described in the European Audiovisual Observatory report (2016).

Reaching young people outside of traditional school settings can be difficult and challenging since they receive information in less structured ways than other age groups do, such as through friends' recommendations, social media algorithms, or just scraps of information coming from the various online places. To reach youth, media literacy interventions need to use new formats and platforms and even new writing styles. One way is harnessing the power of social media to teach about media literacy. UNESCO is one of the pioneers in this approach. Its MIL CLICKS social media initiative spreads MIL knowledge through daily short, educational, and easy-to-digest posts that use examples from everyday life to teach concepts. Similar activities are conducted by The News Literacy Project and others. Such initiatives go hand-in-hand with formal education, moving it out of the classroom and into virtual communities.

Working in partnership with different national or transnational networks is also key to executing an effective media literacy intervention (European Audiovisual Observatory 2016). Cooperating with regulatory and self-regulatory bodies, as well as media (especially public media services), is also central to promoting media literacy.

Policy Perspective

From a sustainability perspective, enduring and widespread media literacy depends on supportive government policies. "[T]he development of media education, as has been observed in many countries, begins with a bottom up movement, [but] its continual growth requires the blessing of the government, with a policy that may directly and indirectly help the development of media education" (Cheung 2009, 5).

A consistent roadblock to a successful top-down-only approach is that while governments often talk about the importance of media literacy, there can be a lack of follow-up "in the form of clearly assessed activities or models of student progression in skills and competencies" (Buckingham and Domaille, in Cheung 2009, 24). Simultaneous top-down and bottom-up approaches are the most effective. Successful grassroots initiatives can be used to convince policy makers that the efforts deserve continued support.

From an intergovernmental policy perspective, encouragement of member states from different parts of the world to include media literacy and media and information literacy into national policies and strategies can be beneficial. For example, the Organization for Security and Co-operation in Europe (OSCE) has highlighted the need to increase support for educational programs on media and internet literacy (OSCE 2015, 59, 64, 67). UNESCO's MIL Policy and Strategy guidelines are another example of a resource that can facilitate policy development and cooperation between civil society and governments.

Empowering Citizens

Media development[6] projects have been focused on developing quality content; supporting freedom of expression and information, independent media, and investigative journalism; and strengthening self-regulatory mechanisms (Kalathil 2017). One area the interventions have largely neglected is the strengthening of the recipients—audiences 'capacities to recognize and appreciate quality content and to understand the functions of the media. Such awareness on the part of the public is an essential part of media literacy. There has been some work done in this area. For example, the European Association for Viewers Interests is a nongovernmental organization (NGO) focused on empowering citizens around issues of media literacy. Among other activities, they advocate for the interests of citizens by engaging EU institutions as media policy stakeholders (European Association for Viewers Interests).

Support for Research and Resource Development

More empirical evidence is needed to better understand both the impact media literacy is having on citizens' actions, participation, and good governance as well as the effectiveness of media literacy policies and initiatives. The research needs to provide insight into how people, on the grassroots level, are making decisions and engaging with information—and how well informed they are and want to be.

UNESCO's MILID network, for example, has already conducted research on the views of educators and young people on issues ranging from data privacy to media and information literacy, but much more needs to be done.

Also, as the majority of innovative practices in MIL are provided by NGOs and in non-formal education settings, research must focus on assessing the effectiveness of these pedagogical approaches. The next section reviews current practices and needed improvements in this area.

Assessing Media Literacy

According to Livingstone and Thumim (2003, 9), measuring media literacy remains a challenge. Due to the variety of research foci, methodologies, and population samples, it is difficult to draw comparisons between people's levels of media literacy. Further complicating the issue is a lack of a common evaluation framework, universally accepted definition of media literacy, and common conception of identifying what "significant" means in terms of ML projects, "which means that a multitude of cultural, social, and political factors are relevant in shaping how the level of significance is understood" (European Audiovisual Observatory 2016, 1). Martens concludes that evaluating and explaining the effectiveness of media literacy education is one of the most profound challenges for current research in the field (Martens 2010, 9). As Abbott (this volume) has noted, "the challenge of measuring the impact of media development assistance is largely attributable to the uncertainty about what it is that we are measuring, and towards what ends."

Nevertheless, evaluations and assessments[7] have been made in different regions of the world by different entities. They are indispensable in policy making through providing information on results and outcomes of the learning process and its efficiency. Assessments, usually led by researchers and institutes, CSOs, academic institutions, and international funding organizations, take into account (through different methodologies) two dimensions: individual competencies and environmental factors, that enable the understanding levels of media literacy. Individual competencies refer to the personal ability to exercise media literacy skills: "the capacity for critical analysis; a creative, problem-solving capacity; and the ability to create and communicate content while participating in public sphere" (Tornero and Pi 2013, 334). Environmental factors focus on the policy and legislation on media literacy and other "contextual factors that affect individuals and relate to media education, media policy, cultural environment, citizens' rights, the roles the media industry and civil society play, etc" (Tornero and Pi 2013, 334).

Environmental factors are important because

> "the media do not exist in a bubble, and media literacy very rarely develops in isolation from its environment. Even the basic availability of media and technical devices is affected by the attitudes of authorities, the existence of non-governmental bodies and their activities, and the initiatives of the media themselves in contributing to the creation of a media-literate audience." (Celot 2009, 45)

In the formal education setting, only countries that have highly developed media education curricula—such New Zealand—have incorporated "clear specifications on the skills and competencies that are expected at different levels and how they are to be assessed" (Buckingham and Domaille 2009, 25). Clearly articulating what is being assessed is crucial; without clear assessment indicators, even in places where media education has been established, media literacy can lose prominence in the school curriculum (Buckingham and Domaille, in Cheung 2009).

In the past several years, two significant MIL research projects have been conducted within the EU (European Audiovisual Observatory 2016) to assess the extent that CSOs are present as stakeholders in media literacy and MIL programs (Kanizaj 2017). The 2014 European Media Literacy Education Study (EMEDUS) assessed formal education (primary, secondary, and tertiary) to determine the curricular status of media education. While it did not investigate individual competencies, it analyzed the curricula to locate where media education is taking place; some responses also provided data about teacher training as well as evaluation procedures and exam requirements (Hartai 2014). This report concluded that while many countries teach media literacy in a cross-curricular way, media literacy outcomes are not assessed at all in most of these countries (Hartai 2014).

There have been a number of other media literacy initiative assessments done over the past several years, a few of which are described here.

IREX recently reviewed Ukraine's pilot media literacy project Learn to Discern (L2D) and reported that the program is "extremely promising: people became more skillful in separating fact from fiction, and they shared what they learned with their family and friends" (Susman-Peña and Vogt 2017). Assessing the long-term impact of this program, IREX's major findings show that citizens were better able to detect disinformation 1.5 years later. In particular, the analysis shows that participants of L2D had "statistically significant higher levels of disinformation news analysis skills, greater knowledge of the news media environment, a stronger sense of agency over the media sources they consume, and were more likely to consult a wider range of news sources" (IREX, 2018).

A second example comes from the United Kingdom's independent communications regulator, the Office of Communications, which regularly evaluates media literacy within the United Kingdom with a focus on both adults and children, to provide evidence on understanding and use of electronic media. It assesses individual competences and behaviors/habits. The 2017 report included a "more in-depth exploration of the critical understanding of media and digital participation." (Ofcom 2017, 1)[8] Among other indicators, it measured critical understanding by assessing people's knowledge about how media outlets are funded, their grasp of online privacy and data security issues, judgment in providing personal information online, and their behaviors and attitudes in content evaluation.

The two-tier approach modeled by UNESCO is another assessment effort worth examining. The first tier is Country Readiness, which provides information on a country's level of media and information literacy and its capacity to implement and uptake MIL-related initiatives (MIL-related education, policy, supply[9], access and use, civil society[10]). The second tier is MIL Competencies, which measure the competencies of all citizens, but in particular those of teachers in service and in training (composed of MIL components, subject matters, competencies, performance criteria, and levels of proficiency) (UNESCO 2013, 18). It allows states to conduct comprehensive assessments of their media and information environments, including the extent to which MIL competencies have been acquired, with teachers in focus. The assessment framework also included a plan for national adaptation, and explanations for how to collect data and conduct analyses. UNESCO has not yet published a case study that makes use of this assessment tool.

Conclusion

There seems to be a significant amount of uncertainty in the media and information landscape today. New media platforms are being introduced faster than formal, and even non-formal, education systems can adapt. Mainstreaming media literacy into international media development efforts is important. Media literacy can bring higher levels of engagement in societies and reduce the gap that exists between everyday experiences and learning. However, as this text shows, the penetration of media literacy into communities is lagging and supporting interventions has not yet become a donor priority. What is needed is a simultaneous top-down and bottom-up approach, which can provide sustainability for media literacy. Strategies and interventions need to address the digital divide and disparities that exist between countries in terms of access to media literacy competencies. An intergenerational aspect to media literacy learning should also focus on parents and caretakers. Research and assessment of media literacy policy and projects must be based on empirical data and assess impact.

It is not a question whether there is a need for more or better media literacy initiatives. Both are needed to produce what is at the heart of this issue—development of critical thinking.

Notes

1. Post-truth refers to circumstances in which objective facts are less influential in shaping public opinion than emotional appeals, as per "'Post-truth' declared word of the year by Oxford Dictionaries," accessed at http://www.bbc.com/news/uk-37995600.
2. Disinformation includes false, inaccurate, or misleading information designed, presented and promoted to intentionally cause public harm or for profit (European Commission, 2018).
3. As reported by CIMA in 2017, media literacy was identified by only one donor, Global Affairs Canada, as a priority (Kalathil, 2017).
4. The research included only actions that have taken place outside schools (European Audiovisual Observatory, 2016).
5. This chapter uses David Buckingham's definition of media education: "the process of teaching and learning about media; media literacy is the outcome—the knowledge and skills learners acquire." (Buckingham, 2003, 4).
6. As reported by CIMA, "not all donors have a common understanding of media development (or "media assistance"). Some donors may include development communication (using media primarily to accomplish development aims rather than seeking to strengthen the media sector itself) and content production in their media assistance figures, while others may not" (Kalathil,, 2017).
7. By *assessment*, we are referring to "a process for obtaining information that is used for making decisions about students; curricula, programs, and schools; and educational policy" (Nitko and Brookhart, 2011, 3).
8. The section on critical understanding shows that "Although the majority of internet users describe themselves as being confident online, around a quarter don't make reliable checks before entering financial details" and that "most internet users make some checks to judge the accuracy of factual information online, but this is a challenge for some," among other findings. (Ofcom, 2017, 8).

9. Media and information supply refers to the "regulatory mechanisms that prevail in a given country that determine the supply of media and the quality of information made available to the population. For example, a specific media law that prohibits ownership by private or public operators can explain why there is a lack of independent private or public media in a country" (UNESCO, 2013, 52).
10. CSOs refer to the "non-governmental organizations and community-based organizations, academic networks, professional associations and, to a certain extent, private entities are important stakeholders that are active, supportive and engaged in the field of media and information literacy" (UNESCO, 2013, 53).

Recommended for Further Reading

European Audiovisual Observatory. 2016. *Mapping of Media Literacy Practices and Actions in EU-28.* Strasbourg, France: European Audiovisual Observatory.

Hobbs, Renee. 2010. *Digital and Media Literacy: A Plan of Action.* Washington, D.C.: The Aspen Institute, Communication and Society Program.

UNESCO. 2013. *Media and Information Literacy: Policy and Strategy Guidelines.* Paris: United Nations Education, Scientific and Cultural Organization,.

References

Buckingham, David. 2003. *Media Education: Literacy, Learning and Contemporary Culture.* Polity Press.

Buckingham, David, and Kate Domaille. 2009. "Making Media Education Happen: A Global View." In *Media Education in Asia,* edited by Chi-Kim Cheung, 19–30. London: New York.

Burgess, John. 2013. "Media Literacy 2.0: A Sampling of Programs Around the World." Center for International Media Assistance. https://www.cima.ned.org/resource/media-literacy-2-0-a-sampling-of-programs-around-the-world/.

Burn, Andrew and James Durran. 2007. *Media Literacy in Schools: Practice, Production and Progression.* London: Paul Chapman Publishing.

Cadwalladr, Carole, and Emma Graham-Harrison. March 17, 2018. "Revealed: 50 million-Facebook Profiles Harvested for Cambridge Analytica in Major Data Breach." *The Guardian,* accessed March 24 2018. https://www.theguardian.com/news/2018/mar/17/cambridge-analytica-facebook-influence-us-election.

Celot, Paolo, ed. 2009. *Study on Assessment Criteria for Media Literacy Levels.* European Association of Viewers' Interest, Brussels.

Center for Media Literacy. 2005. "Five Key Questions of Media Literacy." Accessed at: http://www.medialit.org/sites/default/files/14B_CCKQPoster+5essays.pdf.

Domo. "Data Never Sleeps 5.0." Accessed November 10, 2017, https://www.domo.com/learn/data-never-sleeps-5.

European Audiovisual Observatory. 2016. *Mapping of Media Literacy Practices and Actions in EU-28.* Strasbourg, France: European Audiovisual Observatory.

European Commission. March 12, 2018. *A multi-dimensional approach to disinformation: Report of the independent High level Group on fake news and online disinformation.*

Frau-Meigs, D. 2012. "Transliteracy as the New Research Horizon for Media and Information Literacy" *Medijske studije/Media Studies* 3 (6): 14–27.

Frau-Meigs, Divina, Irma Velez, and Julieta Flores Michel, eds. 2017. *Public Policies in Media and Information Literacy in Europe: Cross Country Comparisons.* London: Routledge.

Hartai, László. 2014. *Report on Formal Media Education in Europe 2014.* https://eavi.eu/wp-content/uploads/2017/02/Media-Education-in-European-Schools-2.pdf

Hobbs, Renee. 2001. "Seven Great Debates in the Media Literacy Movement—Circa 2001." http://www.medialit.org/reading-room/seven-great-debates-media-literacy-movement-circa-2001.

Hobbs, Renee. 2010. *Digital and Media Literacy: A Plan of Action.* Washington, D.C.: The Aspen Institute, Communication and Society Program.

Kalathil, Shanthi. 2017. *A Slowly Shifting Field: Understanding Donor Priorities in Media Development. Center for International Media Assistance.* Center for International Media Assistance. https://www.cima.ned.org/publication/slowly-shifting-field/

Kanižaj, I. 2017. "The Role of Civil Society Organisations in Promoting Media Literacy: Transliteracy and Media and Information Literacy in EU." *Revista Fuentes,* 19 (2): 69–80.

Koltay, Tibor. 2011. "The Media and the Literacies: Media Literacy, Information Literacy, Digital Literacy." *Media Culture and Society,* 33 (2): 211–21.

Livingstone, Sonia, with Nancy Thumim. 2003. Assessing the Media Literacy of UK Adults: A Review of the Academic Literature. http://eprints.lse.ac.uk/21673/1/Assessing_the_media_literacy_of_UK_adults.pdf.

Martens, Hans. 2010. "Evaluating Media Literacy Education: Concepts, Theories, and Future Directions." *Journal of Media Literacy Education* 2 (1): 1–22.

Mihailidis, Paul, and Samantha Viotty. 2017. "Spreadable Spectacle in Digital Culture: Civic Expression, Fake News, and the Role of Media Literacies in 'Post-Fact' Society." *American Behavioral Scientist* 61 (4): 441–54.

Murrock, Erin, Amulya, Joy, Druckman, Mehri and Liubyva, Tetiana. 2018. "Winning the war on state-sponsored propaganda: Gains in the ability to detect disinformation a year and a half after completing a Ukrainian news media literacy program". IREX. https://www.irex.org/sites/default/files/node/resource/impact-study-media-literacy-ukraine.pdf

National Association for Media Literacy Education (NAMLE). "Media Literacy Defined." https://namle.net/publications/media-literacy-definitions/

Nitko, Anthony J., and Susan M. Brookhart. 2011. *Educational Assessment of Students.* Boston: Pearson Education.

Ofcom. 2017. *Adults' media use and attitudes,* Report. https://www.ofcom.org.uk/__data/assets/pdf_file/0020/102755/adults-media-use-attitudes-2017.pdf.

Organization for Security and Co-operation in Europe (OSCE). 2015. *Propaganda and Freedom of the Media.* Non-paper of the OSCE Office of the Representative on Freedom of the Media. https://www.osce.org/fom/203926?download=true.

Pariser, Eli. 2011. *The Filter Bubble: How the New Personalized Web Is Changing What We Read and How We Think*. New York, NY: Penguin Group.

Polizzi, Gianfranco. May 22, 2017. "Tackling Fake News: Towards a New Approach to Digital Literacy." The London School of Economics and Political Science. http://blogs.lse.ac.uk/mediapolicyproject/2017/05/22/tackling-fake-news-towards-a-new-approach-to-digital-literacy/.

Singh, Jagtar, Paulette Kerr, and Esther Hamburger. 2016. *Media and Information Literacy: Reinforcing Human Rights, Countering Radicalization and Extremism*. Paris: UNESCO.

Stony Brook University, Center for News Literacy. "What Is News Literacy?" https://www.centerfornewsliteracy.org/what-is-news-literacy/

Tornero, José Manuel Pérez, and Mireia Pi. 2013. "Media Literacy Policy in European Union." In *Media and Information Literacy and Intercultural Dialogue*, MILID Yearbook 2013, edited by Ulla Carlsson and Sherri Hope Culver, 332, 333. https://milunesco.unaoc.org/wp-content/uploads/2013/04/Media_and_Information_Literacy_and_Intercultural_Dialogue.pdf.

UNESCO. 1982. Grunwald Declaration on Media Education. http://www.unesco.org/education/pdf/MEDIA_E.PDF.

———. "Media and Information Literacy." Accessed November 10, 2017, http://www.unesco.org/new/en/communication-and-information/capacity-building-tools/media-and-information-literacy/.

———. 2011. "Media and Information Literacy Curriculum for Teachers." Accessed February 23, 2018. http://unesdoc.unesco.org/images/0019/001929/192971e.pdf

———. 2013. "Global Media and Information Literacy Assessment Framework: Country Readiness and Competencies." http://unesdoc.unesco.org/images/0022/002246/224655e.pdf

Yildiz, Melda N., and Jared Keengwe, eds. 2016. *Handbook of Research on Media Literacy in the Digital Age*. Hershey, PA: IGI Global.

Yildiz, Melda N., Steven S. Funk, and Belinha S. De Abreu. 2018. *Promoting Global Competencies Through Media Literacy*. IGI Global. https://www.igi-global.com/book/promoting-global-competencies-through-media/179376#table-of-contents

CHAPTER EIGHTEEN

Local News

A Shift to Hyperlocal?

MICHELLE BETZ

The media experience used to be a shared experience—en masse—but with the deluge and velocity of information available today it is becoming fractured and disconnected. In fact, it would seem that there are no longer "masses," rather "only ways of seeing people as masses" (Jarvis 2014). Without masses, what then of mass media, particularly within the context of media development?

With the traditional masses of mass media being splintered into ever smaller segments, hyperlocal news and information is becoming a more important aspect of media sectors around the world. Hyperlocal journalism, sometimes called micro-local journalism, refers to the coverage of events and topics on a small, local scale, frequently linked to a geographic community, though the term applies to online communities as well. Hyperlocal news, which can be delivered on the internet, by phone, via community radio, or through any other medium, is in tune with the growing importance of understanding audiences in their specific contexts, catering to their personalized needs and abilities to access information, and situating them within a global information ecosystem.

The "inverted impact pyramid"—in which hyperlocal news or information can have an impact much higher up in this global system—helps us understand this process. The growing connections to community-oriented media, and their audiences, can be foundational to media systems that more effectively serve the public interest. This chapter examines the increasing relevance of hyperlocal content in a changing media environment and the implications for media development, and considers issues of viability and co-option.

Hyperlocal Journalism

While hyperlocal media are not new phenomena, the term has only recently come into vogue and is still the subject of some debate and disagreement. Metzger, Kurpius, and Rowley (2011), however, see some common features in how hyperlocal media are typically described. According to the authors, "hyperlocal media operations are geographically-based, community oriented, original-news-reporting organizations indigenous to the web and intended to fill perceived gaps in coverage of an issue or region and to promote civic engagement." While this definition explicitly ties hyperlocal media to online platforms, well-established pre-digital iterations of hyperlocal media—small-market newspapers, television stations, and community radio in particular—still occupy a critical place in the conversation.[1] In fact, a traditional news medium like community radio still has significant advantages in developing countries due to ease of access for listeners, the low barrier to entry, and the durability and reliability of the communications infrastructure (Dunbar-Hester 2010). The following case study from Nepal helps highlight the nature and impact of hyperlocal media, in this case community radio, on natural disaster recovery efforts.

The Example of Nepal

The 7.8 magnitude earthquake on April 25, 2015, affected many radio stations across the 14 most affected districts in western and central Nepal. Yet the proximity of many of these small local stations to their communities meant they were the first to be approached by a population desperately seeking information. Many of these stations were struggling to get back on air owing to the loss of both human and technical resources.

The Danish nongovernmental organization (NGO) International Media Support (IMS) sought to address both the immediate needs of the affected communities and the longer-term benefit to the radio sector through a rapid response intervention that provided targeted support to local radio (private and community) so they could further their efforts to report on accountability and governance in the recovery and reconstruction period. The post-disaster issues of governance and accountability are of particular relevance in Nepal as the country does not have elected local bodies to provide oversight on recovery and reconstruction spending.

The IMS intervention was a community radio program called *Jamani* that focused on accountability issues at the hyperlocal level, but the intervention's influence eventually spread throughout the country. Though the stories usually focused on the experience of one person, when others heard them on networked radio stations they began telling their own local stations similar stories of corruption and lack of accountability in their communities. The intervention resonated so well because the population's only way of holding local officials accountable in the post-earthquake environment was to talk to the media, and community radio in particular.

In this case there was evidence of the inverted impact pyramid—issues of relevance that were covered first at the hyperlocal level but ultimately reached regional and national audiences. An assessment of radio program *Jamani* found evidence of impact in the most seriously affected districts:

- A school in one affected district was still closed three months after the quake. After traveling one day by car and one day by foot, a *Jamani* reporter arrived on the scene, interviewed those affected and involved, and aired the story. One week after the segment aired, the school reopened.
- *Jamani* produced a story about people living on what had been deemed unsafe land. One day after the broadcast, district authorities moved the people to a safe place.
- *Jamani* aired a story about people who had received relief funds despite not having been affected by the quake. After the story aired, more than 100 people returned the money they had received.

Both private and community radio play a key role in Nepal, though there is little history of them working together. The earthquake presented an opportunity, and it was decided to experiment by bringing together private and community radio. This was essentially the first time these entities had worked together since 2005.

This example illustrates the importance not only of hyperlocal media but of connecting hyperlocal accountability issues with similar challenges at the regional or national level. It is also important to note that hyperlocal media initiatives are most often grassroots- and community-driven or, at the very least, have substantial community involvement. At their best, hyperlocal media are like community radio by virtue of being participatory in nature, with community members raising hyperlocal concerns and seeking answers to those concerns.

Local Audiences and Access

A crucial element for effective media development is adapting to the local context, which includes understanding the media environment and the audience. Although the audience is particularly critical, it is often a challenge to conduct thorough audience research in many contexts. Knowing and understanding the audience as individuals and localized communities is also a commercial necessity for media outlets so they can better produce content that is relevant to intended audiences and ensure the commercial survival and success of media operations. Ultimately, content providers need to know and understand not only the needs of their audience, but perhaps more fundamentally, who their audience is.

In addition to understanding who the audience is for any particular medium or news outlet, there must be an understanding of how people are accessing information. There are many communities where significant portions of the population do not have access to internet-based content or social media. According to the International Telecommunications Union, known as ITU, nearly four billion people remain cut off from the vast resources available on the internet, and those in developing countries account for the vast majority of them (2.5 billion compared with 1 billion in developed countries). Internet penetration tells a similar story: 81 percent of people in developed countries are connected compared with only 40 percent in developing countries and 15 percent in the least-developed countries, with at least half of the latter being affected by conflict (ITU 2016).

Coupled with issues of accessibility is the fact that more governments have begun to block social media sites and communication apps than ever before. The 2016 *Freedom on the Net* report found that two-thirds of all internet users live in countries where criticism of the government, military, or ruling family is subject to censorship (Kelly et al. 2016).

It is for these reasons that in many contexts, traditional hyperlocal media, including community radio, can play an important role. Hyperlocal media outlets can serve those who still rely primarily on radio and may not have access to the internet yet want to know what is happening in their communities—news and information that is often not carried by the national media outlets.

Global, Glocal, and Horizontal Networks of Communication

On the other hand, there is the potential for significant influence of global media networks on local audiences. The diffusion of internet, mobile, and social media have moved us to "horizontal networks of interactive communication that connect local and global in chosen time" (Castells 2007).[2] These horizontal, interactive networks of communication have led to the glocalization of information, which is characterized by both local and global considerations such as content production, distribution, and sustainability. As a result, information today is often hyperlocal in nature yet can reach and impact audiences around the globe. At the same time, global media networks also significantly influence local audiences, resulting in a blend of global, local, and glocal information systems.

Glocal: A blend of local and global information systems. In this case, it most often refers to content that is produced for a local or hyperlocal audience but may have global reach.

Glocalization: The process of local information moving rapidly across borders to reach audiences around the globe.

Recent research by BBC Media Action in Libya provides a snapshot of this glocalization with both national and international television playing important roles in the nation's media consumption. Libyans were found to watch mostly Libyan channels (the main state channel, al-Wataniya, is the most popular) but also international channels. This was true for all sociodemographic groups. The only exception was in the city of Benghazi, where viewers preferred the local Benghazi station, Libya al-Hurra, the city's first private broadcaster, which was set up during the revolution (Dowson-Zeidan 2015).

Because information today is hyperlocal in nature yet global in reach, it is important to bear in mind how global media networks and audiences interact with local information systems and audiences. This interaction is changing. As one academic writes:

> Where once the journalist was on the inside looking out, telling the audience what was happening to them, it is now the audience telling the story alongside journalists whether that be in their own blogs, participatory journalism ventures such as hyperlocal community sites or user generated content and comment often commissioned, often unsolicited. Editors ask readers to submit their opinions, photos, blogs and videos and journalists are increasingly under pressure to know what is significant and relevant to their readers. (Allan and Fowler-Watt 2013)

Relevance, in this case, can be ascertained only by communicating with the audience, particularly to ensure that local voices and concerns do not get lost in the cacophony of international news and infotainment.

One model that can assist in understanding how relevance at a local or hyperlocal level can have national, regional, or international implications is the inverted impact pyramid, which makes clear the interaction between global and hyperlocal and local.

Hyperlocal and the Inverted Impact Pyramid

One digital strategist suggests that most, if not all, national or international stories are grounded in a hyperlocal community. "The inverted impact pyramid is a model that depicts the way in which a hyperlocal story intended for a small audience can become relevant to ever greater numbers of people, leading to a higher potential for impact" (Galperin 2016). The strategist further suggests the inverted impact pyramid is a "model that considers story framing as a foundation on which to create relevancy for the largest number of potential readers. The greater your pool of potential readers, the more likely you are to secure a larger audience" (Galperin 2016).

The inverted impact pyramid and horizontal networks of interactive communication that connect local and global audiences are relevant here: what is important or relevant to one person may in fact be relevant to one million. It is a matter of accessing the appropriate platform or platforms and engaging audiences through impactful storytelling.

Issues of accountability have the potential to be shared on a larger scale—a story may begin as hyperlocal but can have impact beyond the immediate community. Securing a larger audience is also likely to connect communities possibly in ways they were not before. This is an increasingly important evolution in a media system that encourages either hyperlocal, in-group echo chambers or national-level discourse that is perceived to represent the interests of an elite (Bhandari, Bhattarai, and Deane 2016).

Linking up the hyperlocal efforts of one country or region with others can illustrate or reinforce shared experiences and dilute perceptions of otherness. Such activities could be extremely powerful as relevance goes beyond the individual or even the hyperlocal, illustrating the potential for recognizing or establishing common ground across contexts. The post-earthquake IMS intervention in Nepal is one example that shows how hyperlocal stories can connect distant communities.

Beyond helping hyperlocal media outlets harness their power, partnerships with national, regional, or even international outlets are also important for their economic survival. Furthermore, by meeting their audiences' needs and building trust in the content they produce, hyperlocal media outlets can increase community buy-in and help ensure that their survival also remains in the best interest of the community. When hyperlocal outlets partner with other hyperlocal outlets in the same region or country, they may not only increase reach but can also help show the common ground that exists across communities. Such partnerships can also provide a certain level of protection in cases where governments attempt to target or intimidate media outlets.

Issues of Viability and Co-option

But are hyperlocal news outlets viable? There are several trends that suggest that such media may be at least partly sustainable—depending on context, technology, and strategy.

Context is critical, be it sociopolitical, linguistic, religious, or regulatory. Each context is unique and one size very rarely fits all in media development. Online media pioneer *Malaysiakini* in Malaysia, for example, realized early on that engaging Malaysian diaspora audiences would help ensure a viable revenue stream. Today, 20 percent of this glocal outlet's revenue comes from outside Malaysia.

Technology will also play a significant role in the future of hyperlocal news. Futurist Amy Webb suggests that ambient proximity technology enables content producers and audiences to gather and publish content using users' immediate surroundings thanks to something called a beacon.[3] This technology can allow for the creation of temporary hyperlocal social networks to help communities receive credible reporting. Clearly this has implications not just for content but for the bottom line as advertisers will have access to similar technology and will create targeted advertisements. We are already seeing this on Facebook and some news sites in the United States, and companies like Gimbal and Unacast are capitalizing on this technology.

Another technological example relevant for hyperlocal viability is "call to listen" technology. This technology allows the audience to listen to their favorite radio or TV station simply by making a phone call. This has proved successful for some local radio stations as well as international broadcasters such as Voice of America, BBC, Deutsche Welle, and the United Nations and is likely to have implications for hyperlocal stations that would like to reach audiences (and advertisers) beyond their reach.

Ultimately, the sustainability of hyperlocal media, and media development strategy, will depend largely on a thoughtful combination of context and technology and the identified needs of a community. However, local and hyperlocal media are also vulnerable to co-option and media capture. In a recent review of community media in Nepal, BBC Media Action showed that co-option of community media either by musclemen or NGOs was common, resulting in the media outlets becoming tools for international and/or local (and even hyperlocal) power brokers (Bhandari, Bhattarai, and Deane 2016). Similarly, "donors and international non-governmental organizations (NGOs) have co-opted the airwaves with content that too often means much to their funders but little to their audiences, and have failed to invest in the institutional strengthening of the media" (Bhandari, Bhattarai, and Deane 2016).

Perhaps more than ever, journalism faces a serious crisis of credibility, public trust, and ultimately relevance, while the advent of fake news has made transparent, fact-based journalism more important than ever.[4] But with this challenge comes the need to ensure that journalists know and understand the audiences they seek to reach: without an audience, there is no economic survival.

To understand the needs and demands and interactions of the audience, particularly in this hyperlocal, glocal world, there must be substantive qualitative and quantitative audience research, something that has largely been missing from media development. Until now, much of the literature has tended to examine media as a singular space rather than as part of more complex systems. As such, implementers should consider conducting research that takes a bottom-up approach (Stremlau 2014). Media development practitioners must put the audience first—be it international, regional, local, or hyperlocal—and ensure that content producers know and understand the audience's needs.

Implications for Media Development

It is imperative to look at each context in terms of its political, social, and cultural characteristics as well as its media environment and how these interface with one another. The ways in which communities access information are heavily conditioned by language, literacy, infrastructure, and regulation, and are thus highly variable between contexts, including urban-rural divides and gender demographics (Candan and Reeve 2012). This is further compounded by the changing nature of the media and how they are produced, accessed, and used.

While there continues to be debate about the place of hyperlocal in media development, what is clear is that hyperlocal media outlets can play an important role, particularly in the digital age. For it is precisely this, the role of technology, that can help raise local stories and local issues to the global stage. Yet, media assistance organizations seem to still struggle with how best to ensure inclusion as well as partnerships with national, regional, or international outlets that could be critical for the economic survival of hyperlocals as well as meeting the needs of audiences and building trust in the content. Thoughtful engagement of hyperlocals in the future is crucial not only for their survival, but will likely be beneficial to local and regional media partners.

The complexity of contemporary audiences also has implications for platform choice and suggests the need for ongoing research regarding accessibility—what is being accessed and how as well as how that information is being used. Attention should also be paid to how to best work around or address issues of censorship.

As seen in the Nepal example, relevant journalism can also be journalism that provides solutions. In this case, journalism served the public interest and held officials (from hyperlocal to national level) accountable. This accountability, some believe, is actually a service and "journalists and news media companies are actually in the service provision business" (Lavandera 2017). This essentially takes us full circle to the mission of journalism—that of serving the public, which often entails audience engagement and results in some form of accountability. This can also be good for the bottom line.

Notes

1. For further elaboration on the definition of *hyperlocal media*, see, for example, Sara Leckner, Carina Tenor, and Gunnar Nygren, "What about the Hyperlocals?" *Journalism Practice*, 2017, doi: 10.1080/17512786.2017.1392254.
2. Castells continues: "The communication foundation of the network society is the global web of horizontal communication networks that include the multimodal exchange of interactive messages from many to many both synchronous and asynchronous."
3. Beacons automatically push information back and forth between two connected devices in close proximity. For further discussion of this technology see, for example, the Future Today Institute's 2018 *Tech Trends* report at https://futuretodayinstitute.com/2018-tech-trends-for-journalism-and-media/.
4. The *Oxford English Dictionary* defines post-truth as: "Relating to or denoting circumstances in which objective facts are less influential in shaping public opinion than appeals to emotion and personal belief." See "post-truth," *Oxford English Dictionary*, https://en.oxforddictionaries.com/definition/post-truth.

References

Allan, Stuart, and Karen Fowler-Watt, eds. 2013. *Journalism: New Challenges*. Bournemouth University, BU: Centre for Journalism and Communication Research.

Bhandari, Kiran, Dipak Bhattarai, and James Deane. 2016. *Accountability, Nation and Society: The Role of Media in Remaking Nepal*. BBC Media Action.

Candan, Zuleika, and Richard Reeve. 2012. *Working with Media to Prevent Conflict: Cluster Synthesis Report*. London: International Alert.

Castells, Manuel. 2007. "Communication, Power and Counter-Power in the Network Society." *International Journal of Communication* 1: 238–266.

Dowson-Zeidan, Najla, Tim Eaton, and Karen Wespieser. 2015. *After the Revolution: Libyan and Tunisian Media through the People's Eyes*. BBC Media Action Research Report, Issue 06.

Dunbar-Hester, Christina. 2010. "The History and Future of Hyper-Local Radio." *The Atlantic*, October 5. https://www.theatlantic.com/technology/archive/2010/10/the-history-and-future-of-hyper-local-radio/64058/.

Galperin, Simon. 2016. "How the 'Inverted Impact Pyramid' Can Make a Hyperlocal Story Go International." *Media Shift*, April 27. http://mediashift.org/2016/04/how-the-inverted-impact-pyramid-can-make-a-hyperlocal-story-go-international/.

ITU. 2016. "ICT Facts and Figures 2016." https://www.itu.int/en/ITU-D/Statistics/Documents/facts/ICTFactsFigures2016.pdf.

Jarvis, Jeff. 2014. "No Mas Mass Media," *Geeks Bearing Gifts via Medium*. https://medium.com/geeks-bearing-gifts/no-mas-mass-media-b8a2c240d718.

Kelly, Sanja, Mai Truong, Adrian Shahbaz, and Madeline Earp. 2016. *Silencing the Messenger: Communication Apps under Pressure*. Freedom on the Net 2016. Washington, D.C.: Freedom House. https://freedomhouse.org/sites/default/files/FOTN_2016_BOOKLET_FINAL.pdf.

Kurpius, David D., Emily T. Metzgar, and Karen M. Rowley. 2010. "Sustaining Hyperlocal Media." *Journalism Studies* 11 (3): 359–376. doi: 10.1080/14616700903429787.

Lavandera, Maria Jose. 2017. "News Organizations Need to Find New Ways to Provide Value: Shifting from a Content-Production Frame to a Service-Provider Mindset." *New York University Journalism*, March 15. http://projects.nyujournalism.org/newsliteracy2017/topics/journalism-as-a-service/.

Metzgar, Emily T., David D. Kurpius, and Karen M. Rowley. 2011. "Defining Hyperlocal Media: Proposing a Framework for Discussion." *New Media & Society* 13 (5): 772–87. doi:10.1177/1461444810385095.

Stremlau, Nicole. 2014. "From the Field: In Search of Evidence—Media and Governance in Fragile States." *Global Media Journal* 4 (2): 1–11.

CHAPTER NINTEEN

Solutions Journalism and a Normative Model for Media Development

TOM JACOBSON

A Western liberal model of the press has predominated in media assistance work during most of the post WWII era. This model presumes a privately-owned press. It promotes newsgathering and reporting practices intended to be evidence based, and objective, in the pursuit of truth. And it embodies a set of normative values concerning precisely what journalism has to offer Western-style democratic political systems, opposition to abuses of power.

However, a variety of alternatives to this model has evolved in recent decades, sometimes coupled with assistance efforts and sometimes not. A movement for development journalism during the 1970s and 1980s attempted to advance a form of journalism suitable for new and rapidly changing nations. Public service broadcasting has always advocated an alternative to the standard Western model of journalism. Various models of citizen journalism are being tried around the world. An *ubuntu* approach to journalism based in traditional African values has been advanced in Africa. There are more.

A recent entrant to this terrain of newer journalism models is *solutions journalism*. Solutions journalism is a set of guidelines for reporting that offers some advantages over the standard Western reporting model in countries undertaking rapid social and political change. It has received backing from development research organizations such as BBC Media Action and funders including the Bill & Melinda Gates Foundation. And a growing number of news outlets have employed solutions reporting guidelines around the world.

In addition to different guidelines for reporting, solutions journalism also reflects a set of values that vary from those in the standard Western model. They are concerned with finding solutions to social problems, as well as to uncovering abuses of power. These are values that are reflected in Amartya Sen's capabilities approach to development. This chapter describes solutions journalism, situating it in relation to other current practices. It also places solutions journalism within the normative framework of the capabilities approach. The result is a model of the press that shares some important features with the Western model of reporting but differs from this model in significant ways as well.

Development, the Western Model of Journalism, and Some Alternatives

The most prominent statement of the Western liberal approach to journalism was the *Four Theories of the Press* (Siebert, Petersen, and Schramm 1956). *The Four Theories* was written in the context of the Cold War to articulate a democratic perspective on journalism. But it was also written in the context of post-war era work on development, or modernization. Modernization theory argued that the overriding goal of development was economic growth, accomplished through unfettered markets. Cultural tradition would largely need to be abandoned to make room for new, modern social institutions. Universal rights that prioritized the civic rights of the West would be required. And technologies would be expected to solve social problems as they arose. In short, new post-colonial societies would eventually evolve to assume the form of Western capitalist democracies, largely in the mold of America (Black 1966).

The *Four Theories* presented a normative theory of the press that suited modernization theory's vision of the future. It employed a typology of four different forms of government and the kinds of media systems that were integral to each. The Libertarian label was given to the model used in Western democracies: the essential characteristics of the libertarian press were its opposition to government, its aim to inform the citizenry, and its need to entertain in order to generate the funding base required for independence. In addition to a Soviet Communist theory of the press and an Authoritarian model, a fourth, Social Reponsibility model of the press was included reflecting earlier criticisms of American news reporting (Pickard 2010).

The libertarian model began to suffer widespread criticism at least as early as the 1960s (Nerone 1995). Development Journalism appeared in Asia during the run-up to the period of the New International Information Order, advocating reporting practices that would focus less on corruption, dysfunctional politics, and natural disasters than did Western styled reporting and more on positive social change. Advocates of development journalism believed reporting was needed that would report success stories on industries started, schools built, and health conditions improved. It would continue to employ evidence based reporting on malfeasance, on abuse of government. And it would strive to remain free of governmental control. But it would also publish reports on promising events taking place in still new and struggling nations (Quebral 1988).

Western journalists and media analysts opposed development journalism on the basis that it represented government capture of journalism. They overlooked development journalism's commitment to evidence-based reporting and argued that such reporting would merely serve as advocacy on behalf of government (Ogan 1982). As this debate took place, the shortfalls in Western styled reporting denounced by development journalism were documented by a reporter for the Associated Press. The title of Mort Rosenblum's book pointedly characterized the extent to which Western news agencies and newspapers were preoccupied with news of *Coups and Earthquakes* (Rosenblum 1979).

Other alternatives to the standard Western model followed. Citizen journalism efforts arose around the world to supplement the work of professional reporters with the newsgathering efforts of everyday citizens. Local agency in media management has been advocated to ensure the expression of local voices, representing the needs and interests of marginalized communities (Rodríguez, Kidd, and Stein 2009). Public sphere theory led to a widening awareness of the importance of political public dialog (Habermas 1989). More recently, citizen journalism, non-governmental organizations, and digital journalism start-ups capitalize on social media and other internet utilities to produce a digitally networked reporting ecology that make possible both global awareness and grassroots agency (Beckett 2010).

Some of these alternatives represented not only change in reporting practices but in some cases, change in the normative aims of journalism as well. Alternative media services were encouraged to combat not only authoritarian governments, but hegemonic Western media themselves (Pickard 2007). At least one justification for alternative media advocated them as an expression of political anarchism (Downing 2001). The *ubuntu* approach to journalism, based in Bantu cultural values, emphasizes universal bonds of sharing that bind human beings to one another. Also in Africa, China's growing interest in the region has produced a "constructive journalism" approach to reporting which aims to ensure that China's activities in the region, and China's view of African interests as well, are reported in a specific way. Constructive journalism would largely erase not only the emphasis on private ownership of the press, but would entirely erase the tension between journalism and government embodied in the Western journalism model. On the academic front, prominent statements have argued that normative issues should be addressed on an *ad hoc* basis, analyzing press systems within the context of the social and economic systems where they reside, rather than within the framework of universalistic normative principles (Hallin and Mancini 2004).

Solutions journalism therefore appears not simply as a new set of guidelines for reporting practices. It also appears against a backdrop of contesting views over what journalism is for, and particularly what comprises journalism in settings where rapid improvements in social and political justice are needed, where social and economic problems demand attention. This is the backdrop of development.

The Capabilities Approach to Development

A normative framework for journalism implies not only an approach to politics, but also to culture and other values, to development. If modernization theory doesn't provide a desirable model for development, then where is such a model to be found? The most prominent statement on what comprises development today is Amartya Sen's work.

Sen's capabilities approach to development is strongly normative in its claim that development should be defined as the public's freedom in choosing their policy preferences (Sen 1999). Importantly, he argues that journalism and the media have a key role to play in the process of deciding upon preferred choices. He also believes that the ideas of human rights and free speech have universal relevance, though he emphasizes the importance of understanding the meaning of these ideas within local cultural contexts.

Sen aims to broaden the concerns of development policy beyond wealth, whether wealth is measured in terms of per capita income, gross national product, or some other measure of economic wellbeing. He believes that development must focus on enabling a wide range of *functionings*, or "doings and beings," beyond simply enjoying a paycheck. Sen wants to make the aims of development broader, and more humane. Thus, functionings are treated as the expression of what a flourishing life entails.

> "The concept of 'functioning', which has distinctly Aristotelian roots, reflects the various things a person may value doing or being. The valued functionings may vary from elementary ones, such as being adequately nourished and being free from avoidable disease, to very complex activities or personal states, such as being able to take part in the life of the community and having self-respect." (Sen 1999, 75)

Sen pairs the concept of functioning with the concept of *capabilities*. For Sen, development refers not really to the enjoyment of specific functionings but rather to the choices that are available to actually enjoy possible functionings. For example, material wealth is something that most people want, but some people may want more or less. Some citizens may be willing to qualify gains in immediate financial wellbeing for environmental sustainability or better schools or preservation of traditional arts. "A person's 'capability' refers to the alternative combinations of functionings that are all feasible for her to achieve" (Sen 1999, 75).

The ideas of functionings and capabilities comprise the conceptual basis for Sen's approach to development as freedom. Development is not wealth, nor is it a specific set of social benefits such as education or health. Development, instead, is the *capability to choose* functionings. "Capability is thus a kind of freedom: the substantive freedom to achieve alternative functioning combinations" (Sen 1999, 75).

Sen's approach to development as freedom includes elaborately developed theories of welfare economics, human rights, justice, and rationality (Sen 2004a, 2004b, 2009). It also emphasizes the importance of citizen participation through communication. The envisioning of capabilities requires that citizens discuss freely what are the many things they value and what priorities among them are to be established. "Indeed, one of the strongest arguments in favor of political freedom lies precisely in the opportunity it gives citizens to discuss and debate—and to participate in the selection of—values in the choice of priorities" (Sen 1999, 30).

Thus, Sen makes a strong case for the importance of pubic communication. Nevertheless, a deeper understanding of communication's role within the capabilities approach is required. While his work gives public discussion a central role in advancing citizen agency, this role is sketched rather than analyzed. Nowhere does he criticize the *Coups and Earthquakes* approach to Western reporting widely decried by others. Nowhere does he consider the kind of journalism that might be needed to fully support citizen discussion on preferred development priorities.

Solutions Journalism

If citizens are to be empowered to make choices, then journalism must somehow improve its ability to effectively present choices available to citizens on matters of public importance, choices of which they might otherwise be unaware.

A new brand of reporter is calling for news that enhances public choice not only in low-income countries but in high-income countries as well, "solutions journalism." Solutions journalists argue that journalism should report not only problems, but should also cover promising solutions to those problems: "Solutions journalism is rigorous and compelling reporting about responses to social problems" (Solutions Journalism Network n.d.). It focuses on attempts to address not only social problems, but also outcomes, analyzing why a particular solution might appear to be working, or why not. Solutions journalism embodies the kind of reporting needed to facilitate what Sen calls government by discussion over preferred capabilities in a more effective way than does traditional journalism.

This trend, or movement, in reporting is not entirely new. It began at least as early as the 1990s (Benesch 1998). At the time, reporters and newspapers started experimenting with reporting that provided some positive news in addition to what could often seem to be unrelenting gloom. This was not formulaic, feel-good news, but rather an effort to provide hard hitting analysis. Stories might cover what models are having success in reducing the dropout rate in public schools. How do they work? What are they doing differently from other attempts? In America, the American News Service (ANS) operated for five years, from 1995–2000, under the branding motto "search for solutions." In the early 2000s, *The Nation* magazine published solutions oriented stories in a "What Works," section.

In 2013 a Solutions Journalism Network (SJN) was established, pointing to research suggesting that a steady diet of negative coverage produces news fatigue, turning away readers. Young readers in particular find unrelenting negativity in news coverage discouraging (Associated Press 2008; Curry and Hammonds 2014). The SJN promotes understanding of solutions reporting that is neither formulaic nor mere boosterism. It conducts newsroom trainings, and it promotes models of effective solutions journalism. Today, newsrooms employing the solutions approach include the *New York Times*, the *Boston Globe*, the *Huffington Post*, the Center for Investigative Reporting, and hundreds of other outlets across the United States. Solutions reporting is now pursued outside the U.S. The BBC has ongoing solutions focused journalism (Hare 2016), and news organizations in the Global South are using the solutions approach including South Africa's *Mail & Guardian* and *New Delhi Television.*

Solutions journalism implies a significant shift in journalism's aims. On one hand, solutions reporting remains Western-style journalism. It includes hard-nosed, evidence based reporting intended to serve as a watchdog on government. It is neither advocacy journalism or civic journalism. At the same time, it differs from the Western model in attempting to facilitate government by presenting to the public additional information on matters of common interest. One of the network's founders, David Bornstein (2011) believes that solutions journalism ought to represent the manifold positive social change efforts now underway globally. Thus, solutions journalism complements Sen's emphasis on capabilities. It aims to help the public be aware of choices they might wish government to pursue in addressing social problems.

Exploring Practical and Normative Implications of Solutions Journalism

New journalism models arise from everyday journalism practice. However, if new practices are to be taught on a widespread basis, advanced, and defended when necessary then the normative goals and values they reflect must be clear. Christians makes this case in his introduction to a special issue on *ubuntu* journalism in the *Journal of Media Ethics*.

> Media ethics is a complicated enterprise of many dimensions. But the future of media ethics depends primarily on theory. All aspects of research and professional practices matter, but the vitality of our theorizing is *sine qua non*. We find our pathway now in the future conceptually. (Christians 2015, 61)

The main requirement for a normative theory of the press is that, beyond a description of how reporting operates on a daily basis, it must provide guidance on how the press ought to operate in terms of norms and political aims. If the aims of the standard Western model of the press produce reporting inclined strongly towards negative coverage, then a model is needed that encourages some reporting that is socially productive. This doesn't need to be pro-government propaganda, advocacy for a political regime, or advocacy journalism. But a balance between negative and constructive reporting is needed.

The capabilities approach offers a normative basis for such a new journalism model, or perhaps it is an adjustment of the old model. It prizes the historical role of the press in promoting transparency and holding government to account. At the same time, it calls for the press to facilitate public deliberation on choice. This requires information that goes beyond "gotcha journalism," beyond opposition to abuses of power.

Understanding more fully how solutions journalism could support a capabilities approach to development requires further research. Good and useful reporting alone cannot institute the kinds of capabilities Sen calls for, but monitoring contributions of solutions journalism to political and policy processes would be helpful. At the level of reporting practice this would begin with identifying solutions reporting efforts already underway, and similar ones (Al-Zikri 2017), around the world.

In a historical context, it would be useful to carefully determine where the solutions orientation is similar to what development journalism had attempted to do, and where different. At the level of normative principles, a fuller understanding of how solutions journalism might be seen to complement Sen's thinking is required. For example, running throughout Sen's work is a strong defense of cultural variety. He argues that prioritizing citizen choice includes prioritizing citizen choice over preferred cultural values. Does his framework inform a truly multicultural approach to journalism?

To be sure, not all reporting need be, or should be, solutions oriented. And, just to be clear, all media development work need not be solutions journalism oriented, or even journalism oriented (Nelson and Peña-Susman 2012). However, solutions journalism offers one tool that aims to augment the traditional watchdog role of the press with a more constructive role. This seems an option worth pursuing for those working in the field of media assistance.

Recommended for Further Reading

Benesch, Susan. 1998. "The Rise of Solutions Journalism." *Columbia Journalism Review* 36 (6): 36–39.

Nerone, John C. 1995. *Last Rights: Revisiting Four Theories of the Press.* Urbana, IL: University of Illinois Press.

Sen, Amartya. 1999. *Development as Freedom.* New York, NY: Knopf.

References

Associated Press. 2008. *A New Model for News: Studying the Deep Structure of Young-Adult News Consumption.* New York, NY: Associated Press. http://manuscritdepot.com/edition/documents-pdf/newmodel.pdf Al-Zikri, Yassin. 2017. *Conflict Sensitive Journalism: A Guidebook for Yemeni Journalists.* Studies & Economic Media Center (SEMC). https://www.mediasupport.org/wp-content/uploads/2017/10/Conflict-sensitive-journalism-guide-Yemen_1.pdf

Beckett, Charlie. 2010. *The Value of Networked Journalism.* A Report of Polis. London: The London School of Economics and Political Science.

Benesch, Susan. 1998. "The Rise of Solutions Journalism." *Columbia Journalism Review* 36 (6): 36–39.

Black, Cyril E. 1966. *The Dynamics of Modernization: A Study in Comparative History.* New York, NY: Harper & Row.

Bornstein, David. 2011. "Why Solutions Journalism Matters, Too." *New York Times*, December 20. https://opinionator.blogs.nytimes.com/2011/12/20/why-solutions-journalism-matters-too/?ref=opinion&_r=0

Christians, Clifford G. 2015. "Introduction: *Ubuntu* for Journalism Theory and Practice." *Journal of Media Ethics* (Special issue on Ubuntu for Journalism Theory and Practice) 30 (2): 61–73.

Curry, Alexander L., and Keith H. Hammonds. 2014. *The Power of Solutions Journalism.* University of Texas Engaging News Project. https://mediaengagement.org/wp-content/uploads/2014/06/ENP_SJN-report.pdf

Downing, John D. H. 2001. *Radical Media: Rebellious Communication and Social Movements.* Thousand Oaks, CA: Sage Publications.

Habermas, Jürgen. 1989. *The Structural Transformation of the Public Sphere*. Cambridge, MA: The MIT Press.

Hallin, Daniel C., and Paolo Mancini. 2004. *Comparing Media Systems: Three Models of Media and Politics*. Cambridge, MA: Cambridge University Press.

Hare, Kristen. 2016. "How the BBC's looking for the Solutions to the World's Big Issues." *Worldhacks,* November 18. https://www.poynter.org/news/how-bbcs-looking-solutions-worlds-big-issues

Nelson, Mark, and Tara Susman-Peña. 2012. *Rethinking Media Development: A Report on the Media Map Project*. Washington, D.C.: Internews.

Nerone, John C. 1995. *Last Rights: Revisiting Four Theories of the Press*. Urbana, IL: University of Illinois Press.

Ogan, Christine L. 1982. "Development Journalism/Communication: The Status of the Concept." *Gazette* 29 (1–2): 3–13.

Pickard, Victor. 2007. "Alternative Media." In *The Encyclopedia of Media and Politics,* edited by Todd Michael Schaefer, and Thomas A. Birkland, 12–13. Washington, D.C.: CQ Press.

———. 2010. "'Whether the Giants Should Be Slain or Persuaded to Be Good': Revisiting the Hutchins Commission and the Role of Media in a Democratic Society." *Critical Studies in Media Communication* 27 (4): 391–411.

Quebral, Nora. 1988. *Development Communication*. Laguna: University of the Philippines, Los Baños.

Rodríguez, Clemencia, Dorothy Kidd, and Laura Stein, eds. 2009. *Making our Media: Global Initiatives Toward a Democratic Public Sphere. Volume One: Creating New Communication Spaces*. Cresskill, NJ: Hampton Press.

Rosenblum, Mort. 1979. *Coups and Earthquakes: Reporting the World for America*. New York, NY: Harper & Row.

Sen, Amartya. 1999. *Development as Freedom*. New York, NY: Knopf.

———. 2004a. *Rationality and Freedom*. Cambridge, MA: Harvard University Press.

———. 2004b. "Elements of a Theory of Human Rights." *Philosophy and Public Affairs* 32 (4): 315–56.

———. 2009. *The Idea of Justice*. Cambridge, MA: Harvard University Press.

Siebert, Fred S., Theodore Peterson, and Wilbur Schramm. 1956. *Four Theories of the Press: The Authoritarian, Libertarian, Social Responsibility, and Soviet Communist Concepts of What the Press Should be and do*. Urbana, IL: University of Illinois Press.

Solutions Journalism Network. n.d. *What is solutions journalism?* https://thewholestory.solutionsjournalism.org/what-is-solutions-journalism-c050147bb1eb

CHAPTER TWENTY

The Enduring Place of Investigative Journalism in Media Development

DREW SULLIVAN

The stories that journalism is most famous for—from Watergate to the Spotlight series on priest pedophiles to the Panama Papers—are all investigative series. So, it may come as a surprise to learn how few journalists are dedicated full-time to investigative reporting: their numbers in the mere thousands among the millions of other journalists worldwide who produce the day-to-day content of the news. So much depends on the specialized work of this small group. I have dedicated more than a decade of effort with the Organized Crime and Corruption Reporting Project (OCCRP) to supporting and cultivating this community around the world.

Investigative Reporters and Editors (IRE), a U.S.-based association for members of the profession, defines investigative journalism as "the reporting, through one's own initiative and work product, of matters of importance to readers, viewers, or listeners. In many cases, the subjects of the reporting wish the matters under scrutiny to remain undisclosed" (Houston and IRE 2009, v). This definition is accurate, through excessively modest. Journalists have to decide which events of the day are newsworthy; investigative journalists, through their "own initiative and work product" make the news. They are agenda-setters of the highest order, and because of their commitment to "matters of importance," their agenda frequently is akin to the moral consciousness of the media.

> Their stories call attention to the breakdown of social systems and the disorder within public institutions that cause injury and injustice; in turn, their stories implicitly

> demand the response of public officials—and the public itself—to that breakdown and disorder. Thus the work of these [investigative] reporters calls us, as a society, to decide what is, and what is not, an outrage to our sense of moral order and to consider our expectations for our officials, our institutions, and ultimately ourselves. (Ettema and Glasser, 1998, 3)

Because their work is dedicated to public interest and frequently on topics others would wish to remain "undisclosed," investigative reporters are also responsible for an outsized share of the change that comes about from journalism. If someone is getting fired or law enforcement is starting an investigation because of a news story, it is almost always due to investigative reporters.

"Investigative journalism is absolutely essential," said Nobel laureate economist Joseph Stiglitz. "It's really part of the enforcement mechanism. It provides checks against the abuses. The very fact that there are investigative reporters out there … acts as a deterrent. Its very presence is an important part of successful development … It's a key part of making our democracy work" (GIJN 2017).

As vital as investigative journalism is to democracy, its practitioners still remain scarce in the countries where they are most needed. In the developing world, it's not unusual to a country with less than a dozen full-time investigative reporters. A survey by the OCCRP found that countries like Azerbaijan, Slovenia, Bosnia and Herzegovina and Kazakhstan had single digit numbers of working investigative reporters.

The transition to digital media has created both opportunities and challenges for the practices of investigative journalism to spread and thrive. Sheila Coronel in 2016 predicted the dawn of "a Golden Age of global muckracking," ushered in partly by the spread of digital technologies that have enabled networks of investigative journalists to flourish; the International Consortium of Investigative Journalists, the Global Investigative Journalism Network, and OCCRP are among the largest and most notable, but there are many other smaller, and less formal collaborations. "The era of the lone wolf is over," she declared (Coronel 2016). Many of these initiatives have benefitted from the growth in non-profit funding for journalism.

But the decline of traditional business models in the digital age has also hurt investigative journalism disproportionately, especially in local media markets (Hamilton 2016). In developing democracies, this challenge has been compounded by recent declines in media freedoms; investigative journalists, of course, face the greatest threats in these environments, making their profession untenable without significant expenditure on security and legal protections. And most importantly, news media in developing and authoritarian countries can at times be among the few independent institutions still standing—so that even when investigative journalists uncover wrongdoing, the police, courts, or politicians may not take action. These weak environments also need assistance from the international community to ensure that independent journalism contributes to better governance and accountability.

International Assistance to Investigative Reporting

Investigative reporters have always felt out of place in the media development community. Having to rely on money from governments or even wealthy patrons like George Soros is problematic to many investigative reporters. The results have been predictable. While donors and media development advocates talk a lot about the importance of investigative reporting, it has traditionally received a smaller share of media development assistance, an area that itself receives just a fraction of total international aid. According to a Center for Media Assistance (CIMA) report from 2017, media gets just 0.5 percent of the total international development spending. Investigative reporting gets just 2.5 percent of that smaller pot, according to a 2011 CIMA report.

However, attitudes are changing. The 2017 CIMA report found donors ranked investigative reporting second in their priorities behind freedom of information. While new statistics are not yet available, anecdotally it appears that donor investment in investigative reporting is growing. Multimillion-dollar projects like the U.S. Department of State's Global Anti-Corruption Consortium, USAID's Regional Investigative Journalism Network, and large grants from Omidyar and the Open Society Foundations to investigative reporting networks have been announced in the past few years.

"Only recently has investigative journalism begun receiving a noticeable share of media development funding," said David Kaplan, the director of the Global Investigative Journalism Network and the 2011 CIMA study's author. "This is due in part to those of us in the IJ community making a better case to donors on its impact, return on investment, and importance to development and democracy" (Kaplan n.d.).

"A lot of the greatest work that prosecutors and watchdogs do comes from the work that [investigative] journalists do," U.S. Attorney Preet Bharara told journalists in 2016. "I would encourage anyone who's able to fund investigative journalism to spend money on it because it's money well-spent and it's good for the public" (GIJN 2017).

If the goal of media development is to create positive change, then why not reverse the past and invest 98 percent of all media development funds on investigative reporting? It's not that easy.

Investigative Reporting Challenges

To begin with, investigative reporting is actually quite rare; simply put, there are not a lot of investigative media for donors to invest in. Furthermore, it is very hard to scale those that do exist for reasons that I will make clear here.

This small number of investigative reporters is partly due to costs. An investigative project can easily cost a media organization upwards of a million dollars in Western Media. OCCRP, one of the world's largest investigative reporting organizations by stories published, averages $40,000 per story in developing countries where costs are low. Add in high salaries for the veteran journalists and the risks of being sued and it's not hard to understand that investigative reporting is often the first department cut when money must be saved. Media organizations simply cannot afford to do much investigative reporting. The other problem is that there are few people efficient enough to be cost-effective investigative reporters. You need experienced veterans who have the skills and experience to investigate quickly. A good reporter can do an investigation in three months that might take another two years. This efficiency is an existential issue to investigative reporting organizations. Investigative organizations incur a significant risk each time they embark on a project. Can they do a good enough story in a timely enough fashion that will justify the expense? Will donors think their stories have enough impact or readers to justify the high costs? Will they attract enough readers or viewers to stay in business when they publish just three or four major stories each year? Will slipshod work cause a raft of lawsuits that will drive them out of business? Often, this must be done with young or inexperienced reporters who are still learning their craft. Organizations without efficient journalists will fail and go out of business.

The subtleties of investigative reporting are often lost on people who do not understand the business. There is a tendency to equate journalism and investigative reporting, but they are very different. It takes as long as four years to train a journalist to do investigative reporting. That's about the same amount of time it would take a family practice doctor to become a surgeon.

In the professional community that supports media development, there are some donors, implementers and trainers who have been journalists, but very few are experienced investigative reporters. I am aware of only one investigative reporter in the donor community and a half dozen in the implementer community.

To create a development program for investigative reporting takes trained professionals with experience in the field. From a decade of experience of participating in trainings and conferences, I have found this is happening in a minority of cases. No one would expect a photographer to teach a class on landscape painting, but that is what is frequently done in the field of media development assistance.

Even with good intentions, it is still difficult to still provide useful training. Those seeking to support the growth of investigative journalism must find good (and real) investigative reporters, plan a good training program, and then overcome the challenges of working in repressive media environments.

Lessons Learned

OCCRP's has learned from experience that there are elements which increase the probability of success in doing investigative reporting. Many of these approaches are shared by other organizations like the Stockholm School of Economics, the BBC and others:

- Investigative reporting involves learning procedures and protocols as much as basic knowledge. Classroom training is the beginning, but not the end of investigative reporting training. That's because with an almost infinite number of stories, and hundreds of different countries and cultures, you cannot predict the challenges reporters will have to overcome. Learning requires work on real world problems that cannot be simulated or anticipated.
- Investigative reporting at organizations relies on a set of people that at a minimum includes an investigative editor as well as a reporter. Good investigative editors make their reporters more effective and efficient. Yet there are very few and sometimes no trained investigative editors in a country, and support programs too frequently neglect them. Good investigative journalism requires investigative reporters, investigative editors, and a culture of investigative reporting in the whole newsroom.
- Working on real world problems means organizations facing real-world consequences. In addition to designing an effective program of support, those who support investigative reporting must also have expertise in mitigating risks and challenges of high-profile journalism; investigative journalism needs the protection of a hardened organization that can respond to and resist lawsuits, hacking attempts, intimidation, threats, and the other problems inherent in investigative journalism.
- You need a significant investment from a donor because the work is more expensive. You are hiring the best journalists and they must sometimes travel globally, access commercial data, and spend what needs to be spent to get the story.
- It takes 3–4 years of intense work to develop an investigative reporting and 5–6 years to develop an investigative editor. This takes a significant commitment from an implementer and a donor.

These are just some of the challenges. Investigative reporting can cause huge problems. Investigative reporting has cost people and companies billions of dollars in fines, seized assets and legal fees. There is a lot at stake. It is not unusual for the donors to investigative reporting to be threatened by governments and organized crime. For example, crime figures and governments have hired expensive lawyers and lobbyists to get the organization defunded by its donor governments. It's a deadly serious business that often causes political problems for donors.

Impact of Investigative Journalism

Despite these challenges, the results from successful investigative reporting projects can be immense. Election races have been reshaped, leaders who abuse their power have been driven from power. Thousands have lost their jobs. Many corrupt officials have gone to jail. And that's what we know about. There are likely countless untold stories of governments reversing bad decisions or people being fired that will never be known. That is in part because of the difficulties of monitoring and evaluating the impact of investigative reporting.

In the book Democracy Detectives, economist James T. Hamilton (2016) argues "Each dollar spent on a story can generate hundreds of dollars in benefits." OCCRP's internal analysis of stories estimates that the organization has returned $440 for each $1 invested based on fines or seizures paid by the subjects of its stories. That's in addition to more than 100 investigations started by law enforcement and regulators, more than a dozen politicians deposed and other significant effects. However, it is impossible to plan for such impact and it's difficult to prove the causal relationships to the stories. Another difficulty is determining who should be selected to receive donor funds.

The goal of any media development program should be to create a rich journalism and investigative reporting ecosphere in a country. Often donors select one organization to be the beneficiary of their largess and discourage more than one organization from forming arguing that too many organizations will cause a problem with sustainability. But investigative reporting benefits from having a landscape where multiple organizations are thriving and where people can train and move around within that space. It's better to start three organizations than one because they will create a larger market that will make all sustainable. It's the same logic for putting a new restaurant where they are already a couple restaurants. It attracts diners.

Creating that ecosphere is difficult. The challenges facing a local investigative reporting organization are immense. Threats, intimidation, lawsuits, harassment from authorities, smear campaigns, restrictive laws, and even arrests are not uncommon. But these are well known problems that journalists have faced.

"Investing in Investigative Journalism is not for the faint hearted. The field's high payoffs come with high risks, particularly in countries with weak rule of law where impunity for attacks on journalists is high," said David Kaplan. "We face death threats and murders, lawsuits and intimidation, a lack of resources and funding, surveillance states, corrupt bosses, and more." (Kaplan n.d.).

Then there is the issue of sustainability. From experience of watching centers fail, the greatest threats to these small investigative organizations are journalistic and managerial. Successful centers are often started by inspirational journalists who are very good at investigative reporting or by an entrepreneur who sees the need for a good center. But both must learn to be good managers, fundraisers and business people. And they must build good investigative journalism staffs run by good editors. Most organizations fail because of poor management or poor journalism skills. If an organization does not have a great investigative editor, they cannot do the kind of stories that will attract readers, impress donors and create change. If they don't have good business skills, they will be stuck forever as vanity centers.

Sometimes donors or implementers seek to build their own investigative centers in countries where there is not a center. They argue one is needed and that it can help improve the local investigative journalism. This has not been a successful approach. An informal review of failed or moribund organizations shows that an inordinate number of them were created by media development support organizations. The main reasons they failed were because:

- They failed to appreciate the importance of the quality of the investigative reporting in the success of the project
- They chose people to run the organization who would never be good enough to sustain the organization journalistically.
- They or their charges failed to plan for sustainability and the centers closed when funding ended
- They selected people without the entrepreneurial drive to overcome the litany of problems inherent in setting up a business.

Existing centers, even if formed by an entrepreneurial reporter, can be undermined by the development community. In often well-intentioned attempts to help, donors or media development organizations often encourage local centers to change their focus to get funds that might meet the development organization's needs. This often moves fragile organizations off their central mission or focus and can prove fatal to these organizations.

One way to mitigate these sorts of problems is to team with existing media houses or those few practitioners who specialize in this space. By bringing in investigative journalism expertise, these mistakes can be avoided. Organizations like the Global Investigative Journalism Network (GIJN), Investigative Reporters and Editors (IRE) and successful investigative reporting organizations like the Philippine Center for Investigative Journalism, KRIK in Serbia, Correctiv in Germany and others have a wealth of experience they are willing to share.

Donors should also look at directly funding successful journalism programs, which tend to do the training and scaling naturally. We suggest core support for proven investigative centers as the most cost-effective way to work in this space. "This is long-haul stuff, so it's not ideal for donors with short-attention spans and frequently shifting priorities," said Kaplan. "And it's a rough business. But for those with the vision and the nerve, the payoffs are extraordinary" (n.d.).

Recommended for Further Reading

Coronel, Sheila. 2016. "Coronel: A Golden Age of Global Muckraking at Hand," Keynote, *Investigative Reporters and Editors Conference*. Published by the Global Investigative Journalism Network. https://gijn.org/2016/06/20/a-golden-age-of-global-muckraking/

GIJN. 2017. "Investigative Impact: The Role of Investigative Journalism in Fostering Change—and How to Measure It." *Global Investigative Journalism Network*. https://drive.google.com/file/d/1o5G6O__lZ6NkWmqcY1T0APV-9xDhPhb2/view

References

CIMA. 2011. "Continental Shift: New Trends in Private U.S. Funding for Media Development." *Center for International Media Assistance*. https://www.cima.ned.org/resource/continental-shift-new-trends-in-private-u-s-funding-for-media-development/

———. 2017. "A Slowly Shifting Field: Understanding Donor Priorities in Media Development." *Center for International Media Assistance*. https://www.cima.ned.org/publication/slowly-shifting-field/

Coronel, Sheila. 2016. "Coronel: A Golden Age of Muckraking at Hand," Keynote, *Investigative Reporters and Editors Conference*. Published by the Global Investigative Journalism Network. https://gijn.org/2016/06/20/a-golden-age-of-global-muckraking/

Ettema, James S. Theodore L. Glasser. 1998. *Investigative Journalism and Public Virtue*. New York: Columbia University Press.

GIJN. 2017. "Investigative Impact: The Role of Investigative Journalism in Fostering Change—and How to Measure It." *Global Investigative Journalism Network*. https://drive.google.com/file/d/1o5G6O__lZ6NkWmqcY1T0APV-9xDhPhb2/view

Hamilton, James T. 2016. *Democracy's Detectives*. Cambridge, MA: Harvard University Press.

Houston, Brant and Investigative Reporters and Editors. 2009. *The Investigative Reporter's Handbook: A Guide to Documents, Databases and Techniques*, 5th ed. Boston, MA: Bedford/St. Martin's.

Kaplan, David. n.d. Interview.

CHAPTER TWENTY-ONE

Public Service Broadcasting and Media Development

MINNA ASLAMA HOROWITZ AND DAVOR MARKO

Public service broadcasting (PSB)—television or radio that is partly or wholly funded by the public money (budget, license fee, or tax) but independently operated in the public interest—has long been one of the institutional and structural foci of media development and international media assistance. Despite the predictions of the demise of PSB as an ineffective and costly form of media, it has endured as a means of providing content and services. At its most idealistic reiteration, PSB is thought to provide diverse, independent, and universal service and content, that, in turn, supports a democratic public sphere. Given the increasing challenges of the current private media landscape, international donors are looking at public service models to provide a path to independent media and journalism (Abbott 2016). Yet, donors and development agencies face several substantial challenges while designing and applying strategies to support PSB, and its digital variant, public service media (PSM). This chapter outlines some of those challenges around the world.

Similar and Different: Challenges for Development

When an international media assistance strategy for post-war Bosnia and Herzegovina (BiH) was designed in the late 1990s, it was believed that the establishment of an umbrella public broadcaster would contribute to democratization and social cohesion. It was also thought that such a broadcaster would overcome local ethno-national and political divisions. Radio-Television in BiH was modeled after the British Broadcasting Corporation (BBC) and heavily supported by the international community. More than 15 years after the intervention, however, the state broadcaster is not a trusted media organization, its programming does not attract audience attention, and it lacks funds for sustainable operation. Even worse, local stakeholders—from politicians to ordinary citizens—do not feel ownership over this institution. It seems that the project has generally failed.

On the other side of the globe, South Africa's public broadcaster also inherited the British model (as did many other institutions). It is a state-owned broadcaster funded by public resources. Yet, as Berger (2010) points out, "the theoretical correspondence of public ownership, public financing and public service was never quite there from the start." Following the post-colonial period, the broadcaster started to serve governments rather than the public, and public funding was phased out in favor of advertising-driven economics.

The experience and outcome of media support in Iraq do not show more success. Heavily supported externally, the local broadcaster hardly managed to move from a state- to public-interest broadcaster in the post-Saddam Hussein era.

The key similarity between these cases is the hampered ability of these broadcasting organizations to remain independent, operate with stable funding, and produce quality and trustworthy content. This tendency, apparent in many emerging public service broadcasting countries in the Global South, has resulted in skepticism. In addition, digitalization is creating new demand to apply the principles of public service broadcasting to a range of digital media platforms, with a new set of challenges. Those involved in assistance efforts have noted that the experience from Iraq in particular brings up "the important question of whether there really is any alternative to supporting PSB aspirations" (Abbott 2016, 18–19). But, as Abbott notes, "for many countries, PSB offers the best means of reflecting the values, norms, and public policy preferences that are enshrined in the socio-legal systems and constitutional cultures for their countries" (2016, 5–6). As a consequence, public service broadcasting continues to be a major focus of many media development efforts.

This chapter outlines aspects of international support to reform public broadcasting, main shortcomings and lessons learned, as well as open questions and dilemmas that could serve as guidelines for future strategies and support tactics.

Foundations of Public Service Broadcasting

In its ideal form, a PSB is a model of media organization that is independent in its operation from both political control and private interests. It has the highest possible autonomy when it comes to governance and program production, is funded at least in part through public funds (license fees, taxes, budget line items, or a combination), is transparent in its operation, produces programs of the highest quality that do not need to be popular, and is directly accountable to the citizens (UNESCO 2001, Syversten 2003).

Advocates of PSB, including some in the media development community, believe that PSB represents an ideal form of media organization that provides citizens with reliable and quality information, and serves as a trusted source and public forum for discussion and dialogue. As part of the so called Reithian legacy, named after the BBC's first director, it is believed that PSB has to carry out three essential tasks—to inform, to educate, and to entertain—and can perform these tasks in distinct and different ways compared with commercial media.

Still, PSB is today a contested concept, and its existence is not taken for granted, either by commercial competitors or in some cases governments. Its legitimacy, mandate, structure, models of funding, and relation to the audience in the multiplatform, globalizing media landscape have been extensively debated. There are two main approaches to PSB, one that could be labeled as the "market failure approach" and the second as the "social responsibility approach." The market failure approach aims to limit PSB services to those domains that are not adequately served by the market or by private media content producers and distributors of news, educational, and cultural programs (Thomass, Moe, and d'Haenens 2015). Some advocate for its de-institutionalization and believe missing content should instead be subsidized on a competitive basis (Elstein and Cox 2004) or defined by consumers' tastes (Peacock 1986, 2004).

Advocates of the social responsibility approach (Donders 2012; Jakubowicz 2004; Lowe and Bardoel 2007; van den Bulck 2008) believe PSB is a valuable asset to society and something that should function outside market logic. This belief has driven the creation of public service media which applies its tenets to media platforms beyond broadcasting. PSB has essentially been a national project, and even in mature PSB countries in Western Europe, how PSBs function across countries differs greatly. Differences are also evident in how PSBs are transitioning to multimedia environments (Aslama and Syvertsen 2007).

International actors heavily supported privately-funded independent media worldwide to provide an alternative voice to state media and empower citizens in their right to be informed. However, many of these externally supported media did not survive the departure of donors owing to weak business models and unsupportive environments for financial sustainability. In this environment, international organizations, primarily those from Europe, have favored public service media as a sustainable model. As highlighted by the European Broadcasting Union (2012), "only organizations of sufficient size and scale, such as PSM, can guarantee a long term, sustainable, high quality and independent information and entertainment offer that is universally available." In practice, though, despite significant external effort, supporting and developing functional and independent PSM that are distinctive and trusted has been a challenge.

Due to different historical, economic, political, and cultural contexts, emerging PSB/PSM countries have different starting points than mature PSBs in the Global South. As Rahman (2016a), documenting public service media in the Global South, notes, in those contexts the potential and practice of PSM has to be seen as "contextual, relative, and plural ontology, in which the degree of public service and nature of ownership may vary among enterprises and across regions."

Transforming former state-controlled broadcasters into public service broadcasters or creating public media organizations from scratch in the context of developing democracies was meant to be one of the most visible changes in the third wave of democratization.

Policy makers in developing countries have looked for role models in established democracies to provide guidance on reconstructing their media systems (Voltmer 2013). While describing this process, scholars have usually referred to it as an "imitative transformation" (Splichal 2001), in which local institutions were either completely or partly modeled after successful institutions in the West. Such efforts, however, neglected to take into account the local contexts and environments, including countries' historical junctures and local context, when "transplanting" the Western models (Berkowitz, Pistor, and Richard 2003).

Applying Western standards and principles to create independent, professional media institutions in developing environments has characterized the so called normative approach in media reform. Yet, the results of the normative approach have been inadequate media policies and often dysfunctional legal and institutional solutions, resulting in institutions that do not meet the standards and principles after which they were designed, nor do they function as envisaged within their new contexts (Marko 2017).

Taking a purely normative approach to PSB reforms has been recognized as the main shortcoming of PSB-related media assistance. Such an approach has resulted in "hybrid" models of public media (Irion and Jusić 2013; Voltmer 2013). Even though the institutional structures of established public service broadcasting organizations, such as supervisory bodies and license-fee funding schemes, were implemented, the resulting organizational forms have resembled the old system of state broadcasting rather than, for example, the BBC (Voltmer 2013). Differences between the hybrid institutions and their Western role models are usually perceived as deviances, flaws, and shortcomings.

Public to State to Public: Political Will May Not Adhere

Around the world, trends in public service broadcasting vary. In South Asian and Southern African countries, for example, the colonial public media generally became state-administered media after independence. Often de facto controlled by the political elite, the media markets in these countries are also usually heavily commercialized (Rahman 2016a).

For example, in Pakistan, state-owned Pakistan Television was first a mega media operator that monopolized the airwaves till 2002, after which the government liberalized the media market. This marked what some call a shift from "monopoly to cacophony." A similar progression to market commercialization happened in Bangladesh. Bangladesh Television (BTV) is now responding to these media market developments with multiplatform strategies. However, the lack of autonomy is a primary obstacle to BTV functioning as a public service media operator. BTV lacks credibility due to its structural and on-air bias in favor of ruling parties, coupled with politicization of the management and polarization of most of the journalistic staff along party lines (Rahman 2016b).

The core issue in these cases is that, instead of being the key arbiter, the state becomes the subject of political competition (Zielonka and Mancini 2011). This can lead to the colonization of state and public institutions, including public service broadcasters, by political parties and business groups—generated through economic underdevelopment and illiberal and authoritarian tendencies in local politics.

In such circumstances, public service media become vulnerable, easily captured, and instrumentalized by local political actors. Regulations and laws protecting their independence are ineffective against populist and increasingly authoritarian elites who adjust laws as they wish in a bid to turn these broadcasters into instruments of political power or to minimize their influence as independent and democratic voices.

This politicization can be observed on several levels:

- In management, where politicians directly influence the management nomination process for the main governing bodies
- When programming is characterized by a lack of plurality of political views, and where dominant positions are reserved for the governing political parties
- Through funding—for example, when a broken funding model based on license fees is used. Funding from companies in some cases has also resulted in subtle and indirect pressure on PSB programming. Such was the case in Serbia where Radio Television of Serbia received funding from the country's

> leading marketing agencies, all owned by persons tied with political parties governing the state, and mostly operated in nontransparent ways.

Such politicization, either on its own or coupled with political interests and high commercialization, such as in Latin America, leaves little room for genuine public media initiatives to grow. The case of Mexico illustrates this. First, despite the long history of broadcasting in the region, there is no consensus about what "public media" means in Mexico, or in Latin America generally. This corresponds with the situation in many developing countries, where there is no consensus on what constitutes public values in broadcasting. In addition, not only are real PSM legacies lacking, but the audiences are fragmented, the infrastructure is poor, and there is a great need for capacity-building for media management. It is difficult, then, to compete with or even complement the dominant players in Mexico's highly commercialized media system (Brambila 2016).

In addition, there are examples where the international community has tried to set up a private media with a public mission, aiming to break the monopoly of the state over public service media. An apt example is TV B92, established in 2000 in Serbia with significant support from the U.S. Agency for International Development and European Union. Modeled after British Channel 4, this private broadcasting outlet was meant to serve the public interest by demonstrating a new, professional approach, experimenting with new formats and remaining independent from political and commercial influences.[1]

Another significant example can be found in Ukraine, where Hromadske TV was introduced in 2013. It started as an online community TV channel run by a group of local journalists with an innovative approach and young staff. The purpose was to counter state-controlled media, propaganda (spread by media linked with Russia and pro-Russian politicians), and media systems enacted and controlled by local oligarchs. The initial effort was substantially supported by international donors. While its importance within the wider media system remains a matter of debate, Hromadske TV continues to attract donors. And given the major reforms the public broadcaster in Ukraine is undergoing, it has the potential to become a special production unit within the PSB system.[2]

Commercial competitors alone do not challenge public service. Lack of clear understanding of what public service means, especially in the digital environment, hampers opportunities for public service broadcasting and public service media to flourish. For example, in South Africa, the "indefinability" of public service principles and the muddled distinctions between public, private, and community broadcasting challenges South Africa's PSB (Fourie 2013). This, in turn, has recently led to politicization of the broadcaster's content (Ciaglia 2015).

This is also the case with Radio Television Afghanistan (RTA). A state broadcaster that is known to show government bias, it also has a clear educational mandate that it does not live up to. However, it does tend to promote national unity and social cohesion because of its respect for minority groups. Indeed, in Afghanistan, the terms "public" and "national" are used synonymously. (Wakili 2014).

Similarly, in the case of Indonesia, the absence of a clear state media policy to regulate the commercial and profit-driven logic of the media industry has resulted in displacement by the ever-growing media privatization due to market forces, symptomatic media monopoly and oligopoly, gradual liberalization of the public sector, and weakening of the public sphere. In this environment, the public may get more channels but fewer content options. Therefore, it is still an uphill climb for the PSB in Indonesia be fully realized or even move towards PSM (Latif and Hassan 2016).

Digitalization: High Hopes, Meek Results

European donor agencies and media development organizations have recognized the potential offered by digitalization and multimedia platform strategies to deliver public services in developing regions through PSM. For example, with funding from the British government, BBC Media Action uses television, an interactive English-learning website, as well as mobile, social media, and newspapers to educate and promote public dialogue in Bangladesh (Rahman 2016b).

Yet, in general, it seems that the great hope that digitalization and increased choice would lead to greater demand for more diverse, independent news and an irresistible groundswell of pressure to either reform the state broadcaster into an independent public service provider or create a new PSB is not happening anywhere in the world. However, digitalization is challenging both mature and emerging public service media (Tambini 2015). It is safe to say that the public service broadcasting model is now being reappraised and reevaluated around the world against the backdrop of radical changes in the way content is created and accessed digitally.

These challenges are particularly acute in the Arab world, where the digital revolution has coincided with (and some would argue, triggered) political uprisings and power shifts. The Arab Spring was instrumental in putting media reform on government agendas across the Southern Mediterranean region. In response to demands for freedom of speech and the lifting of state control, steps have been taken to enshrine these notions in national constitutions—to encourage the growth of private media and promote public broadcasting models that respond to perceived audience needs (Dabbous 2015). Yet, for example, more than half a decade after uprisings in Egypt, there is no real difference between the concepts of public service and state-controlled broadcasters. The main broadcaster is dubbed Egyptian Television to indicate its official status. Its funding comes directly from the government and it has significant human resources. Some efforts to form a new public broadcaster with new funding were quashed when the initiative could not get a broadcasting license (Abdulla 2017).

Conclusion: Knowledge, Innovation, and Support

The challenges to public service broadcasting and public service media may seem enormous, but they also indicate clear needs and opportunities for media development. The past two decades have expanded the meanings of "public service" and "broadcasting," as globalization and the digitalization of media have enabled media outlets to reach vastly more people around the world At the same time, the world is faced with a number of discouraging trends, including diminishing journalistic and media freedom around the world and the much-discussed phenomena of filter bubbles and fake news. The need to support independent, robust, and public interest and public service media is obvious, especially in light of widespread "media capture," where both governments and commercial interests seem to align against public-interest media (Schiffrin 2017).

Many public service media organizations are indeed embracing their role as stakeholders that can help remedy challenges in the increasingly complex media landscape. In domains of production and collaboration, public service media in mature PSM countries are improving their services by leveraging multiplatform opportunities, through efforts such as the 60-second news in the interactive BBC Minute CatchUP player, or the Flemish public media's collaborations with start-ups and other private initiatives through their VRT Sandbox. In addition, public service media in Europe are taking seriously the fight against "information disorder" (Wardle and Derakhshan 2017) and innovating fact-checking projects and other activities to counter the so-called fake news.

Moreover, even in the age of instantaneous social media content dissemination, public service media are especially crucial—for access to and accuracy of information—in times of crisis. For example, Japan's NHK (Japan Broadcasting Corporation) during the 2011 earthquake and corresponding Fukushima nuclear disaster exemplified the important role public service media and the use of different media platforms can play as part of a nation's disaster management system

(Tanaka 2013). But it is commitment to public service rather than technological advancement that matters most. This was evident during Hurricanes Irma and Maria in the Caribbean in 2017, when public radio was able to provide information and support both when other connections failed during the storms and in the storms' aftermath (Porter 2018).

Despite the challenges, mature public service media organizations are surprisingly resilient. However, community initiatives just may be the future of PSM in supporting democratic development in the Global South. For example, in Bangladesh and other South Asian countries, bloggers have played a key role in political movements and various multiplatform initiatives (such as the web and mobile content of BBC Media Action) and have gained visibility and popularity as proxy public media (Rahman 2016a).

In sum, public service media is currently an undefined and uncertain project, but holds promise for media development. Support for public media innovation is needed by professionals and institutions, as well as scholars and media development experts. That similar challenges exist in very different contexts points to the need for comparative knowledge and collaborative action, which seem to be the best ways to strengthen and innovate PSB/PSM, outside and within media development. There are efforts like this underway. In 2016, for example, seven Latin American countries—Chile, Uruguay, Peru, Mexico, Paraguay, Costa Rica, and Colombia—signed a joint agreement to create the first Public Television Network in Latin America[3] (Rahman 2016a). Examples by other stakeholders include:

- Comparative research on emerging PSB countries by scholars and research centers, such as the study on policies in the Western Balkans by the research center Analitika in Bosnia and Herzegovina, or the comparative study on Public Service Media Initiatives in the Global South, published by the Simon Fraser University Public Knowledge Project in Canada (see further reading)
- Research by the Center for International Media Assistance and Deutsche Welle that is specifically geared toward PSB and media development (see further reading)
- The work of the nonprofit Public Media Alliance as a global capacity-building and advocacy organization, with many members outside of the global North,[4] or the Global PSM Experts Network, an informal project to broaden knowledge exchange for emerging PSB countries, initiated by the RIPE Network, a nonprofit network of scholars and practitioners involved in research and development that supports the advancement of public service in media.[5]

Notes

1. B92 gradually lost its fiercely independent stance, and eventually rebranded itself as O2 television, but its importance in the Serbian media sphere nonetheless makes it a stand-out case of success in international media assistance. For more on B92's rebranding, see Maja Zivanovic, "Serbia's Iconic B92 TV Officially Becomes History: http://www.balkaninsight.com/en/article/iconic-serbian-tv-b92-officially-goes-to-history-08-25-2017.
2. For a summary of media reforms in Ukraine, see "Roadmap of Reforms for Ukraine: Media Reform." http://cedem.org.ua/wp-content/uploads/2017/01/media_eng_final.pdf
3. CNTV, http://www.cntv.cl.
4. "The Largest Global Association of Public Broadcasters," Public Media Alliance, https://publicmediaalliance.org/.
5. Ripe @ 2018, http://ripeat.org/.

Recommended for Further Reading

Abbott, Susan. 2016. *Rethinking Public Service Broadcasting's Place in International Media Development*. Washington, D.C.: Center for International Media Assistance, National Endowment for Democracy.

Lublinski, Jan, Merjam Wakili, and Petra Berner. 2014. *In the Service of the Public Functions and Transformation of Media in Developing Countries*. Edition DW Akademie. http://www.dw.com/en/new-publication-transforming-state-media/a-18082898.

Marko, Davor. 2018. "Feasibility of a Public Service Orientation in the Western Balkans *Complications for a 'Networked Society'", in Lowe, G.F, H. van den Bulk and K. Donders. Public Service Media in Networked Society, Nordicom. http://www.nordicom.gu.se/sites/default/files/kapitel-pdf/08_marko.pdf*

Rahman, Anis, and Gregory Ferrell Lowe. 2016. *Public Service Media Initiatives in the Global South*. Burnaby, Canada: Simon Fraser University, Public Knowledge Project.

Keywords: Public Service Broadcasting, Public Service Media, State Media.

References

Abbott, Susan. 2016. *Rethinking Public Service Broadcasting's Place in International Media Development*. Washington, D.C.: Center for International Media Assistance, National Endowment for Democracy. http://www.cima.ned.org/wp-content/uploads/2016/02/CIMA_2016_Public_Service_Broadcasting.pdf.

Abdulla, Rasha. 2017. *What Does Egypt Need to Have a Proper Public Service Broadcaster?* (Unpublished Panel Presentation). Broadcast Education Association.

Aslama, Minna, and Trine Syvertsen. 2007. "Public Service Broadcasting and New Technologies: Marginalisation or Re-monopolisation?" In *Media Between Culture and Commerce*, edited by Els de Bens, 167–178. Bristol, England: Intellect Books.

Bardoel, Johannes, and Leen d'Haenens, eds. 2007. *Western Broadcast Models: Structure, Conduct and Performance.* Berlin, Germany: De Gruyter Mouton.

Berkowitz, Daniel, Katharina Pistor, and Jean-Francois, Richard. 2003. "Economic Development, Legality, and the Transplant Effect." *European Economic Review* 47 (1): 165–195.

Berger, Guy. 2010. *Beyond Broadcasting: The Future of State-Owned Broadcasters in Southern Africa.* Bonn, Germany: Friedrich Ebert Stiftung.

Brambila, José Antonio. 2016. "Public Media Service in Mexico and Latin America: Recent Improvements and Future Challenges." In *Public Service Media Initiatives in the Global South,* edited by Anis Rahman, and Gregory Ferrell Lowe, 53–72. Burnaby, Canada: Simon Fraser University, Public Knowledge Project.

Ciaglia, Antonio. 2015. "Explaining public service broadcasting entrenched politicization: The case of South Africa's SABC." *Journalism* 18 (7): 817–834. doi: 10.1177/1464884915614245.

Dabbous, Dima. 2015. "Assessment of Public Service Broadcasting in the Southern Mediterranean Region." *MedMedia,* European Union.

Donders, Karen. 2012. *Public Service Media and Policy in Europe.* New York, NY: Palgrave Macmillan.

Elstein, David, and David Cox. 2004. *Beyond the Charter: The BBC after 2006.* London: Broadcasting Publishing Group.

European Broadcasting Union. 2012. *Vision 2020.* https://www.ebu.ch/files/live/sites/ebu/files/Publications/EBU-Vision2020-Full_report_EN.pdf.

Fourie, P. J. 2013. "The Rise and Fall of Public Service Broadcasting in South Africa." *Communitas* 18 (1): 1–20.

Irion, Kristina, and Tarik Jusić. 2013. "International Assistance and Media Democratization in the Western Balkans: A Cross-National Comparison." (Sarajevo: Center for Social Research Analitika). *Working Paper* 1. https://www.ivir.nl/publicaties/download/International_Assistance.pdf.

Jakubowicz, Karol. 2004. "Ideas in Our Hands: Introduction of PSB as Part of Media System as Part of Media Change in Central and Eastern Europe," *European Journal of Communication* 19 (1): 53–74.

Latif, Roslina Abdul, and Badrul Redzuan Abu Hassan. 2016. "PSM Initiatives in the Southeast Asian Region: A Comparative Study between Malaysia and Indonesia." In *Public Service Media Initiatives in the Global South,* edited by Anis Rahman, and Gregory Ferrell Lowe, 73–92. Burnaby, Canada: Simon Fraser University, Public Knowledge Project. http://monographs.lib.sfu.ca/index.php/sfulibrary/catalog/book/1.

Lowe, Gregory Ferrell, and Johannes Bardoel, eds. 2007. *From Public Service Broadcasting to Public Service Media.* Gothenburg, Sweden: Nordicom.

Marko, Davor. 2017. *Media Policies in Western Balkans: Between the Normative Requirements and Local Specificities.* Analitika, Regional Research Promotion Programme. http://www.policyhub.net/en/politics-and-standards/201.

Moe, Hallvard. 2011. "Defining Public Service beyond Broadcasting: The Legitimacy of Different Approaches." *International Journal of Cultural Policy* 17 (1): 52–68.

Peacock, Alan. 1986. *Report of the Committee on Financing the BBC.* London: His/Her Majesty's Stationery Office.

———. 2004. *Public Service Broadcasting without BBC*. London: The Institute for Economic Affairs.

Porter, Kristian. 2018. *Broadcasters, Hurricanes and Recovery in the Caribbean*. Public Media Alliance. https://www.publicmediaalliance.org/broadcasters-hurricanes-recovery-caribbean/.

Rahman, Anis. 2016a. "Introduction." In *Public Service Media Initiatives in the Global South*, edited by Anis Rahman, and Gregory Ferrell Lowe, 1–16. Burnaby, Canada: Simon Fraser University, Public Knowledge Project. http://monographs.lib.sfu.ca/index.php/sfulibrary/catalog/book/1.

———. 2016b. "Public Media Initiatives in Bangladesh and South Asia: Politics and Prospects." In *Public Service Media Initiatives in the Global South*, edited by Anis Rahman, and Gregory Ferrell Lowe, 17–36. Burnaby, Canada: Simon Fraser University, Public Knowledge Project. http://monographs.lib.sfu.ca/index.php/sfulibrary/catalog/book/1.

Schiffrin, Anya. 2017. "Introduction." In *In the Service of Power: Media Capture and the Threat to Democracy*, edited by Anya Schiffrin, 1–8. Washington, D.C.: Center for International Media Assistance, National Endowment for Democracy. https://www.cima.ned.org/resource/media-capture-introduction/.

Splichal, Slavko. 2001. "Imitative Revolutions Changes in the Media and Journalism in East-Central Europe." *Javnost-The Public* 8 (4) -: 31–58.

Syvertsen, T. 2003. „Challenges to public television in the era of convergence and commercialization," Television & New Media 4 (2): 155–175.

Tambini, Damian. 2015. "Five Theses on Public Media and Digitization: From a 56-Country Study." *International Journal of Communication* 9: 1400–24.

Tanaka, Takanobu. 2013. "NHK's Disaster Coverage and Public Value from Below: Analyzing the TV Coverage of the Great East Japan Disaster." *Keio Communication Review* (35): 91–104. http://www.mediacom.keio.ac.jp/publication/pdf2013/takenobu.pdf.

Thomass, Barbara, Hallvard Moe, and Leen d'Haenens. 2015. "Renewing the Public Service Media Remit." In *European Media in Crisis: Values, Risks and Policies,* edited by Josef Trappel, Jeanette Steemers, and Barbara Thomass, 182–99. New York, NY: Routledge.

Van den Bulk, Hilde. 2008. "Can PSB stake its claim in a media world of digital convergence? The case of the Flemish PSB management contract renewal from an international perspective," The International Journal of Research into New Media Technologies, Volume 13, Issue 3: 335–349.

Voltmer, Katrin. 2013. *The Media in Transitional Democracies*. Cambridge, England: Polity.

Wakili, Merjam. 2014. "Afghanistan: Reform Fear, Limited International Support, Failed Transformation." In *In the Service of the Public- Functions and Transformation of Media in Developing Countries*, edited by Jan Lublinski, Merjam Wakili, Petra Berner. Edition DW Akademie, 36–50. http://www.dw.com/en/new-publication-transforming-state-media/a-18082898.

Wardle, Claire, and Hossein Derakhshan. 2017. *Information Disorder: Toward an Interdisciplinary Framework for Research and Policy making*. Council of Europe. https://rm.coe.int/information-disorder-toward-an-interdisciplinary-framework-for-researc/168076277c.

Zielonka, Jan, and Paolo Mancini. 2011. "Executive Summary: A Media Map of Central and Eastern Europe." Report of Project Media and Democracy in Central and Eastern Europe. London: The London School of Economics and Political Science and ERC Project, University of Oxford, 8.

CHAPTER TWENTY-TWO

Media Development and Media Reform

Time for Change

DES FREEDMAN AND JONATHAN A. OBAR

The "Stickiness" of the Development Frame

Media development theory is plagued by definitional confusion. In what ways is it different to "media for development" and does it refer exclusively to structural rather than behavioral issues? To what extent should media development be understood in relation to external interventions to assist capacity-building in specific countries or to internal pressure to democratize media systems? Does it refer to a developmental process or to a desired state of development, an outcome or "as activities towards that outcome" (Berger 2010, 551)? Who sets the parameters for what is considered "developed" and does this apply to all countries that lack a fully independent and pluralistic media system underpinned by legal guarantees of freedom of expression (in which case we are talking about most countries in the world)? Little wonder that Martin Scott (2014, 75) argues that defining media development is like "nailing jelly to a wall" and that unless we resolve this conceptual turbulence, both the status and the effectiveness of the field will be undermined.

That may be true but we believe that it is nothing compared to a more fundamental problem: that media development remains intimately, and unhelpfully, associated with the modernizing paradigm in which it was originally conceived. This relates not just to how it is understood, but how it is practiced and it shapes the identity of the agents, methods, and objectives of the entire exercise. There is little argument that the field has moved on dramatically from the neo-colonialist mode of thought that marked its origins and now embraces an ethical commitment to participatory communication; there is, nevertheless, concern that discursive shifts have not been accompanied by more material transformations in terms of agenda-setting, resource allocation, and accountability. So for Hemer and Tufte (2012, 234), "agency has largely remained in the institutions and organizations that have 'invited' citizens to participate, mobilize and to act" just as Arsenault and Powers (2010, 2), while noting that modernization theory is outdated, nevertheless argue that "the roots of this paradigm are still evident in much current thinking about media development and implementation of media development." Thinking about media development may have changed, but *doing it* differently may be lagging behind.

In reality, media development continues to be dominated not by user communities, but by donor-led initiatives aiming to increase the capacity of journalists to fulfil their democratic role, to build sustainable media markets, and to nurture legal frameworks to guarantee media rights (Arnold 2010; CIMA n.d.). This is the universe of UNESCO, the United Nations Development Program, the World Bank and the international development wings of western governments. It is an environment in which "expertise" flows from North to South, while resources and capital continue to flow in the other direction: a deficit of some $2 trillion worth of all goods and services in 2012 alone (Hickel 2017). While the motivations and alliances may be somewhat different than they were when Daniel Lerner first described the media as a "mobility multiplier" (1958, 52) that would usher developing nations into the modern age, the operating logic of contemporary media development seems rather similar to approaches to modernization that have been critiqued by, for example, Freire (1983/1970) and Escobar (1995) for reproducing existing structural imbalances. Peter Golding, in an early rejection of development frames, argues that they were a means through which "calibrated indices of underdevelopment can be constructed" (Golding 1974, 39)—indices that rely on quantitative instruments that even Everett Rogers, himself intimately associated with the modernizing "diffusion of innovations" approach, later described as the "deceitful simplicity of measurement" (1993, 37). Yet how different to that dominant paradigm are today's training programs or metrics such as UNESCO's Media Development Indicators, IREX's Media Sustainability Index, or the European Union's Media Pluralism Monitor in their attempt both to acknowledge systemic inequality and to address these pernicious divisions through a recognition that "static societies are brought to life by outside influence, technical aid, knowledge, resources, and financial assistance" (Golding 1974, 43).

Some practitioners explicitly acknowledge the historic integration of media development programs into soft power exercises driven by foreign policy considerations. For example, Ricardo Trotti, the director of press freedom at the Interamerican Press Association, maps out in detail how development objectives have "generally followed the focus of U.S. and European foreign policy" (Trotti 2013, 2). Indeed, he attacks the attempts of populist left-wing governments in Ecuador, Bolivia, Argentina and elsewhere to enact structural change and argues that democratization is explicitly tied only to *neoliberal* policies. "It is the freedom of the private sector, the market expansion, its needs and competition—with minimal state regulation—and the new technologies, which allows democratizing communication" (2012, 12). While this certainly doesn't reflect the views of all media development theorists, Trotti nevertheless raises awkward questions about the extent to which international assistance—whatever the motivation—can be pursued independently of established relations of power.

So, media development is indeed a fraught and contested field. Reflecting on this gap between the theory and practice of media development, many critical theorists argue that we need to "refocus our attention" (Hemer and Tufte 2012, 235) and to "change the lens" (Raboy in this volume). However, they appear to want to achieve this *within* the field of media development, rather than to accept that its compromised history may suggest that we need a rather more radical break. Jan Servaes, one of the pioneers of the participatory communication approach, argues that while social change will involve the redistribution of power, "many communication experts agree that structural change should occur first in order to establish participatory communication policies" (Servaes 2008, 27). If this is true, then to what extent is media development, with its roots in modernization discourse and its connections to existing centers of power, an effective means with which to pursue structural change? And if development frames remain trapped in a paternalistic mode of operation, can media reform movements—with a reputation for more localized and activist forms of organizing—provide either inspiration or a potential solution to this dilemma?

Media Reform to the Rescue?

Given that contemporary iterations of media development are so often preoccupied with questions of pluralism, governance, independence and funding—precisely the areas of policy and regulation with which media reform movements are involved—it is often hard to see a conceptual difference between the two spheres. And yet, there is a sense in which the two communities are quite distinct:

the former tied to agencies in the North working on behalf of communities in the South, while the latter is more likely to be seen in terms of struggles that take place exclusively in the North; the former is linked to top-down strategies developed outside the frame of conflict, while the latter is viewed in relation to initiatives developed and executed by grass-roots movements (Segura and Waisbord 2016).

This would be a huge over-simplification, not simply because it dismisses the contradictions inherent in development campaigns, but also because it exaggerates the organic, bottom-up character of media reform. Indeed, a substantial amount of media reform work—from net neutrality to anti-monopoly campaigns—is carried out by "experts," lobbyists and professional NGOs with battlegrounds in law courts and parliaments that are well outside the everyday realm of user communities. There is, therefore, a "developmental" character to media reform just as there is a "reforming" character to media development; media reform movements are far from immune from paternalistic and pragmatic assumptions while development campaigns can be shaped by the activities on the ground of communities who are supposed to be the recipients of the development.

While we believe that there are similar tensions within both approaches and that dialogue between the two communities is likely to be productive for both, it may be easier to open up these contradictions inside reform, rather than development environments because of the former's *relative* distance from elite groups and their connections to other democracy movements. This is precisely what we believe is necessary: to shift the debate within the theory and practice of media reform better to focus on activities that are developed and implemented by publics rather than on behalf of publics, and to engage in struggles that confront power rather than seeking simply to ameliorate its effects.

We have previously argued that media reform movements "are a response to expressions of concentrated media power and develop in the context of ongoing struggles over the distribution of communicative resources" (Freedman and Obar 2016, 25). We ought to have said that movements are at their most effective when they relate to, and draw on, wider social struggles for redistribution and that it is these struggles that can help to discipline and orientate media reform campaigns along productive, participatory lines. Of course, this is just as appropriate to media development projects—that, for example, literacy campaigns, training projects for journalists and efforts to amend legislation to increase pluralism, will be all the more effective when they are directly connected to ongoing democracy and social justice movements—but it may be these connections are more difficult to foster given the structural constraints placed on development projects by funders.

Indeed, many media reform efforts can be placed on a spectrum between media development efforts that perpetuate a "modernizing" paradigm, and a normative ideal of autonomous, independent, bottom-up groundswells. The fact that many well-meaning media reform efforts struggle with the constraints of the former and the impossibility of realizing the latter should come as no surprise as many such efforts, especially in the West, are organized by activists wielding traditional tactics for influencing policy and policymakers. Guo and Saxton (2010) identify eleven such tactics that include: direct lobbying, research, public events and direct action, media advocacy, judicial advocacy, coalition building, administrative lobbying, expert testimony, public education, voter registration, and grassroots lobbying. Many of these tactics, especially those that aim to influence technocratic decision-making, emphasize reliance on experts, think tanks, donors, public relations professionals, and political operatives.

Sometimes, the distinction between media reform and media development strategies is blurred. For example, in Qatar, the non-profit Doha Centre for Media Freedom organizes media and information literacy training programs designed to train journalists and media producers with the goal of "defending media freedom in the Arab world" (Townson 2016, 312). Specific emphasis is placed on supporting journalists in the Middle East who are persecuted for their dissent while also developing future media professionals who value critical thinking. The ideal is that such efforts may foster media systems that "promote quality journalism and guarantee access to impartial information" (2016, 316).

The New America Foundation (NAF) presents another interesting example of an organization heavily involved in various aspects of media reform, while clearly maintaining connections to aspects of the media development paradigm. Its Open Technology Institute "works at the intersection of technology and policy to ensure that every community has equitable access to digital technology and its benefits" (OTI n.d.). Initiatives address common media reform themes such as international efforts to promote universal access to secure and private broadband technologies (including community broadband efforts), advocacy in support of network neutrality and modernization of the U.S. universal service fund, as well as advocacy in opposition to media mergers. At the same time, in 2016–2017 the organization received funding from a variety of large corporations and corporate owners, some with vested interests in the current media landscape. The New America Foundation received more than $1 million in funding from the Bill and Melinda Gates Foundation, Google, the William and Flora Hewlett Foundation, Eric and Wendy Schmidt and others, as well as between $250,000 and $999,999 from Bloomberg, the Carnegie Corporation of New York, JP Morgan Chase & Co., Microsoft, the Rockefeller Foundation and others. The current board of directors for the Foundation includes individuals with connections to established industry and politics, including Reihan Salam, executive editor of the National Review, David Bradley, chairman of Atlantic Media, Michael Crow, president of Arizona State University, Fareed Zakaria, a host on CNN and columnist for the *Washington Post* and various individuals involved in financial management and real estate businesses. Indeed, the New America Foundation exemplifies an organization working to reform the media system at the same time as being heavily implicated in corporate agendas and networks of influence. The scandal in which Barry Lynn, head of NAF's Open Markets initiative was ousted after making critical comments about Google, one of NAF's funders, is just one such example of these tensions (Vogel 2017).

On the other hand, media reform promotes mobilizations beyond traditional policy-making institutions and seeks to foster activities implemented by publics, rather than on behalf of publics. For example, in 2012 the activation of a digitally-mediated Fifth Estate was instrumental in halting the Stop Online Piracy Act (SOPA) in the United States (Reitman 2016) while in 2013, similar efforts by Open Media's Stop Online Spying Coalition temporarily stopped the cyber-surveillance Bill C-30 in Canada (Obar and Shade 2016). In 2014, a massive mobilization, coordinated by Free Press, the Electronic Frontier Foundation and others helped achieve a victory for net neutrality in the United States. Indeed, approximately four million public comments were submitted to the Federal Communications Commission's (FCC) net neutrality docket, the most submitted to any proceeding in the Commission's history (Sohn 2014). When the FCC decided at the conclusion of the 2014 review to strengthen net neutrality protections, FCC Chairman Tom Wheeler referred to the digital mobilization, noting "a shout out to four million Americans who took their time to share with us their views" (Stuart 2015). According to Wheeler: "Your participation has made this the most open process in FCC history. We listened and we learned" (Rushe 2015). In each of these cases, massive online mobilizations confronted institutional power structures. Whilst these examples do reflect significant moments of popular participation, each campaign was, of course, shaped and facilitated in part by established media reform organizations as opposed to publics alone. In the case of the 2014 net neutrality battle, the use of digital form letters as a primary method of online mobilization suggests that only a semblance of the public's voice was directly connected to the deliberations (Obar 2016). While this shouldn't minimize the public interest victory, it does problematize the normative ideal of activities being developed and implemented by publics themselves as distinct from qualified intermediaries.

Other media reform efforts aim to mobilize autonomous publics by involving them in social movements that are directly connected to the pursuit of a more democratic communications environment. These are the "media movements" analyzed by Segura and Waisbord (2016, 3)—the "networks of citizens and associations that aim to achieve social transformations through collective actions such as advocacy, education and protest"—that have been so influential in recent years in Argentina, Ecuador, Mexico, and Uruguay. We can also point to efforts by community radio broadcasters that provide alternative examples of bottom-up reform. Unauthorized community stations aiming to strengthen Indigenous rights and opportunities in Guatemala (Camp 2016), and pirate broadcasters in the 1990s responding to U.S. markets dominated by ownership consolidation (Sassaman and Tridish 2016), provide unique examples of media reformers working with local communities to establish popular communication resources.

Policy-hacking efforts in Germany, Iceland, and Argentina provide examples of reform groups and their publics developing regulatory agendas and frames with the aim of influencing not only the topics being addressed by policymakers but the ordering of importance and framing of those topics (Hintz 2016). Similarly, the Internet Rights and Principles Coalition (IPRC), which worked to develop a Charter of Human Rights and Principles for the Internet, did so through coalition-building and then sought to influence internet policy throughout the world (Franklin 2016).

While the distinction between media reform and development may sometimes be blurred, this should not prevent advocates of democratic media from either camp from maximizing the involvement of publics themselves in both agenda-setting and campaigning exercises. There is no pure version of media reform in which publics spontaneously and independently come together to demand communication rights, but a focus on building media movements that are aimed at citizen participation and resource redistribution is surely the most effective route to meaningful change.

Recommended for Further Reading

Artz, Lee, ed. 2017. *The Pink Tide: Media Access and Political Power in Latin America*. London: Rowman & Littlefield.

Freedman, Des, Jonathan A. Obar, Cheryl Martens, and Robert W. McChesney, eds. 2016. *Strategies for Media Reform: International Perspectives*. New York, NY: Fordham University Press.

Hackett, Robert, and William Carroll. 2006. *Remaking Media: The Struggle to Democratize Public Communication*. London: Routledge .

Segura, MariaSoledad, and Silvio Waisbord. 2016. *Media Movements: Civil Society and Media Policy Reform in Latin America*. London: Zed Books.

References

Arnold, Anne-Katrin. 2010. "Media Development vs. Communication for Development: Structure vs. Process." *People, Spaces, Deliberation*, May 8, 2017. http://blogs.worldbank.org/publicsphere/media-development-vs-communication-development-structure-vs-process.

Arsenault, Amelia, and Shawn Powers. 2010. "The Media Map Project: A Resource on the Impact of Media Development Worldwide." https://mediamapresource.files.wordpress.com/2010/12/literature-review-the-media-map-project.pdf.

Berger, Guy. 2010. "Problematizing 'Media Development' as a Bandwagon Gets Rolling." *International Communication Gazette* 72 (7): 547–65.

Camp, Mark. 2016. "Cultural Survival: Media Reform in Guatemala." In *Strategies for Media Reform: International Perspectives*, edited by Des Freedman, Jonathan A. Obar, Cheryl Martens, and Robert W. McChesney, 319–24. New York, NY: Fordham University Press.

CIMA. n.d. *What is Media Development?* https://www.cima.ned.org/what-is-media-development/.

Escobar, Arturo. 1995. *Encountering Development*. Princeton, NJ: Princeton University Press.

Franklin, M. I. 2016. "Mobilizing for Net Rights: The IRPC Charter of Human Rights and Principles for the Internet." In *Strategies for Media Reform: International Perspectives*, edited by Des Freedman, Jonathan A. Obar, Cheryl Martens, and Robert W. McChesney, 72–91. New York, NY: Fordham University Press.

Freedman, Des, and Jonathan A. Obar. 2016. "Media Reform: An Overview." In *Strategies for Media Reform: International Perspectives*, edited by Des Freedman, Jonathan A. Obar, Cheryl.Martens, and Robert W. McChesney, 3–18. New York, NY: Fordham University Press.

Freire, Paulo. 1983 [1970]. *Pedagogy of the Oppressed*. London: Continuum.

Golding, Peter. 1974. "Media Role in National Development: Critique of a Theoretical Orthodoxy." *Journal of Communication* 24 (3): 39–53.

Guo, Chao, and Gregory D. Saxton. 2010. "Voice-In, Voice- Out: Constituent Participation and Nonprofit Advocacy." *Nonprofit Policy Forum* 1 (1): 1–25.

Hemer, Oscar, and Thomas Tufte. 2012. "ComDev in the Mediatized World." *Nordicom Review* 33: 229–38.

Hickel, Jason. 2017. "Aid in Reverse: How Poor Countries Develop Rich Countries." *The Guardian*, January 14. https://www.theguardian.com/global-development-professionals-network/2017/jan/14/aid-in-reverse-how-poor-countries-develop-rich-countries.

Hintz, Arne. 2016. "Policy Hacking: Citizen-Based Policy-Making and Media Reform." In *Strategies for Media Reform: International Perspectives*, edited by Des Freedman, Jonathan A. Obar, Cheryl Martens and Robert W. McChesney, 223–38. New York, NY: Fordham University Press.

Lerner, Daniel. 1958. *The Passing of Traditional Society: Modernizing the Middle East*. New York, NY: Free Press.

Obar, Jonathan A. 2016. "Net Neutrality: Closing the Technocratic Divide? Activist Intermediaries, Digital Form Letters, and Public Involvement in FCC Policy Making." *International Journal of Communication* 10: 5865–88.

Obar, Jonathan A., and Leslie Regan Shade. 2016. "Activating the Fifth Estate: Bill C-30 and the Digitally Mediated Public Watchdog." In *Strategies for Media Reform: International Perspectives*, edited by Des. Freedman, Jonathan A. Obar, Cheryl Martens, and Robert W. McChesney, 39–57. New York, NY: Fordham University Press.

Open Technology Institute. n.d. "About us." New America Foundation website. https://www.newamerica.org/oti/about-us/

Reitman, Rainey. 2016. "Electronic Frontier Foundation: Lessons from the SOPA Fight." In *Strategies for Media Reform: International Perspectives*, edited by Des Freedman, Jonathan A. Obar, Cheryl Martens, and Robert W. McChesney, 92–99. New York, NY: Fordham University Press.

Rogers, Everett. 1993. "Perspectives on Development Communication." In *Perspectives on Development Communication*, edited by K. Sadanandan Nair, and Shirley A.White, 35–45. New Delhi: Sage.

Rushe, Dominic. 2015. "Net neutrality activists score landmark victory in fight to govern the Internet." *The Guardian*, February 26, 2017. http://www.theguardian.com/technology/2015/feb/26/net-neutrality-activists-landmark-victory-fcc

Sassaman, Hannah, and Pete Tridish. 2016. "Prometheus Radio Project: The Battle Over Low-Power FM in the United States." In *Strategies for Media Reform: International Perspectives*, edited by Des Freedman, Jonathan A. Obar, Cheryl Martens, and Robert W. McChesney, 182–89. New York, NY: Fordham University Press.

Scott, Martin. 2014. *Media and Development: Development Matters*. London: Zed Books.

Segura, Maria Soledad, and Silvio Waisbord. 2016. *Media Movements: Civil Society and Media Policy Reform in Latin America*. London: Zed Books.

Servaes, Jan. 2008. "Introduction." In *Communication for Development and Social Change*, edited by Jan Servaes, 14–28. New Delhi: Sage.

Sohn, Gigi B. 2014. "FCC Releases Open Internet Reply Comments to the Public." *Official FCC blog*, October 22, 2017. https://www.fcc.gov/news-events/blog/2014/10/22/fcc-releases-open-internet-reply-comments-public.

Stuart, Matthew. 2015. "Watch the FCC Chair's Impassioned Defense of Net Neutrality." *Business Insider*, February 27, 2017. http://www.businessinsider.com/fcc-chair-tom-wheeler-defends-net-neutrality-2015–2.

Townson, Peter. 2016. "Doha Centre for Media Freedom: Media Reform through Capacity Building." In *Strategies for Media Reform: International Perspectives*, edited by Des Freedman, Jonathan A. Obar, Cheryl Martens, and Robert W. McChesney, 312–18. New York, NY: Fordham University Press.

Trotti, Ricardo. 2013. "Media Development in Latin America: How the U.S. Government should redirect its efforts." Speech at Harvard University, May 1. https://programs.wcfia.harvard.edu/files/fellows/files/trotti.pdf.

Vogel, Kenneth P. 2017. "Google Critic Ousted from Think Tank Funded by the Tech Giant." *New York Times*, August 30. Retrieved from https://www.nytimes.com/2017/08/30/us/politics/eric-schmidt-google-new-america.html.

PART FIVE

Digital Media and Convergence

CHAPTER TWENTY-THREE

Digital Convergence and Its Implications for Media Development

DANIEL O'MALEY

The internet was not designed to be primarily a mechanism for news distribution. However, in many countries digital platforms are now the primary source of news and information. In places with extremely closed media environments, the internet is often the only way for individuals to access news and information. Increasingly news content, whether it be audio, video, or text, is being converted into the zeros and ones that allow it to be transmitted via the digital network that is the internet. There is no doubt that legacy media like radio, television, and newspaper will continue to play an important role in terms of reaching audiences. However the so-called "digital convergence" means that the internet will be the primary means through which all others forms of media are transmitted (Mueller 1999). Moreover, in addition to being an important transmission mechanism, the internet and related digital technologies are now central to how journalists communicate with sources and conduct reporting. This means that how the internet develops and is governed as a technological platform will undoubtedly impact both the dissemination of news as well as the reporting capabilities of news outlets.

The digital networking standards that enable the internet to function as a global system, like all forms of technology, are socially shaped and inherently political. This means that their development is circumscribed by a specific socio-political context, and that once created, the way they are configured impacts social processes (Winner 1980). For example, the TCP/IP networking standards, which allow diverse computing systems to communicate, and the Domain Name System (DNS), which is a decentralized database that connects internet names to internet numbers, were both originally developed by a network of computer scientists and academics who prized openness and decentralization (Castells 2003). In contrast, the alternative computer networking standard x.25, which was largely championed by European, state-owned telecommunications agencies, would have produced a nationally-centralized, government-managed inter-networking system quite different from the internet we now know (Castells 2003, 26). The triumph of TCP/IP over x.25 in the "protocol wars" of the 1980s and 1990s led to the development of a truly open and decentralized global network in which any two connected computers are able to exchange information (DeNardis 2009). This essential openness is what enabled the internet to reshape how information circulates and thus transform our media ecosystems.

Yet, the internet is a constantly evolving network of networks that changes as new technologies are created and as people go about using it in different ways. This means that current internet governance debates involving topics like net neutrality, encryption standards, and digital rights management (DRM), to name just a few, will potentially reshape the overall environment of media ecosystems for decades to come. For example, whether net neutrality—the principle that internet service providers (ISPs) must treat all data on the internet the same, and not discriminate or charge differently by user, content, or platform—remains the global standard will have massive implications for the way the internet develops (Wu 2003). An environment in which ISPs are able to prioritize content for purely economic reasons poses a threat to all types of content producers, including news media organizations, as it makes it potentially more costly to reach audiences. Likewise, without net neutrality, the type of information end users can access will be constrained in ways determined by market forces as opposed to the public interest. In this scenario, both efforts to promote media pluralism and to access to information would be fundamentally undermined (McChesney 2013). Even ostensibly benevolent efforts to subsidize access to specific internet platforms, so-called "zero-rating" arrangements prevalent in developing countries, can run up against long-standing international human rights frameworks depending on how they are implemented (Carrillo 2016). In short, how data flows over the internet and who is able to control those flows will substantially impact the circulation of news and information worldwide.

The global nature of the internet sets it apart from older communications technologies, which are more easily regulated on a national or even local level. The development of transnational social media platforms run by private companies has further complicated issues of legal jurisdiction and sovereign control. In many regards, the decentralized nature of the internet has been beneficial to freedom of the press because it has made it more difficult for governments to censor content. At the same time it has created new challenges for media development as decisions that impact circulation of news are often made in highly technical internet governance bodies far flung from the field were media development projects have traditionally been implemented. While technical discussions about internet governance often seem distant from the work of local media development practitioners, in actuality they will have an enormous impact in determining whether or not societies have access to an environment conducive to a vibrant and diverse media ecosystem (Cath, ten Oever, and O'Maley 2017).

The Public Sphere Rewired—News Media Implications

One of the hopes of the internet in the 1990s was that its decentralized nature would facilitate more entrants into the public sphere. The fact that it would create an inexpensive way for people to communicate was associated with its potential to democratize media systems that had been either dominated by state monopoly or privately-owned media oligopolies (Diamond 2010). In the 1990s and early 2000s the spread of the decentralized internet was heralded by media scholars as potentially ushering in a radical democratization in the communications space. For some, the internet was a nearly "ideal" communications system because of how it allowed for "rapid and inexpensive access for any political party or point of view" (Price 2002, 7). The possibility for increased pluralism online and the ability of individual bloggers and citizen bloggers to cover their own realities was seen as destabilizing to entrenched information monopolies—both corporate and governmental, depending on the context. In this way it would empower individuals and marginalized groups and engender more media pluralism.

However, over the past decade or so cyber optimism has quickly given way to growing pessimism as the internet has also been used for mass surveillance and the political mobilization of non-democratic actors (Morozov 2011). This is particularly true in an era when access points to the internet are becoming increasingly centralized in a smaller number of corporations (Benkler 2016), and when many governments are actively pushing for "internet sovereignty" policies that would effectively fragment the global internet by breaking it up into nationally controlled computer networks (MacKinnon 2013). Indeed, a number of countries are now emulating China's so-called Great Firewall, which allows the regime to monitor users and censor content (Kalathil 2017). Nonetheless, what both the optimists and pessimists share in common is a belief that the internet as a medium is an increasingly important factor in social life, particularly in the way it has impacted the circulation of the news and information that shapes public dialogue.

Reframing the Boundaries of the Enabling Environment in the Digital World

Much like the broader development field, media development has traditionally been conceptualized as operating within the framework of nation-states. The national focus of media development interventions is evident in the way that the field evaluates media systems. For example, Freedom House's World Press Freedom Index and IREX's Media Sustainability Index perform analysis based on the national context. This frame of reference made sense at a period in time when media organizations and their channels of distribution were largely geographically circumscribed within national boundaries. Yet, the emergence of the global internet on which new media content is distributed has given a new scale to the work of media development. Evaluating the state of the media and news circulation in a specific country can no longer be done without taking into account the broader context. The ability of news media outlets to reach audiences is now so dependent on both the policies of large technology and telecommunications companies as well as the technical standards set by international bodies that it is impossible to evaluate a national context without taking this into account. This national frame of analysis neglects the way that changes to the global internet standards and structure *or* the content platforms that exist on top of it can have uneven impacts on different types of media, and across borders.

The spatial reconfiguration of media environments occurred at the same time a theoretical shift in the media development occurred that significantly altered the focus of development interventions. Since the late 1990s researchers and practitioners have stressed that effective media development efforts must include more than just training and capacity building for journalists. Rather, they argued, the focus should be on creating an enabling legal and regulatory environment that fosters news production and circulation. This new focus entailed an increase in attention paid to media policy and laws that would enable media freedom and access to information more broadly (Price 2002). These were the ingredients necessary for a vibrant media ecosystem to thrive. These types of interventions differed significantly from journalist training activities, and often involved a broader set of stakeholders from society that included more than just media professionals.

The focus on the enabling environment has reshaped media development from being a merely technical development project aimed at capacity building, to one that is increasingly attuned to the political work inherent in fostering media ecosystems (Nelson and Susman-Peña 2012; Rothman 2015). This understanding has imbued media development efforts with a more proactive focus that necessitates engagement in broader governance debates. Since the decisions that are now having the most impact on media environments are now related to internet and technology policy, the logical next step is for media development stakeholder to become much more actively engaged in internet governance.

Multistakeholder Internet Governance as a New Site of Media Development

The development of the internet as a patchwork of computer networks using shared software protocols and which is largely operated by private entities has led to a unique multistakeholder governance model. This means that it involves the participation of governments, the private sector, and civil society. This model has been embraced by internet governance bodies like the ICANN as well as through the United Nation's World Summit on the Information Society (WSIS) process that led to the creation of the internet Governance Forum (Raymond and DeNardis 2016). This multistakeholder model of governance sets the internet apart from previous worldwide communications technologies, such as the telegraph and telephone, that were largely controlled and regulated by governments or government-controlled monopolies which owned the physical infrastructure. Moreover, it is quite different from multilateral governance, which relies solely on the participation of representatives from governments. Civil society actors are now able to help determine the policies that shape the internet on a global scale. Media development stakeholders, which have previously been largely absent or, even excluded, from these governance discussions, are now able to be active participants who are able to help set policy (Cath, ten Oever, and O'Maley 2017). This is an important shift, and one that empowers advocates of media freedom and media development.

The current multistakeholder model of governance is based on lofty ideals of equal participation and broad consensus. In practice, however, power is not always distributed among the various stakeholders as corporations and governments have an outsized influence. Moreover, representatives from the Global North have largely dominated these discussions (Cath and Floridi 2017; Hintz and Milan 2014; Hofmann 2016). Nevertheless, the nascent multistakeholder model does create a mechanism for more broad-based decision-making process that can lead to policy solutions that are more durable because they incorporate diverse perspectives and needs. Indeed, there is a growing body of research that documents how multistakeholder internet governance processes have created better policy and with wider societal buy-in in places as diverse as Brazil, Kenya, and South Korea (van der Spuy 2017). On a global scale, the work of the Internet Corporation for Assigned Names and Numbers (ICANN) in effectively maintaining the Domain Name Server (DNS) since 1998 is evidence that international multistakeholder bodies are capable of handling technically complex governance processes. Moreover, the transferring of formal stewardship of the Internet Assigned Numbers Authority (IANA) functions associated with DNS maintenance from the U.S. government to the global community via ICANN in 2016 demonstrated confidence in the robustness of multistakeholder governance processes to negotiate geopolitically contentious issues in an effective and transparent way (Strickling and Hill 2017). ICANN is just one example of the various multistakeholder bodies currently making decisions that impact the digital media ecosystem. The challenge now is to work toward making internet governance bodies more representative of global diversity while at the same time ensuring that their policy outcomes benefit the public interest and uphold internationally-recognized human rights.

How will media development efforts engage with internet governance? Given that this sector is already woefully under supported in financial terms, trying to engage in global policy and technical standards discussions alongside well-funded representative from other sectors appears daunting. Yet, the media development community has a lot to offer. For starters, the focus on media pluralism and incentivizing high-quality information are issues that need championing in the realm of internet governance. For example, returning to the example of net neutrality, policy decisions that disregard its impact on news circulation and media concentration will be needlessly flawed and quite detrimental to media ecosystems. The down-stream impacts of internet governance discussions on news media environments means that it is incumbent upon media development stakeholders to make sure they have a seat at the policy-making table.

Recommended for Further Reading

MacKinnon, Rebecca. 2013. *Consent of the Networked: The Worldwide Struggle for Internet Freedom*. New York, NY: Basic Books.

Benkler, Yochai. 2016. "Degrees of Freedom, Dimensions of Power." *Daedalus* 145 (1): 18–32.

DeNardis, Laura. 2009. *Protocol Politics: The Globalization of Internet Governance*. Information Revolution and Global Politics. Cambridge, MA: MIT Press.

References

Benkler, Yochai. 2016. "Degrees of Freedom, Dimensions of Power." *Daedalus* 145 (1): 18–32.

Carrillo, Arturo J. 2016. "Having Your Cake and Eating It Too? Zero-Rating, Net Neutrality and International Law." *Social Science Research Network*, January 3, 2018. http://papers.ssrn.com/abstract=2746447.

Castells, Manuel. 2003. *The Internet Galaxy: Reflections on the Internet, Business, and Society.* Oxford, England: Oxford University Press.

Cath, Corinne, and Luciano Floridi. 2017. "The Design of the Internet's Architecture by the Internet Engineering Task Force (IETF) and Human Rights." *Science and Engineering Ethics* 23 (2): 449–68.

Cath, Corinne, Niels ten Oever, and Daniel O'Maley. 2017. *Media Development in the Digital Age: Five Ways to Engage in Internet Governance.* Washington, D.C.: Center for International Media Assistance.

Diamond, Larry. 2010. "Liberation Technology." *Journal of Democracy*, 21 (3): 69–83.

DeNardis, Laura. 2009. *Protocol Politics: The Globalization of Internet Governance.* Information Revolution and Global Politics. Cambridge, MA: MIT Press.

Hintz, Arne, and Stefania Milan. 2014. "In Multistakeholderism We Trust: On the Limits of the Multistakeholder Debate." *CGCS Media Wire* (blog). September 19. http://www.global.asc.upenn.edu/in-multistakeholderism-we-trust-on-the-limits-of-the-multistakeholder-debate/. Accessed 3 January 2018.

Hofmann, Jeanette. 2016. "Multi-stakeholderism in Internet Governance: Putting a Fiction into Practice." *Journal of Cyber Policy* 1 (1): 29–49.

Kalathil, Shanthi. 2017. *Beyond the Great Firewall: How China Became a Global Information Power.* Washington, D.C.: Center for International Media Assistance.

MacKinnon, Rebecca. 2013. *Consent of the Networked: The Worldwide Struggle for Internet Freedom.* New York, NY: Basic Books.

McChesney, Robert W. 2013. *Digital Disconnect: How Capitalism Is Turning the Internet Against Democracy.* New York, NY: The New Press.

Morozov, Evgeny. 2011. *The Net Delusion: The Dark Side of Internet Freedom.* New York, NY: PublicAffairs.

Mueller, Milton. 1999. "Digital Convergence and Its Consequences." *Javnost—The Public* 6 (3): 11–27.

Nelson, Mark, and Tara Susman-Peña. 2012. "Rethinking Media Development: A Report on the Media Map Project." *Internews,* April 26.

Price, Monroe. 2002. "The Enabling Environment for Free and Independent Media: Contribution to Transparent and Accountable Governance." *USAID Office of Democracy and Governance Occasional Paper Series.*

Raymond, Mark, and Laura DeNardis. 2016. "Multistakeholderism: Anatomy of an Inchoate Global Institution." In *Who Runs the Internet?* 18–43. Ottawa, Canada: Centre for International Governance Innovation.

Rothman, Paul. 2015. *The Politics of Media Development.* Washington, D.C.: Center for International Media Assistance.

Spuy, Anri van der. 2017. "What If We All Governed the Internet? Advancing Multistakeholder Participation in Internet Governance." *UNESCO Series on Internet Freedom*, January 3, 2018. https://en.unesco.org/sites/default/files/what_if_we_all_governed_internet_en.pdf.

Strickling, Lawrence E., and Jonah Force Hill. 2017. "Multi-stakeholder Internet Governance: Successes and Opportunities." *Journal of Cyber Policy* 2 (3): 296–317.

Winner, Langdon. 1980. "Do Artifacts Have Politics?" *Daedalus* 109 (1): 121–36.

Wu, Tim. 2003. "Network Neutrality, Broadband Discrimination." *Journal of Telecommunications and High Technology Law* 2: 141–79.

CHAPTER TWENTY-FOUR

The Revenue Paradox of Digital News Media

MICHELLE J. FOSTER

A tense paradox has formed that, unless it is resolved, will continue to undermine independent news producers and stymie broader efforts of media development. Audiences are moving to digital, particularly mobile, in wholesale numbers, creating opportunities for increased reach and new ways of engaging that have amplified the potential impact of news media. Yet, for many reasons, independent media outlets have struggled to win large digital audiences, and even when independent news outlets do break through, their success with the public is not rewarded commensurately by advertisers.

The benefits of digital media technologies to independent news outlets are real. Media outlets that previously reached an audience of thousands can now reach tens or hundreds of thousands of people, if not more, and at a lower expense than in a previous era. Gone are the structural limitations of reach, such as the logistics of distributing newspapers or the confined range of broadcast towers. Gone too are the legacy media costs of customer acquisition (such as sampling, discounted subscription offers or telemarketing) or audience development (replaced with those specific to digital environments such as SEO, direct sales, social marketing, and channel sales).

With an expanded potential audience and reduced cost structure, it would seem almost inevitable that independent journalism could hone its focus on reporting while generating a better bottom line through digital advertising. But it has not been inevitable, least of all for media outlets in development countries.

Particularly vulnerable are those operating in exile, owned by ethnic or religious minorities, or facing unfair competition from government-aligned media.

Smaller media outlets operating in restrictive environments are especially vulnerable because the spread of digital technologies has also globalized media and advertising markets, bringing local news producers into competition against the content of media giants such as Disney Channel Worldwide, and putting them at a disadvantage in a "distributed content" market that is now dominated by platforms like Google and Facebook, the two of which in 2017 collectively took over 60 percent of global online advertising revenue, according to figures from the World Advertising Research Council (Richter 2017).

The paradox is that digital media have given small, independent voices the chance to reach new audiences, but they can't get noticed. And where these voices have managed to stand out and have a public impact, they are not necessarily getting paid. Digital should have been a lifeline to independent journalists in repressive environments, but too frequently it has become an additional burden.

As documented by other chapters in this volume,[1] there are growing efforts to build coalitions to reform media laws and change internet governance in ways that might gradually level the playing field. Yet in the meantime, news media outlets must continue to embrace a digital transition. If that's where the audience is, that's where the reporting must be. This chapter looks at how media outlets themselves are trying to resolve the contradictions of the digital news market.

While continuing to distribute their content via mobile and other digital platforms in order to have impact, news media are adopting additional and diverse strategies for generating revenue. Those include such approaches as event management, product diversification, niche marketing, targeted emails and SMS, among others. For news media operating under threat, many continue their whole or partial reliance on philanthropic, investor or donor support, as well. Bharat Anand, author of *The Content Trap*, has succinctly summarized the challenge, noting that in a world with nearly unlimited competition, there are two issues facing media: the problem of getting noticed and the problem of getting paid (Anand 2016). To that, one can add the managerial aspect of getting it all done.

Getting Noticed

While all media compete in an increasingly crowded market that is often dominated by well-branded global media, local and alternative voices face significant obstacles to getting noticed, including both environmental and operational challenges. In repressive environments, these obstacles are becoming even greater as authoritarian leaders learn to use market forces against journalists with a similar effect to overt forms of censorship or harassment (although those remain sadly abundant).

Local media compete with an entire world of content. Somalis follow Premier League football. Cambodians watch Korean soaps. Burmese have BBC. These glossy shows with high production values are often more interesting, entertaining, and compelling than local reporting created with cell phones, voice-overs, and shaky images.

Governments stack the deck. Authoritarian states have modern-day propaganda machines that fully exploit the potential of social media and leverage well-crafted story-telling. In addition, media is captured by oligarchs and others friendly to repressive regimes that use it to dazzle audiences with such riches of content that the absence of local news, local reporting and governmental accountability is masked (Schiffrin 2017). This in effect adds to the well-oiled machines of state propaganda that are backed with the resources and influence of the ruling government.

Social media used as platforms put publishers at risk. Publishers who use Facebook or other social media platforms as primary distribution channels are at risk to the algorithm. Although they offer low-cost and fast ways to share news reports, content isn't searchable, is presented out of context, and can be counterfeited. Social media platforms, moreover, harvest the lion's share of revenue. And perhaps deadlier, content producers don't own the platform and are hostage to its updates and shifting priorities: they are deeply vulnerable to decisions beyond their control.

A good example of this disruption was Facebook's experimental "Explore Feed" tested during the fall of 2017 in six countries (Flynn 2017). It moved organic, branded content, except ads, off the main news feed, leaving only ads and posts from friends visible. Most affected were content producers who relied either heavily or exclusively on Facebook as a distribution channel. Immediately, locally produced news content dropped out of sight. Lana Lu, the producer of a web-based television series in Serbia, summarized, "It feels like I was painting a mandala, grain by grain, only to see it blown by the wind in a single stroke" (Šajkaš 2017).

Facebook claimed it was just an experiment and there were no plans to further implement the approach—until there were. In January 2018, Facebook announced that it would roll out the approach to its entire network. "Facebook has introduced sweeping changes to the kinds of posts, videos and photos that its more than two billion members will see most often, saying … that it would prioritize what their friends and family share and comment on while de-emphasizing content from publishers and brands" (Isaac 2018).

Journalists inadvertently play a role in limiting their reach and influence among audiences when hewing to a narrow editorial focus. Sites with unrelenting coverage of politics, opposition and conflict often contain limited information on other topics. This focus can also limit revenue growth: businesses want brand-safe environments for their ads, and placing a car ad adjacent to pictures of dead bodies is not typically considered "brand-safe."

Conversely, there are topics people care deeply about that support frequent, engaged visits to a site. Local news, sports, health, education, and personal finance news are often appealing. They can also stimulate commenting and sharing, generating longer visit durations and more pages visited; all metrics that are rewarded by search engines.

Independent news sites are sometimes invisible, or poorly visible, to search engines. Those typically reward fresh content and "responsive" formats that scale automatically to mobile devices. They reward lightweight, fast and well-optimized sites. Unfortunately, among many news organizations served by the media development community, there remain low internal levels of expertise in these areas.

They are also invisible to audiences. Behind all of this are key gaps in the ability of independent news media to know their audiences, appeal to them with relevant content, and market that content in targeted and effective ways. Even with free tools such as Google Analytics and Facebook Insights, few small, independent outlets have the background or resources (either staff or time) to assess those data and use them to inform content and marketing strategies. Many also lack robust targeting and messaging skills. Yet collectively those are the tools that build the bridge between good journalism and audiences and, thus, create impact.

Getting Paid

The exciting potential of creating audiences online is tempered by the realities of supporting those efforts with digital ad revenues. It is abundantly clear that even when a digital news brand can create a broad audience, this doesn't mean it will get paid.

While outlets increasingly look toward digital platforms for their audiences, many factors can limit their ability, at least at present, to generate digital ad revenue. Audience realities, such as how they gain access to and pay for content is one factor. Publishers' participation in ad networks and markets is another.

Consumer Access to Content and Ads

In many parts of the world, particularly in rural areas, many citizens still lack access to the internet, often due to poor infrastructure and/or cost-prohibitive devices, data and networks. Potential subscribers to email, text and other content services may also be unable to pay because of undeveloped mobile and digital payment systems.[2]

The presence of Facebook Free Basics[3] in a market can also affect how local news producers do—or don't—get paid. The service offers users, largely living in poor and under-developed markets, access to an all-you-can-eat smorgasbord of content without incurring data charges, as long as it is consumed within the Facebook environment. Yet audiences wandering off that platform immediately incur those charges, leading to the perception that they pay extra for branded news content.

At the same time, audiences that do enjoy regular access to online platforms frequently employ ad blockers, especially where data costs are high, download speeds are slow, and ads consume significant data. Web browsers like Google Chrome and Safari have announced plans for automatic blocking of some ads in future versions, and one estimate finds that as many as 615 million devices around the world already have ad-blocking software installed (Willens 2017). Though publishers and consumers alike welcome a better user experience, ad blocking inevitably limits a prime source of digital revenue.

Attracting Advertising

Although each of these can be addressed individually, in aggregate they pose substantial challenges. Yet the larger challenge is on the demand side of advertising.

For digital media, size matters. Attracting robust digital ad revenues is a function of three factors: audience size, geographic location, and the strength of the local consumer economy. Advertisers want to reach a large enough audience in the markets they serve, where people can afford to buy their products. If these don't align, they don't buy ads.

Without audience scale in targeted markets, it is impossible to generate meaningful digital revenues from the advertising networks that deliver programmatic ads. Ad networks enable advertisers to buy ads across multiple platforms in a cost- and time-efficient manner. They aggregate advertising inventory across multiple sites and then deploy advertisers' ads. They also target, optimize, and report results for those campaigns. Certainly, it's possible to sell ads locally or through ad agency arrangements, but for media with low audience reach, or that some may consider alternative or oppositional voices, it's often an uphill climb.

Yet it's not just size that matters. So does geography. Assuming that a news site achieves around a million views a month, a level which might make it revenue-ready (Lambert 2017a), the real estate adage of "location, location, location" holds true. Ad spending is linked to the potential for consumer spending, and that is highest in developed countries.

Typically, digital ad rates are based on CPMs, or the cost per thousand ad views (cost-per-mille).[4] They are highest for audiences in the West and significantly lower elsewhere.

For example, a recent comparison of the programmatic CPMs between the United States and a sampling of African websites highlights the gap. For the uppermost ad unit across all device types, U.S. audiences achieved a CPM of $1.70, while a sampling of African audiences achieved between $0.13 and $0.42 (Lambert 2017b). Stated differently, at a CPM of $0.13, an ad would need to be displayed about 77,000 times to generate $10. At that CPM level, it would require substantial traffic to support an on-going operation (Caribou Digital 2017).

These price levels are unlikely to improve in the near-term. In developing countries, where there are relatively few advertisers and plenty of ad availabilities, ad pricing tends to become commoditized and seek the lowest level.

Diversifying Revenue Sources

As media companies around the world have come to grips with the disconnect between audience size and their ability to generate digital ad revenue, many have developed diverse sources of revenue, some of which are linked to their news reporting, some not.

Increasingly, consumer-generated revenue is a much bigger piece of the pie. For example, the *New York Times* generates revenue from events, sponsored content, and affiliated sources such as The Wirecutter and The Sweethome. It considers itself a subscription-first business operation. During the first quarter of 2017, the company's digital-only subscription revenue was up 40 percent over the same period in 2016, reaching $75.8 million … and exceeded digital advertising revenue of $49.7 million (up 19 percent over the prior year).

Audience scale also matters in attracting non-ad revenue. Media organizations with strong brands have the tools to promote and support diverse lines of business. Those can be used to cross-subsidize news-gathering efforts. A recent study by SembraMedia of digital native news media in Latin America showed that those with the largest monthly traffic were also successful at generating revenue from multiple sources, and two-thirds of digital native organizations reported generated revenue from three of more sources – see Table 24.1 below (SembraMedia 2017). Its report broke those organizations into four tiers of business maturity.

In its research, SembraMedia identified "two paths to growing these businesses: building audience to drive traffic and advertising, or leveraging the loyalty of the audience to inspire micro-donations and the 15 other ways they are making money" (SembraMedia 2017). Those other methods included events, training, membership, crowdfunding and native advertising.

Table 24.1. Four tiers of business maturity among digital news outlets in Latin America.

Tiers (Based on 2016 revenues)	Percentage*	Median annual revenues	Median monthly traffic	Median years in business
Stars & Standouts $500,000 or more	12%	$512,821	3,750,000	7
Steadfast & Striving $100,000-$499,999	17%	$205,128	182,800	4.5
Struggling & Steady $20,000 - $99,999	23%	$40,513	45,500	5
Startups & Stagnants $100-$19,999	32%	$7,383	10,300	3
Reported $0 in revenue	17%	—	—	—

*Percentage in each tier based on 84 responses; 10 declined to provide private financial data, 6 were removed because they were extreme outliers. Source: data.SembraMedia.org

The report also concluded that sales and marketing capacity are also essential to the success of advertising-supported media as those that don't hire salespeople, don't make sales.

Bottom line, whether revenue comes from consumers or businesses; subscriptions, events, newsletters or advertising; media organizations need to get paid. And their best chance of doing so is to cultivate multiple revenue streams.

Getting It Done

Creating great journalism is just one part of the job. And it can be argued that for some newsrooms, such as those that are close to the government or generating entertainment-influenced news programming, it might not even be an essential part of the revenue mix. But serious news organizations also need serious business skills. What are some of those?

To compete in a digital world, any successful content producer needs to offer a clearly differentiated product. For example, producing local news in local languages can be attractive to both audiences and potential advertisers while also setting one's news apart from others'.

Startling only to journalists steeped in the evangelical "separation of church and state" approach to journalism is the increasing realization that all people who report and create content must be well-versed in understanding audience behavior. This requires a deeper understanding of audience insights: how people use different media sources, what they expect, and how well their needs are met.

The *New York Times*, in its assessment of its own business and how it must adapt to the challenges of a global media world, found that bringing together the newsroom and product teams, informed by user data, is an essential aspect of competitiveness. It concluded, "For the Times to remain a destination—a high bar in an age of social-media platforms—the experience of reading, watching and listening to our work needs to be as compelling as the journalism itself. Achieving this goal will be far easier if our journalists and our product teams ... work more closely together. We need both journalists and product specialists to understand reader behavior, to develop a sharp view of the competition and to understand how different areas of coverage fit into the broader Times experience."[5]

Solid media management mandates the need for strong self-marketing and promotional skills since content only has impact when it is seen, shared, or otherwise engaged with. Essential to that is having the right people in-house supporting technological development. In-house technology and IT skills are as important to contemporary news media as platemaking and carrier routes were to newspapers. A media company can't be fast if it relies entirely on volunteers, contractors or part-timers for tech support—and typically, media companies need to be fast.

Success also requires strong day-in, day-out business management. Independent local news media are often started by activists or journalists; often, these are not the people who fall in love with business and pursue it with a passion. To survive, organizations also require committed leadership, financial rigor and entrepreneurial speed.

Conclusion

The globalized, digital media environment is presently an uneven playing field for smaller, independent news outlets, especially those operating in repressive environments. Efforts to level that playing field are essential, but in the meantime, independent news outlets and the media development community have little choice but to adapt to current conditions by strengthening the quality of journalism and the ability of outlets to reach and retain audiences.

Internally, news outlets must ensure that their content is surfaced, reaches large enough audiences to have impact, and can be monetized. To do so will require understanding and employing audience analytics and metrics to generate clear audience insights. Those insights will inform stronger news-gathering and reporting and yield deeper engagement with their content and, thus, greater impact.

But beyond reporting and journalism, media organizations must have disciplined management to survive in fast competitive environments. At present, strong local reporting can be drowned out by the louder voices of entertainment and captured media (Foster 2017). They need internal strengths in technology, sales force management, business planning and strategic thinking to create market momentum.

These media must become brands that are stronger than just their news offerings or unique points of view. Brand strength, engagement and vitality will open the doors to multiple revenue sources if these other components are firmly in place.

Notes

1. See, for instance, chapters in this volume by Mark Nelson, Des Freedman and Jonathan Obar, and Daniel O'Maley.
2. For further insight into the issues surrounding digital advertising, a recent report offers in-depth analysis. Paying Attention to the Poor: Digital Advertising in Emerging Markets; Caribou Digital Publishing; 2017; http://cariboudigital.net/new/wp-content/uploads/2017/07/Paying-Attention-to-the-Poor.pd
3. Facebook Free Basics is a service provided by Facebook in a number of countries with cooperation of local governments and telecoms. It is loaded on users' mobile phones, allowing people to access a limited number of internet sites and services free of data charges, as well as a variety of Facebook offerings, such as Facebook and Messenger. This has generated controversy since it could potentially lead to restricted internet access among poor or marginalized communities. In the author's experience in Myanmar, it was seen to limit traffic outside the Facebook environment because whenever users followed links to content outside the Free Basics environment, they were notified that data charges would apply, thus limiting their willingness to follow links to independent news media and other sites.
4. What is a "Cost Per Thousand—CPM"; Investopedia; http://www.investopedia.com/terms/c/cpm.asp "Cost per thousand (CPM) is a marketing term used to denote the price of 1,000 advertisement impressions on one webpage. If a website publisher charges $2.00 CPM, that means an advertiser must pay $2.00 for every 1,000 impressions of its ad. The "M" in CPM represents the Roman numeral for 1,000."
5. Journalism that Stands Apart, the Report of the 2020 Group, New York Times Company; January 2017; https://www.nytimes.com/projects/2020-report/

Recommended for Further Reading

Anand, Bharat. 2016. *The Content Trap: A Strategist's Guide to Digital Change.* New York, NY: Random House.

Caribou Digital Publishing. 2017. *Paying Attention to the Poor: Digital Advertising in Emerging Markets.* Farnham, Surrey, United Kingdom: Caribou Digital Publishing. http://cariboudigital.net/new/wp-content/uploads/2017/07/Paying-Attention-to-the-Poor.pdf

Foster, Michelle J. 2017. *Media Feast, News Famine: Ten Global Advertising Trends that Threaten Independent Journalism.* Washington, D.C.: Center for International Media Assistance. https://www.cima.ned.org/wp-content/uploads/2017/01/CIMA-Media-Feast-News-Famine_REV_web150ppi.pdf

Journalism that Stands Apart—the Report of the 2020 Group. January 2017. *New York Times*. https://www.nytimes.com/projects/2020-report/

SembraMedia. 2017. *Inflection Point: Impact, Threats, and Sustainability.A Study of Latin American Digital Media Entrepreneurs*. http://data.sembramedia.org/download-the-study/

References

Anand, Bharat. 2016. *The Content Trap: A Strategist's Guide to Digital Change*. New York, NY: Random House.

Caribou Digital. 2017. *Paying Attention to the Poor: Digital Advertising in Emerging Markets*. Farnham, Surrey, United Kingdom: Caribou Digital Publishing. http://cariboudigital.net/new/wp-content/uploads/2017/07/Paying-Attention-to-the-Poor.pdf

Flynn, Kerry. 2017. "Facebook Tests Removing Publishers from News Feed—Unless they Pay." Mashable, October 23. http://mashable.com/2017/10/23/facebook-explore-publisher-post-organic-reach-drop/#hlqOOIQpjPq7

Foster, Michelle J. 2017. *Media Feast, News Famine: Ten Global Advertising Trends that Threaten Independent Journalism*. Washington, D.C.: Center for International Media Assistance. https://www.cima.ned.org/wp-content/uploads/2017/01/CIMA-Media-Feast-News-Famine_REV_web150ppi.pdf

Isaac, Mike. 2018. "Facebook Overhauls News Feed to Focus on What Friends and Family Share," *New York Times*, January 11. https://www.nytimes.com/2018/01/11/technology/facebook-news-feed.html?hp&action=click&pgtype=Homepage&clickSource=story-heading&module=first-column-region&region=top-news&WT.nav=top-news&_r=0

Lambert, Jason. 2017a. Newsgain ApS: Partner, Digital Media, Interview with the Author via Skype. May, Newsgain.com.

———. 2017b. Newsgain ApS: Analysis of DoubleClick Ad Exchange (AdX) Data. August, Newsgain.com.

Owen, Laura Hazard. 2017. "The New York Times Just had a Pretty Stellar First Quarter, Thanks to the Wirecutter and 308,000 Net New Digital Subscriptions." *Nieman Lab*, May 3. http://www.niemanlab.org/2017/05/the-new-york-times-just-had-a-pretty-stellar-first-quarter-thanks-to-the-wirecutter-and-a-ton-of-new-digital-subs/

Richter, Felix. 2017. "25 Percent of Global Ad Spend Goes to Google or Facebook." *Statista*, December 7. https://www.statista.com/chart/12179/google-and-facebook-share-of-ad-revenue/.

Šajkaš, Marija. 2017. "Facebook's 'Explore Feed' Experiment Threatens Independent Voices in Serbia." *Center for International Media Assistance*, November 3. https://www.cima.ned.org/blog/facebooks-explore-feed-experiment-threatens-independent-voices-serbia/

Schiffrin, Anya, ed. 2017. *In the Service of Power: Media Capture and the Threat to Democracy*. Washington, D.C.: Center for International Media Assistance.

SembraMedia. 2017. *Inflection Point: Impact, Threats, and Sustainability. A Study of Latin American Digital Media Entrepreneurs. http://data.sembramedia.org/download-the-study/*

Willens, Max. 2017. "The Global State of Ad Blocking." *Digiday*, June 15. https://digiday.com/media/cheatsheet-global-state-ad-blocking/

CHAPTER TWENTY-FIVE

Media Development in the Digital Age

TARA SUSMAN-PEÑA

This chapter explores how organizations that implement media development programs have tried to adapt to the new realities of news in the digital age, which is an era of complexity and constant change. Summarizing key components of digital transformation, it considers the impact on the news industry, and on media development overall. Using two examples of building new approaches to media development implementation in which the author was intimately involved at different phases—U.S.-based NGOs IREX and Internews—this essay narrates how the organizations are adapting to better meet an uncertain, changing reality.

Media Development Confronts Technology

The heyday of media development assistance in the post-Soviet democratization period held up a clear normative model that donor funded interventions aspired to achieve. During that foundational era, donor supported programs intended to strengthen the quality, independence, and sustainability of the news media. Long-term impacts from that period appear to be mixed,[1] and the undertaking itself was extremely complex, but at least the end goal was clear.[2] Media development strived to make real, a thriving news media sector that provided people from all walks of life with trustworthy, timely, relevant, fact-based information that people need to inform their most crucial decisions; offered diverse perspectives on a variety of issues; as well as held government, the private sector, and other powerful entities and people to account.[3] U.S. media development also emphasized that media outlets should function as profitable businesses, largely through an advertising model. This meant that media outlets had to be able to measure and understand their audiences' characteristics, needs, and desires. According to the logic of the commercial news model, the long-term social value provided to audiences by news would in return give media outlets financial sustainability.

While the role of a well-functioning news media in democracy is broadly accepted,[4] media development assistance has long had some deeply embedded problematic characteristics. As a sector, it was slow to define its key theories of change,[5] and thus has been handicapped in its ability to measure progress or detect flaws (Gagliardone 2010). The difficulty of measuring results of media assistance has long bedeviled its practitioners and has impeded them from being able to more strongly make the case for its importance. Thus, media development assistance has long been beset not just by the difficulties of individual programs and projects (the news media is a highly complex system under the best of circumstances), but by challenges of an existential nature. Especially after the initial post-Soviet democratization boom, media development practitioners periodically gathered together to collectively wring their hands. At such gatherings, it was common to hear sentiments such as: "How can we demonstrate that our work is absolutely essential to democratic and development progress? Why do so few understand this?"

Technological advances before the advent of digital have always impacted the flow of information, of course, from the printing press to television, facilitating wider distribution of information, offering more personal agency and choice, and creating interesting new formats to present information. The rise of digital technology did not immediately transform media assistance practices, but new opportunities began to bubble up, which were not integrated well into the media sector-focused practices honed in the 1990s. (For example, the story goes that IREX ran programs in the mid-1990s with unfortunate names such as Faxes for Freedom and Modems for Freedom. Documentation for such programs is not easy to locate).

Media development practitioners had been incorporating digital formats to different extents since the technologies became available, but this had not changed the basic way they conceptualized their work. In many ways, they clung to the values, norms, and forms of the conception of the media as Fourth Estate, even as the media industry was transforming right in front of them, and their own work was changing. Looking back at the circa 2015 description of an implementer's approach to media development on the website of IREX, one of the primary U.S. media development implementers, reveals this tense state of being unsettled—neither here nor there in media development practice. "… IREX's work with local partners advances media professionalism, sustainability, sound media laws, and the local institutions that support independent media and journalists. We work across all media—television, radio, online, print, and mobile. Recognizing the shift to interactive and multiplatform media and the role of citizen journalists, IREX works to provide and integrate new technologies that democratize the flow of information. …"

About 15 years after the fall of the Soviet Union, the so-called Arab Spring became the next regional phenomenon that crystallized hope in the U.S. for a broad path to democratization in which new free flows of information would play a pivotal role.[6] The media development implementer and donor community awakened to a new promise of digital as a means for social organizing and political change, and donors began to pour money into digital projects. The first waves of spending were strongly marked by a techno-deterministic tendency, or funding technical solutions in search of problems. Welcome support was also provided for internet freedom initiatives, such as anti-censorship activities and digital security skills-building for journalists. As technology has developed, become more accessible, smaller, cheaper, and more widespread, it has offered new ways to exchange information (e.g. social media) and present information (such as virtual reality). Different aspects of these new technologies were incorporated into traditional media development projects (e.g. training print journalists in multimedia techniques using smartphones). They were also taken on by media development practitioners outside of a traditional media development context (e.g. training so-called citizen journalists, a term whose short life span is indicative of just how quickly things are changing).

As technology continued to quickly evolve, newsrooms and journalists began to experiment with new technologies, technology became more central as organization and communications tools for civil society. Media development practitioners debated whether work with technology should be considered as something woven throughout its practices or as a standalone organizational function. But the rapid evolution of technology itself, as well as its increasing integration into and shaping of journalistic practices, eventually made these kinds of debates obsolete. Nonetheless, understanding how these various elements fit together, and which ones media developers should focus on, and how, were the burning questions. Where once we could talk of strengthening a news media sector in isolation, now media developers confront a complex system in which the media sector interacts continually with other elements of the system, and changes in information systems are highly unpredictable.

The news media sector, especially since the rise of social media and the proliferation of mobile smart phones and devices, has been rapidly and continuously changing—to the extent that it has become hard to isolate the media sector from other people that perform acts of journalism outside of formal media outlets. In 2015, for example, led by over 1400 volunteers, Global Voices, a global network of bloggers, turned ten years old; Greenpeace hired a team of veteran investigative journalists; Facebook shot past Google as the top provider of traffic referrals to news sites (Ingram 2015).[7]. At the same time, journalism itself was expanding, shifting, and experimenting. Data-driven journalism, while not a new phenomenon, has increased in visibility with the astronomical rise in the production of data, as well as better and more widespread tools to process and analyze data. ProPublica, the U.S.-based non-profit investigative journalism organization, broke with its own norms and fired off a Tweetstorm in late November 2016, debunking president-elect Trump's claims of voter fraud (Borchers 2016). Solutions Journalism, which focuses on identifying and exploring solutions to social problems, has slowly been gaining ground.

At the same time that the digital age has brought about powerful new formats for reporting, producing, and sharing information, journalism has been beset by crisis. A key buzzword in development is sustainability: helping to make local organizations able to survive and thrive without assistance from international or other external organizations. However, the news media has been in economic crisis for a decade, since the global economic recession of 2008. Traditional media revenue models are falling apart as advertising dollars have gone online or disappeared altogether.[8] In 2018, the news media globally increasingly has to defend itself, and differentiate itself, from so-called fake news. Hoaxes and propaganda are as old as the news. However, the increasing sophistication, along with professional production values, enabled by accessible and inexpensive technology, and potential for wide and rapid distribution, enabled by social media, make fake news more powerful and threatening than ever. More broadly, authoritarianism and populism are on the rise globally, even in stable democracies, which threatens the legal, political, and social dimensions of journalistic practices.

There were of course increasingly important practical conditions associated with the rise of digital information and news. Donor funding for media development, already a tiny portion of overall donor funding to begin with, was becoming further dispersed into related areas such as internet freedom and training for citizen journalists (Mottaz 2010). Such digital components of media development projects were becoming ubiquitous.[9] Of great concern to the long dominant U.S. media development NGOs, other implementing organizations without a strong journalistic foundation, such as Chemonics, FHI360, and Creative Associates were beginning to implement large media projects. Fresh opportunities also appeared on the horizon, as a new crop of private foundations built from digital media wealth began to appear, such as Bill & Melinda Gates Foundation,

Omidyar Network, and Google (through its Foundation and other mechanisms), among others. Lastly, in everyday life, the lines were clearly blurring between what for a time was called "old" and "new" media.

U.S. Media Developers Reframe Their Work

This extremely complex situation has arisen at the same time that across the global development landscape, analysts have been considering how complexity theory and systems thinking might be useful to help understand change, including the forces that stand in the way of aid interventions having the positive consequences that were intended.[10] Embracing complexity means taking into account that media development problems do not have a linear logic and cannot be solved by trying to fix one aspect of the problem in isolation. It means acknowledging that as information systems behave like complex systems, such as natural ecosystems: they are dynamic (often changing in unpredictable ways); nonlinear, contain networked relationships; and are impossible to understand in their entirety.

In this context of upheaval and uncertainty, Internews and IREX—the two largest U.S. media development non-profits, both of which grew up during the post-Soviet democratization period and both of which gain the majority of their funding from U.S. government grants—have been reckoning with how they conceptualize the work they do. While the work is more relevant than ever—witness the rise of closing spaces where information is scarce, falling trust in institutions, the ongoing need to hold power to account—it is also significantly broader than before, and hard to pull together into a single, coherent framework. The problem of understanding how the rise of digital technology fits into media development is not a problem of digital per se; it is once again an existential problem. The problem is about defining exactly what media development does, why it exists, and proving that it contributes positively and substantially. The conundrum: how best to design a normative model when the norm is no longer clear? How to create a clear approach to implementation in a world of complex systems? What is media development in the digital age, exactly? In this context it should come as no surprise that both Internews' and IREX's new frameworks incorporate ideas and framing from complexity theory and systems thinking.

Internews has recently been through a process to redefine its strategic framework, which it defines according to four goals: access, inclusion, content, and engagement.[11] Internews' approach evolved organically out of its origins as an innovative news organization in the 1990s focusing on creating stronger links between the U.S. and then-Soviet Union. Giving the organization a fully articulated shared language and vision was important in a rapidly changing world. The new strategy was created to respond to a world in which "The whole industry has changed … it has been a rapid sea change. The old models were broken, new models are emerging, and no one has the answers yet" (Rouse 2017). The new definition evolved through a very inclusive process garnering input from across Internews' global programs, starting with defining the organization's core values. None of the four goals are new, but the definitions are clearer, the institutional commitment to them more intentional. Access and content have always been front and center of Internews' work, while the focus on engagement and inclusion is newer. Notable is the absence of the word media from the language of the strategy, which reflects the global state of affairs. The framework is supported by a robust theory of change that enables Internews to better measure progress toward the four goals, resulting in four expected areas of impact:

- Greater freedom of expression and access to information
- Increased knowledge and understanding around critical development issues
- Improved environment for informed decision-making and action
- Increased civic participation and progress toward SDGs[12] (the United Nations' Sustainable Development Goals)

IREX's approach to media development was defined in the 1990s as a holistic media sector approach, featuring four pillars of media development (based on the model of a traditional media sector): professional journalism, sound business management of media outlets, a supportive legal enabling environment, and strong supporting institutions. This model is reflected in IREX's Media Sustainability Index,[13] which has been measuring these pillars, plus media pluralism, since 2001. In 2015, IREX undertook an 18-month long collaborative research and visioning exercise to re-conceptualize its approach to be able to design for an unknown future. IREX works across other areas of global development, supporting civil society, education, leadership, and youth, and it incorporated aspects of each of these areas into its approach.

IREX conceives of its new approach as Vibrant Information systems: content that matters, multiple channels, dynamic engagement, and transformative action. IREX conceptualizes its own work as increasing people's opportunities and improving their abilities, and puts a stronger emphasis on people than on media or information. An increased emphasis on people has to do with values: an acknowledgement that information does not exist for its own sake. The point of information is that it should be useful to people, so that they can improve their own lives and communities. Information is the lifeblood of human relationships and exists only between and among people. An emphasis on people also means increased emphasis not just on teaching people hard skills (e.g. how to edit video) but on increasing people's skills and tools to be able to adapt to changing times.

This means an emphasis on soft skills like critical thinking, communications, leadership, reflection, and learning.

A shift to an emphasis on people also acknowledges shifts in power in information and media systems: whereas, news creation and distribution was once only in the hands of a few, now it is potentially spread much wider throughout the population. This potential does not automatically mean a more equitable distribution of power to include marginalized groups. Thus IREX's approach commits "to gaining an understanding of the prevailing political and economic institutions and powers that affect information, the social and cultural norms, the resource constraints, and incentives, paying special attention to the relationships and power dynamics among different groups and individuals" (Susman-Peña 2016, 20). A commitment to try to analyze power dynamics is a pivotal aspect to a systems approach to media development.

IREX's Vibrant Information Approach is underpinned by four core practices: listening, adaptive learning, knowledge gathering and sharing, and employing a gender lens. IREX is currently undergoing a process of revising its Media Sustainability Index to be able to diagnose and measure the degree to which a system is endowed with Vibrant Information. The vision for supporting a vibrant information system is to support a more just, prosperous, and inclusive world.

What's the Same? What's New?

Currently, the goals for media development practitioners are broader and more ambitious than during the traditional period of media development, and they do not strive to achieve an ideal type of system. For both organizations, it seems clear that while goals have widened, and type of activities has proliferated, they share basic, mostly information-related values that have remained the same:

- Respect for the value of all people
- Access for all to a broad range of information
- Freedom of expression
- Diverse sources of information
- Truth-based, accountable journalism
- All voices can speak truth to power
- Critical thinking skills embedded throughout the population

So, what do these tectonic shifts mean in practice? An illustrative (but not exhaustive) chart below (Table 25.1) demonstrates changes taking place during the digital age. There are several notes of caution about the chart. First, it is important to remember that many activities are much the same (e.g. traditional: training journalists using principles of impartiality and ethics) but the approach to the activity may be quite different (e.g. digital age: long-term coaching instead of a one-day workshop; including bloggers and others without formal training; etc.). Further, it is impossible to pin down a precise moment in time when "traditional" shifted to "digital age" (big changes began after the economic collapse of 2008; Internews and IREX began formally reframing their approaches around 2015). Lastly, the chart depicts shifts in emphasis, not always complete transformations. Outdated practices may continue side by side with innovative ones, particularly when looking at the media development field overall. Some of the digital age practices are still more ideal than real.

Table 25.1. Some illustrative examples of changes to media development in the digital age.

Traditional Media Development Focus	Digital Age Focus
Media sector	Information from a systems perspective (media sectors are a *part* of the system)
Training; capacity building (which sometimes means giving organizations the skills to better define and complete their missions and grow over time; and sometimes it is just code for training)	Capacity building; *plus* increasing opportunities and improving abilities; improving performance (i.e. helping organizations do their work better and achieve results by looking at other factors such as relationships; political economy, etc.)
Professional journalists, editors, etc.	Information producers including professional journalists, activists, and other citizens "Infomediaries" such as librarians
The audience	Information consumers of all types, who also can potentially produce, curate, share information
Single, universalized definition of journalism that includes being impartial, professional	Recognition of and support for acts of journalism performed by a wide range of actors including (but not only) professionally trained journalists. Includes solutions journalism, advocacy journalism, and others; includes new formats such as Tweetstorms, virtual reality films, blogs.

Advocacy for access to information laws; media reform; telecommunications regulations	Advocacy for access to information laws; media reform; telecommunications regulations *plus* participating in internet governance conversations; supporting advocates for internet freedom
Measuring press freedom; measuring media sustainability	Measuring the vibrancy of information; the health of information ecosystems; the health of the internet
Improving monitoring and evaluation practices, especially activities at the beginning, middle, and end of programs to better understand the impact of projects and programs	Consistently employing theories of change; putting continual learning practices into place that enable programs to better adapt based on what is learned, as well as sharing knowledge more broadly
Diagnosis of the progress and success of media development interventions against a fixed model based on a U.S. ideal of how a media sector should function	Diagnosis of interventions based on whether they yield any positive impact on society; Cultivating an analytic mindset; valuing research and striving to embed it into practice and learning; acknowledging and analyzing multiple levels of power dynamics at all phases of implementation
Value technology for tech's sake: creating apps/running hackathons/striving for innovation without ensuring that these approaches are addressing specific problems	Value the importance of context, inclusion, and effectiveness over the tech itself. Tech should solve problems; different types of innovation exist; innovation is not always the best approach

Readying for an Unknown Future

Rather than aspire to achieve a traditional media sector model, both organizations emphasize flexibility and adaptability, being driven by realities on the ground. Both organizations emphasize information (which encompasses journalism but is not limited to it) rather than media. Both stress the many directions in which information moves, and a focus on the people that consume and use information, not just those that produce it. This new framing allows IREX and Internews to work in a more uncertain and changing environment. In the old days, the organizations worked to achieve a previously defined and proven model (such as that of a newspaper financed by subscriptions and advertising). If an intervention did not achieve this model, the only options were to try other methods to build the same model, push harder with the same methods, or admit failure. By hewing to agile management and adaptation—an acknowledgement of complexity and uncertainty as integral to current information systems—IREX and Internews have created space for creativity in which new models can arise. The models may be new, but they still adhere to the information-related values listed above. As these models are very new as of this writing, it remains to be seen what the differences will be across the two organizations.

Even committing to remain adaptable and context-driven does not necessarily buffer these organizations against unanticipated broader shifts in the complex global system. For example, Facebook's dominance—including its Free Basics platform which provides limited free internet currently to a billion people in the global south—will certainly impact the role of media development. Facebook supports some of the basic values of media development at least on the surface—access to information, freedom of expression, and increasingly, critical thinking skills to separate truth from fiction—but its market-driven model is unlikely to help create Vibrant Information systems or reach Internews' four strategic goals. Continual social, political, and technological change is likely to continue to exert existential pressures on media development practitioner organizations. The donor organizations that support them tend to be quite slow to adapt to these broader global trends. Thus, the difficulty of being able to fully put their new approaches into practice is perhaps the only future challenge that can be predicted with any certainty. Ongoing dialogue with donors and policymakers about these changes, as well as broadening funding sources and conditions will be necessary for IREX and Internews to realize their powerful ambitions for approaching the digital age.

Notes

1. Three resources analyzing the mixed outcomes and impacts of a wide range of media development with a U.S. donor focus are Ellen Hume, "The Media Missionaries: American Support for Journalism Excellence around the Globe," Miami, FL: John S. and James L. Knight Foundation, 2004; Krishna Kumar, "Promoting Independent Media: Strategies for Democracy Assistance." Boulder, CO: Lynne Rienner, 2006. https://www.rienner.com/title/Promoting_Independent_Media_Strategies_for_Democracy_Assistance; and Mark Nelson with Tara Susman-Peña, "Rethinking Media Development: A Report on the Media Map Project." Washington, D.C.: Internews, 2012. https://www.internews.org/sites/default/files/resources/Internews_1-9_Rethinking_Media_Dev-2014-01.pdf
2. This essay represents a North American practitioner perspective, which is mostly aligned with Western European and other perspectives, but has some differences. In particular,

most U.S. sponsored interventions focus on a commercial media sector, while practitioners from countries with strong public service media, such as the U.K. and Germany, emphasize the public service model.

3. These are still media development goals, but much has changed, as we will see.
4. See for example, Mary Myers, "Is There a Link Between Media and Good Governance? What the Academics Say," Washington, D.C.: Center for International Media Assistance, 2012. This report reviews half a dozen often- cited studies on how the news media contributes to good governance and democracy.
5. A theory of change spells out how people think that their actions will contribute to a desired change. A simple theory in one USAID example was, "If I add more fuel to the fire, then it will burn hotter." http://pdf.usaid.gov/pdf_docs/Pnads460.pdf See also: Ann-Murray Brown, "What is this thing called 'Theory of Change'?" Washington, DC: USAID Learning Lab, 2016. https://usaidlearninglab.org/lab-notes/what-thing-called-theory-change
6. U.S. government donor funded-programs had some role in facilitating the protests and revolutions, including training bloggers and citizens on digital tools. See for example, Ron Nixon, "U.S. Groups Helped to Nurture Uprisings," *New York Times*, April 14, 2011. http://www.nytimes.com/2011/04/15/world/15aid.html?mcubz=0
7. See also Barthel, Micheal, et al. "The Evolving Role of News on Twitter and Facebook. Washington, DC: Pew Research Center, 2010. http://www.journalism.org/2015/07/14/the-evolving-role-of-news-on-twitter-and-facebook/
8. Media development practitioners have taken note of these threats to sustainability, and publications analyzing potential ways forward have mushroomed without agreeing on any solutions. For example, Michelle Foster, "Matching the Model and the Market: The Business of Independent News Media," Washington, DC, CIMA, 2011; "Financially Viable Media in Emerging and Developing Markets," SIDA and WAN-IFRA, 2011; Robert G. Picard, "Mapping Digital Media: Digitization and Media Business Models," London, Open Society Foundations, 2011.
9. Ibid.
10. See Algoso, Dave, "Which of these three books on complexity and development are right for you? Review/user's guide," From Poverty to Power, 2016, http://oxfamblogs.org/fp2p/which-of-these-three-books-on-complexity-and-development-is-right-for-you-reviewusers-guide/
11. The new strategy process follows Internews' 2014 research and strategy initiative defining Information Ecosystems to support resilience (the ability to survive, adapt, and even thrive in the face of change), which the author led. Internews created a diagnostic tool created from the information ecosystems research was created to help assess information needs, analyze challenges and gaps (such as who is vulnerable and excluded), and design strategies for effective information production, distribution, and engagement. This diagnostic was meant to help focus decision-making in an increasingly complex world. At present the relationship between the Information Ecosystems framework and the strategic framework is unclear. However, the fact that these two existential processes happened in succession illustrates the ongoing challenge for media development organizations to conceptualize the work that they do in a way that is adequate to the complicated, confusing times they operate in.

12. See https://www.internews.org/theory-change.
13. All of the Media Sustainability Index studies can be found at https://www.irex.org/resource/media-sustainability-index-msi.

Recommended for Further Reading

"Citizens as Agents of Change." 2017. *World Development Report 2017: Governance and the Law.* http://www.worldbank.org/en/publication/wdr2017

International Center for Journalists. 2017. "ICFJ Survey: The State of Technology in Global Newsrooms." *ICFJ.* http://www.icfj.org/sites/default/files/ICFJTechSurveyFINAL.pdf

Lee, Panthea, Nonso Jideofor, and Kate Reed Petty. 2016. "People-Powered Media Innovation in West Africa." *Reboot.* http://westafricamedia.reboot.org/

SembraMedia. 2017. "Inflection Point: Impact, Threats, and Sustainability. A Study of Latin American Digital Media Entrepreneurs." *SembraMedia.* http://data.sembramedia.org/

Webb, Amy. 2017. "The Global Survey on Journalism's Futures." *Future Today Institute.* https://futuretodayinstitute.com/global-survey-on-journalisms-futures/

References

Borchers, Callum. 2016. "ProPublica channels Donald Trump, calls out voter fraud 'lie' in first-ever tweetstorm." *Washington Post,* November 28. https://www.washingtonpost.com/news/the-fix/wp/2016/11/28/propublica-channels-donald-trump-calls-out-voter-fraud-lie-in-first-ever-tweetstorm/?noredirect=on&utm_term=.3b665442686e3

Gagliardone, Iginio. 2010. *From Mapping Information Ecologies to Evaluating Media Interventions: An Experts Survey on Evaluating Media Interventions in Conflict Countries.* Paper presented for the workshop: "Evaluating Media's Impact in Conflict Countries." Caux Conference Center, Switzerland. December 13–17, 2010 http://www.global.asc.upenn.edu/fileLibrary/PDFs/iginiocaux.pdf

Ingram, Mathew. 2015. "Facebook has taken over from Google as a traffic source for news." *Fortune,* August 18. http://fortune.com/2015/08/18/facebook-google/

Mottaz, Laura. 2010. *U.S. Government Funding for Media Development: A Special Report to the Center for International Media Assistance.* Washington, D.C.: Center for International Media Assistance.

Rouse, Marjorie. 2017. Senior vice president for programs, Internews. Personal communication, September 8.

Susman-Peña, Tara. 2017. *Vibrant Information for Just, Prosperous, and Inclusive Societies.* Washington, D.C.: IREX. https://www.irex.org/sites/default/files/node/resource/vibrant-information-paper.pdf

CHAPTER TWENTY-SIX

How Scholarship on Media Development Can Make a Difference

GUY BERGER

In the international community, an early link between research and media development was stimulated by concerns about international media imbalances. This led to the appointment at UNESCO in 1977 of the International Commission for the Study of Communications Problems, which gave rise to the "MacBride Report" three years later. The UNESCO Member States' response was to set up the International Program for the Development of Communication (IPDC) to secure resources for actors requesting assistance in this area. Over the years, IPDC raised more than $100 million for over 1,500 media development projects in more than 140 developing countries and countries in transition.[1]

Research into media development in this case elicited significant policy responses.[2] In the early years, IPDC gave out grants to grow the capacity of state-owned news agencies in developing countries. After the 1991 Windhoek Declaration, the focus switched to supporting independent media and the requisite national enabling environment of law and professional capacity.

In more recent decades, research into media development has had less impact, and the context has also evolved significantly. Media development, itself, has grown, but in a piecemeal way. It embraces practices that are often fragmented and sometimes embedded in wider "development" activities (e.g., democratization, anti-corruption, and behavior change regarding HIV.) Within the broader "development industry," there is not a unified community, site, or identity for interventions that might be considered broadly to deal with strengthening the media. For a decade or more there has not been a regular global gathering of a sizeable body of media donors, nor of media development scholars, (although at country-level there is sometimes a degree of coordination by Western media donors). Competition for donor funds and competition between donors, has complicated the construction of a community in this space.

Research into media development reflects this fragmentation and is likely compounded by the complex location of the subject in academia—somewhere at the interface of development studies, media studies, and journalism studies. A further factor is the absence of related momentum in academic journals and the low visibility of informal documentation about the practice—for instance, project reports and evaluations go into the archives of donors, rather than being availed publicly online with search-friendly meta-data.

At the same time, it is exactly for these reasons that research into media development is far from being a crowded arena, and that opportunities exist for researchers, scholars, and practitioners to work to more systematically advance knowledge in this area. This is not a quest to establish a field of knowledge for the mere sake of it. Rather, the issue is about making sense of the diversity of experiences in terms of the broad objective of advancing media development. This current volume is a praiseworthy step in this direction.

However, the opportunity is not as straightforward as simply increased engagement and cooperation among interested academics and practitioners. To start, there is no clearly agreed conceptualization of what "media development" actually means. An earlier article by this author (Berger 2010) pointed to the implicit circularity in the UNESCO Media Development Indicators, which equated media development to a series of features in a media landscape, and vice versa, without venturing a more generic conceptualization. Indeed, such a conceptualization could allow for recognitions of salient changing features, particularly in these digital times. It could also assist in foregrounding the values and norms necessarily implicated in any conceptualization of media development. From one point of view, there is some value in treating "media development" as if it were a technical, neutral term, aligning it with the broader notion of "development" in general, which assumes a universal consensus that it's a "good thing." However, as any unpacking of development will show, things are often more controversial than the positive connotations would suggest. For example, if development is about gender equality or reversing climate change, it is also fully evident these goals are not equally shared by many actors. Likewise, if media development is, when made more explicit, about free, pluralistic, and independent (news) media, it is also similarly evident that many actors do not favor such an orientation.

Still, without an explicit normative component, it is difficult to assess the meaning of the word "development." When businesses invest in media domestically or internationally, is that part of "media development"? Or is the phrase only when there is a development agenda and policy at work (as distinct from a money-making or political rationale)? A linked issue is that media development interventions imply a power dynamic: there are developers ... and developees (notwithstanding references to development "facilitators" and development "partners"). Yet, much community media around the world relies on volunteers; if they are "developers," contributing to thc growth and viability ("development") of the related media outlets, who then are the "developees"? A further question is: if the aim of "media development" is to improve an enabling environment for pluralistic media, is it not questionable to perceive policy makers (power holders considered as objects of an intervention) as "developees"?

Much discussion and practice of media development is about initiatives with expressed interests in media's potential democratic role. But when there is technical training or equipment provided for journalists who work in government-controlled media, is this media development? What about when non-traditional donor agencies and actors enter the scene and seek to strengthen even privately-owned media as a tool of government? Without a definition, we cannot easily perceive whether these kinds of interventions should also be part of a common research focus. To add further nuance, when any state puts resources into expanding its own media holdings internationally—treating these as instruments of foreign policy—does this count as media development? And what are the implications when the erstwhile "developers" themselves are arguably now in need of development, such as for capacity-building towards intercultural sensitivity and inclusive global coverage? Today, many "developed" media systems appear to need support to protect press freedom, preserve Net Neutrality, and fight back against disinformation and troll attacks on journalists (especially women journalists). Media that were once role models, hosts of foreign interns, or examples of best practice reporting, are now themselves struggling to find sustainable business models which can inter alia support local and investigative journalism.

As elaborated later, today's context includes the UN's Sustainable Development Goals (SDGs) holistic package of envisaged targets focused on universal issues that include climate change, migration and gender equality—which are relevant to all countries, notwithstanding in different degrees. These re-conceptualizations of what development is for, and who it is for, constitute a fertile topic for interested scholars of media development worldwide. In short, exciting work can be done today into exploring the meaning of "development" in media development in the current era, the normative values entailed, and who is involved in what roles.

New Actors and the Institutions Formerly Known as "the Media"

As if all the questioning of development were not complex enough, the issue also arises as to what is encompassed by "media" in media development. Generally speaking, the assumption is that media development is aimed at the development of media institutions, which in turn depends on developing an enabling environment, particularly at a legal level. Media development therefore requires both direct and indirect activity. But what complicates understanding here is the variety of relevant end-beneficiary institutions identified to be "enabled" (e.g., entertainment media, news media, hybrid enterprises, advertising agencies, printing plants, signal distributors, internet connectivity actors, journalism schools, professional associations, self-regulatory institutions, fact-checking NGOs, press freedom watchdogs, etc.)

In most of these cases, the "intention" of the development intervention is not ultimately to develop the institutions/actors involved, as an end in itself, but as a means to other ends, such as a particular political role, cultural significance, impact on gender equality, climate change policy, improved health, etc. In this way, "media development" is an instrumentalized practice, and the connections between the "enabling environment," the institutions/actors affected (whether directly or indirectly targeted) and the ultimate desired societal outcome are not so straightforward. Evidently, this makes monitoring and evaluation particularly challenging, and the variety of variables in any given instance is at odds with the ever-present hope that analysis can simply identify "what works" and transpose it to other contexts.

Another issue to consider is the changing character of "media." Most internet companies today play media roles in varying degrees. As well as mediating the connection between media institutions and their audiences, they also and overwhelmingly control the communications channels between members of what was formerly a mass audience that was only vicariously represented in national information exchange and conversation. In some respects, other historic linkages—such as between political actors as news sources, and the news media as conveyer of their messages—are also increasingly being disintermediated. Many politicians nowadays bypass the news media conduit to interact directly with their constituents, raising the question of news media's changing strategic role vis-à-vis elections for example. In this light, it is hard to see the development of media institutions in isolation, especially insofar as the intention of many interventions is to ultimately impact on the public, and when single-purpose dedicated media institutions (while still influential) no longer constitute the gatekeepers they once were.[3]

Few observers today would want to see internet giants as beneficiaries of media development support, given that these behemoths seem more than capable of developing themselves, and given that their very strength is increasingly an obstacle to the development of news media institutions. In token recognition of this trend, however, a number of the internet giants are themselves playing a significant role in supporting the news media—partly to ward off regulation that might, for example, otherwise restrain them from occupying positions of such market dominance. On the other hand, in the views of some media development actors and stakeholders, competition regulation should apply, as well as common carrier/net neutrality rules as well so as to ensure fair market opportunity for news media actors. However, one misconception is a refrain sometimes heard from traditional broadcasters that because they face costly regulation (e.g., local content quotas, cross-ownership limits), it would only be fair for internet companies to be subjected to the same. Such an approach ignores the argument that broadcasters use a scarce public resource (airwave frequencies) which justifies these obligations. More significantly, it mistakenly seems to assume that restrictions on internet actors will somehow translate in advertising spend returning to the legacy media institutions.

Better to Focus on "Journalism Development"?

In the face of these dynamics in media and internet realms, one response is to discard the notion of "media" development, and instead focus more directly on "*journalism* development" (as one particularly key dimension of media, which is also often privileged by certain donors). This perspective provides a clear and democratically important focus, and it also opens up the vision to recognizing the significant examples and potentials of journalism carried out outside of media institutions. This signals that journalism, done by individuals, academia, and NGOs for instance, can also benefit from external assistance (whether local, foreign, tax-breaks, loans, grants, subsidies, training and equipment, etc.). Yet, it is also apparent that the bulk of journalism still relies on institutions which can provide processes, brands, consistency and scale of operation, and this reality ought not to be side-stepped by the notion of "journalism development." Irrespective of the source of journalism, however, "journalism development" faces limits if there are not enough attempts to make progress in other aspects of the enabling environment (e.g., political, legal, fiscal, electrical, infrastructural, etc.). Hence, a holistic perspective is still needed even if the focus is on assisting the practice of journalism.

Even while considering all this, whether the main objective is on journalism development or news-media development, the fact is that the proverbial elephants in the room, called Facebook and Google in many countries, increasingly play editorial gatekeeping roles. In addition, they do this by means of algorithmic selection and prioritization which can marginalize media institutions. It would therefore appear difficult to develop journalism in this context, in isolation of the power of the distribution channels and the way that these and other actors outside news media contribute to, and interact with, original journalistic output.

A further point to consider about a focus on *journalism* development is that it risks isolating news and information as such from other classic media functions (entertainment, education), and as such can "miss a trick." In the same way that disinformation ("fake news") cannot be countered by simply "news literacy," but needs a wider set of literacies that include literacy about the issues of narrative and the construction of identities, so too "journalism development" can inadvertently lead to blinkers about the value of support for the wider complementary functions and genres of communications. While news naturally plays a key role, we should still nevertheless avoid a version of Habermas' original vision which implied that the public sphere is and can be comprised of rational individuals who somehow transcend ideology, as well as be exempt from the way that narratives marshal facts into particular meanings. The rise of influential political comedy, "listicule" formats (Buzzfeed), and immersive formats that come close to journalism—and affect the genre too—also need to be considered within the purvey of both media and journalism development. What is further evident today, is a world where trust in what news to generate, believe, and share is strongly affected by online networks of family and friends. The scope of media development efforts should, therefore, logically expand to include developing the capacity of individuals at large through all-round media and information literacy as an essential part of an enabling environment.

Research Challenges

In the light of all these observations about "development" and about "media," as much as we need a common broad conception of what media development designates, we should avoid narrowing our concerns to a tightly-defined, static, and exclusive research object. Instead, "media development" needs a level of shared meaning at the level of mass communications in general (and especially journalistic communications) about what this field entails in terms of improving democracy and sustainable development. What is needed, therefore, is intellectual work to build some consensus around generic elements in search of a basic coherence that could underpin "media development" as a viable research field.

The conceptual issues discussed above are certainly engaging enough. But there is also a long road to strengthening actual research in the area and connecting the conceptual and the empirical.

Knowledge depends on information which, in turn, relies on data. Data availability, or the capacity to generate data, is, therefore, a key issue in the quest to make more sense of "media development" and what is happening to the object under focus. Today, the biggest holders of data about communications are private internet companies who hold their assets close to their chests. When it comes to data about development initiatives and experiences, there are also issues such as in the breadth of the field and the diversity of experiences, which makes it difficult to collect and aggregate data. It was in an attempt to tackle this challenge that UNESCO' IPDC worked in 2012 with the World Bank Institute, Catholic Media Council (CAMECO), Deutsche Welle, and the Center for International Media Assistance (CIMA) under the rubric of "knowledge driven media development" (UNESCO, n.d.c.). A series of discussions resulted in seven "Media Development Data Sharing Principles" (UNESCO, WAN-IFRA, and World Bank Institute, n.d.) premised on the idea of transparency and sharing of information about media development. This was aimed to help promote research and knowledge generation within the media development community of practice. The intention was to develop a wider learning cycle whereby information arising from media development projects could generate knowledge, which, in turn, could enhance future project selection and learning.

However, it proved difficult for the media development actors involved at the time to take the initiative further, given that each was already caught up in its immediate and more specialized media development work. CIMA did explore whether a common search engine could be developed to aggregate data held in dispersed holdings by the various actors, but without success. This cautionary experience suggests that overcoming fragmentation and developing meaningful collaboration is challenging, and therefore, that building a broad-based academic research agenda may encounter similar challenges. At the same time, there are some realistic opportunities in the current period for researchers and practitioners to build closer ties and create knowledge synergies, for example, creating special interest groups in bodies such as the International Association for Media and Communications Research, and publishing further compendia such as this one.

Global Opportunities: Sustainable Development

Various studies, including UNESCO's *World Trends in Freedom of Expression and Media Development* (2018a), and ARTICLE 19's The Expression Agenda Report

2016/2017, signal the tightening environment globally for freedom of expression and the implications this has for media development. It is evident that the news media, besides its many challenges related to digital development and internet actors, is especially impacted by broader polarization, populism, nationalism, war, migration, disinformation, commercialization, and instrumentalization. In addition, wider economic and political policies set the scene for the media landscape in many places. Examples are falls in funding for a genuine public service media sector in numerous countries, and the resilience of political capture of public media institutions in many others.

At the same time, there is also a significant opportunity in the overall broad "development" consensus of the SDGs rubric, agreed at the UN in 2015 with 2030 as the target date for achievement. UNESCO and the Global Forum for Media Development (GFMD) combined forces in the evolution of the goals, seeking to secure recognition of free and independent media as part of the agenda. In the end, this was not successful, but the Member States of the UN agreed on a broader formulation which is still directly relevant to media development. This is within the framework of SDG 16 which is to promote "peaceful and inclusive societies, access to justice for all, and effective institutions." The particular resonance within this is located in SDG Target 16.10: "Ensure public access to information and fundamental freedoms, in accordance with national laws and international agreements."

This reference represents an advance, from a media development point of view, over the earlier blind spot in the earlier Millennium Development Goals (2000–2015.) It is an explicit recognition of communication issues as being integral to the wider development "package." It evokes the need for States to make information available, while coupling this with fundamental freedoms in the same breath. The clear inference is that the exercise of freedom of expression (amongst other rights) is bound up with providing public access to information. The significance of media institutions and journalism as a contributor to the provision of public information through the exercise of expression on mass communication platforms flows logically from this.

Symbolically, this means that importance of media development as part of broader development, is embedded in what is now known as the 2030 Development Agenda. As such, there is a strong basis to argue that this mainstreamed status of media development should also be recognized with appropriate funding for both practice and research within wider development thrusts. This kind of perspective is what informs the recent UNESCO initiative called IPDCtalks, the staging of which in various countries worldwide marks the Organization's International Day for Universal Access to Information each 28 September. The expanded point made in these commemorations is that "public access to information" is not only one target amongst others within the SDGs, but additionally a means towards achieving many of the other targets. Without "public access to information" and the role of media therein, it is rather hard to envisage societies having the information and communications needed to ensure realization of, for example, gender equality, combating climate change, ending corruption, etc. In this regard, there are numerous linkages between individual SDG goals and media development.

A related point to make is that information and media are also vital to assessing progress, or lack thereof, in achieving the SDGs. In this regard, it is significant that advocacy by UNESCO and the GFMD secured two particular indicators to measure changes in regard to "public access to information." These indicators (as with others) were initially approved by the UN Statistical Commission and were subsequently recognized by the UN General Assembly in 2017. Indicator 16.10.1 covers the "number of verified cases of killing, kidnapping, enforced disappearance, arbitrary detention and torture of journalists, associated media personnel, trade unionists and human rights advocates in the previous 12 months." Indicator 16.10.2 is the "number of countries that adopt and implement constitutional, statutory and/or policy guarantees for public access to information." A key aspect of media development—the safety of journalists—is embedded in the first indicator, while the second one relates to freedom of information laws and their implementation which are a key part of the enabling environment for effective media development. These two indicators are significant bridges for monitoring and evaluation that is relevant to media development.

In varying degrees of data partnership with GFMD members, UNESCO now contributes to the global monitoring and reporting on these two indicators. The results are recorded in the UN Secretary General's annual progress report, as well as an accompanying database open to researchers. The UN Member States have agreed that all indicators should be refined annually, reviewed in 2020, and complemented by indicators at the regional and national levels, to be developed by Member States' national statistics systems. The metadata for the current indicators states that what exists is a start, opening the door to further elaboration and expansion. The year 2019 will see particular attention to assessing progress on Goal 16 via its related indicators.

What all this means for media development stakeholders is that there is a global reference point to which they could profitably link their work in terms of relevance and even resources. Furthermore, there are opportunities to either domesticate the global indicators or to work towards alternative indicators at national level (for example, assessing and supporting uptake by investigative journalists of Freedom of Information laws as part of advancing public access to information). In sum, the SDGs open new possibilities to secure recognition and resources for media development, and research dimensions, at both global and national levels.

Global Opportunities in Relation to Internet Issues

An additional opportunity for media development scholars and practitioners is the World Summit on the Information Society (WSIS), a UN initiative begun in 2003 with a mandate renewed to 2025. It focuses on ICTs but includes recognition of an Action Line on the role of media.[4] UNESCO has further advanced the concept of "knowledge societies" as an enrichment of the concept of Information Society for which the pillars include freedom of expression and access to information. Conceptually, this implies the need to treat media development not as a silo, separate from the worlds of e-governance, e-learning, etc., but as part of the wider society. Significantly, the WSIS recognises the interdependence of different aspects of the internet, and accordingly continues to support multi-stakeholder governance modalities. This is also the position of UNESCO Member States who have agreed the concept of "internet universality," which embraces four "R.O.A.M principles." These are *human rights, openness, accessibility* and *multi-stakeholder participation* (UNESCO, n.d.b.). Media development is implicated in all this.

Although links between media development actors and internet-related actors have been underdeveloped, and the media sector has been largely absent from multi-stakeholder engagements, the annual Internet Governance Forum increasingly highlights the crucial intersections between internet governance and media development. One example is digital safety, something which particularly affects journalists; another is anonymity and encryption, which directly impacts on the confidentiality of journalistic sources.[5] Questions around big data are mainstreaming in much media, both in terms of content production and business planning. Online privacy, as in the so-called *Right to Be Forgotten*, has importance for media. Such intersections between digital and media development matters means that media institutions ignore the governance around these issues at their peril. In effect, the potential exists for media development practitioners to exercise a strong educational, advocacy and bridge-building role that can impact on the far-reaching decisions that are being taken in the internet space. Having been left behind by the internet juggernaut, the media sector and its supporters have a lot of catch-up work to do.

Evidently, many media actors see the internet companies as rivals and threats to existing media models and status, but the big companies are recognizing the need for better synergies. They are being held increasingly accountable for content on their platforms and are improving their self-regulation systems in order to stave off state intervention that could cost them money. In this regard, media development, with its concern about independence of institutions up against threats of state control, can find some common political ground with potentially powerful allies. The internet companies also have to increasingly deal with their users' concerns about toxic communications environments and fraudulent news. Seen in this light, journalism appears to be an asset that they could do more to support. This is partly why, as noted earlier, several of them operate media development initiatives. Beyond the public relations benefits, these initiatives could become genuine partnerships in hard mutual interest. In some celebrated cases, a number of tech barons have also become investors or benefactors by buying and resourcing media institutions which constitutes another potential area for synergy (and research), particularly around the extent to which editorial independence is respected.

As it becomes more and more clear that the internet giants have won the contest for advertising, thanks to big data and their leadership of the attention economy, many media institutions will rely more and more on partnerships that provide them a share of the pie. There are some signs of collaboration developing, albeit on highly unequal and erratic terms. Besides a common interest in resisting regulation that restricts free expression, what independent news media offers internet actors is a range of other value-adds: fact-checking and credible content; experience in self-regulation; and news brands that have greater or lesser degrees of recognition and/or trust. In this environment, space exists for new initiatives in media development, particularly if the media institutions also urge internet actors to open up more media-related data, including transparency of their media support work and its assessment. All this is potentially useful material for research and analysis.

Concluding Remarks

Media development today continues to encompass a number of long-standing issues, albeit often with added dimensions. One is securing the safety of journalists, physically, psychologically and digitally. Strides have been made with the UN Plan of Action on the Safety of Journalists and the Issue of Impunity. To be part of this flourishing initiative, an academic network (the Journalism Safety Research Network) has been formed to bolster research into journalistic safety, and the topic of safety is also set to be integrated into the Worlds of Journalism research initiative during 2018. Supporting gender equality in and through media continues to be an issue that attracts research attention. The Global Alliance for Media and Gender and the linked UNITWIN research network (UNESCO, 2017a; UNESCO UNITWIN, 2018) are studying this subject, and various actors are using the UNESCO Gender Sensitive Indicators for Media (UNESCO, 2017b.)

A new issue that calls out for urgent attention by media development supporters is that of *media and information literacy*. This has become ever more topical as internet penetration increases, and ordinary people have ever more opportunities to produce, as well as consume, public (and private) information. The gamut of desired competencies continues to expand, from understanding the protocols of news and how advertising works, through to identifying and countering hate speech, as well practicing digital security, protecting privacy, and evaluating what is "fake news" (UNESCO, 2018b.)[6] Many academics are now involved in the Global Alliance for Partnerships in Media and Information Literacy. The paradigm of "media development" today has to embrace the issues of user/audience development, and the intersection of social media and news media.

As noted above, internet governance is another issue facing media development. The integration of the internet into so much of life means that media institutions, and media development practitioners, are willy-nilly stakeholders in the governance of digital affairs. The complex interdependence of the "Net" is recognized in UNESCO's concept of *internet universality*, which interprets "internet development" as progressive alignment to human rights, openness, accessibility and multi-stakeholder participation. To provide a better understanding of how this plays out in a given society, UNESCO is developing indicators along the model of its Media Development Indicators (UNESCO, n.d.a.). The resulting research tool will help many stakeholders—and not least media development actors—gain a holistic picture of the particular internet dynamics in a given society, and of gaps for particular governance changes and development interventions (whether policy, capacity-building, institutional, financial, etc). How the internet and its governance impacts on media development going forward merits intensive monitoring, and the Internet Universality Indicators could be helpful in this regard..

In recapping, it is evident that news media institutions and journalism—the heart of media development—are facing increasing stresses in the new context, with growing challenges to their role and indeed their very survival in some cases. The challenges facing scholarship about media development are also profound. But, there is a framework of possibilities in regard to conceptualizing and researching media development in relation to the SDGs, internet actors, the internet governance agenda, the safety of journalists and media and information literacy. In this context, the people interested in studying the dynamic concept of media development have a window of opportunity to make a distinctive knowledge contribution.

Notes

1. Disclosure: The author has served as Secretary of the IPDC since 2011.
2. In addition to the developmental response, there was major political impact, with the "MacBride Report" being used as a justification by the US and UK to leave UNESCO at

the time, even though the US itself was highly instrumental in the creation of IPDC. See: Nordenstreng, Kaarle. (2010). The New World Information and Communication Order: Testimony of an actor. In Round Table at International Colloquium "30 Years of Communication Geopolitics: Actors and Flows, Structures and Divides." http://www.uta.fi/cmt/en/contact/staff/kaarlenordenstreng/publications/Paris.pdf.

3. Disintermediation is especially evident in regard to advertising, which has historically been vital to the sustainability of the media sector in many countries, and where Internet companies have increasingly become the vectors linking sellers and potential buyers, both symbolically and also transactionally.
4. UN General Assembly resolution /RES/70/125 on the 15 year review of the WSIS. This says that States note "with concern serious threats to freedom of expression and plurality of information, and we call for the protection of journalists, media workers and civil society space. We reaffirm Article 19 and underscore the need to respect the independence of media."
5. See Posetti, J. 2017. *Protecting journalism sources in the digital age*. UNESCO Series on Internet Freedom, Paris: UNESCO. http://unesdoc.unesco.org/images/0024/002480/248054e.pdf.
6. The Paris Declaration on Media and Information Literacy in the Digital Age assesses some of these issues. http://www.unesco.org/new/en/communication-and-information/resources/news-and-in-focus-articles/in-focus-articles/2014/paris-declaration-on-media-and-information-literacy-adopted/.

Recommended for Future Reading

Carlsson, Ulla. 2003. "The Rise and Fall of NWICO, From a Vision of International Regulation to a Reality of Multilevel Governance." *Nordicom Review 2/2003.*

Hoboken, Joris Van, and Wolfgang Schulz. 2016. "Human Rights and Encryption." *UNESCO Series on Internet Freedom*. Paris: UNESCO.. http://www.unesco.org/new/en/media-services/single-view/news/human_rights_and_encryption_unesco_launches_the_eighth_titl/.

References

ARTICLE 19. 2017. *The Expression Agenda Report 2016/2017: The State of Freedom of Expression and Information.* London: ARTICLE 19. https://www.article19.org/wp-content/uploads/2017/12/Expression-Agenda-Report-2017-for-web-_30.11.17.pdf.

Berger, Guy. 2010. "Problematizing 'Media Development' as a Bandwagon Gets Rolling." *International Communication Gazette* 72 (7): 547–65.

UNESCO. n.d.a. "Developing Internet Universality Indicators." https://en.unesco.org/internetuniversality/indicators.

———. n.d.b. "Internet Universality Indicators: Online Consultation Phase II." https://en.unesco.org/internetuniversality/.

———. n.d.c. "Knowledge-Driven Media Development." https://en.unesco.org/programme/ipdc/initiatives/kdmd.

———. 2017a. "Global Alliance on Media and Gender."
http://www.unesco.org/new/en/communication-and-information/crosscutting-priorities/gender-and-media/women-make-the-news-2016/join-the-global-alliance/

———. 2017b. "Global Alliance for Partnerships on Media and Information Literacy." http://www.unesco.org/new/en/gapmil/.

UNESCO UNITWIN Network on Gender, Media and ICTs. 2018. "Who We Are." http://www.unitwin.net/who-we-are/.

UNESCO, WAN-IFRA, and World Bank Institute. n.d. "Media Development Data Sharing Principles: Preamble." https://en.unesco.org/sites/default/files/media_development_data_sharing_principles_final.pdf.

UNESCO. 2018a. *World Trends in Freedom of Expression and Media Development Global Report 2017/2018*. Paris: UNESCO and University of Oxford. https://en.unesco.org/world-media-trends-2017.

UNESCO. 2018b. *Journalism, Fake News and Disinformation. Handbook for Journalism Education and Training*. UNESCO series on journalism education. Paris: UNESCO http://unesdoc.unesco.org/images/0026/002655/265552e.pdf

About the Contributors

Marc Raboy is full professor and Beaverbrook chair in ethics, media and communications in the Department of Art History and Communication Studies. A former journalist in a wide variety of media, educated at McGill, Professor Raboy taught previously at the Université de Montréal and Laval University.

Monroe E. Price is an adjunct full professor at the Annenberg School for Communication and the Joseph and Sadie Danciger Professor of Law and Director of the Howard M. Squadron Program in Law, Media and Society at the Cardozo School of Law. He directs the Stanhope Centre for Communications Policy Research in London, and is the Chair of the Center for Media and Communication Studies of the Central European University in Budapest.

Mark M. Nelson is the senior director of the Center for International Media Assistance (CIMA). A former journalist and development specialist, he has written extensively on aid effectiveness, governance and the role of media in development.

Silvio Waisbord is a professor in the School of Media and Public Affairs at the George Washington University, editor-in-chief of the Journal of Communication and former editor-in-chief of the International Journal of Press/Politics.

Nicole Stremlau is head of the Programme in Comparative Media Law and Policy at Oxford University's Centre for Socio-Legal Studies. Her research focuses on media and governance, particularly in areas of conflict and insecurity in Africa.

Douglas Griffin the director of business development at Albany Associates. He is a lawyer specializing in media and communications strategy and policy.

Carolyn Byerly is graduate professor and chair of the Department of Communication, Culture & Media Studies (CCMS) at Howard University's Cathy Hughes School of Communication.

Marius Dragomir is the director of the Center for Media, Data and Society. He previously worked for the Open Society Foundations (OSF) for over a decade.

Shanthi Kalathil is director of the International Forum for Democratic Studies. Her work has focused primarily on issues pertaining to democratization, development, and media.

María Soledad Segura is a professor at Facultad de Ciencias de la Comunicación and Facultad de Ciencias Sociales of Universidad Nacional de Córdoba, and researcher at the Consejo Nacional de Investigaciones Científicas y Técnicas.

Savyasaachi Jain is a senior lecturer in JOMEC, specializing in journalism and documentary. His specific areas of interest encompass international journalism, global media systems, and the influences that shape journalistic practices and standards.

Gillian McCormack is Internews' regional director for Europe and Eurasia Programs. She has 20 years of experience in media development, electoral assistance and training, including three years working for Internews in Russia from 2004 to 2007.

James Deane is the director of policy and learning at BBC Media Action where he oversees the organization's research, technical assistance and policy activities. He has spent more than 30 years working in the field of media development.

Tatjana Ljubic is an expert in media and information literacy (MIL) research, policy development, and project implementation. She collaborated with UNESCO, Council of Europe, Media Diversity Institute and other international and domestic organizations in the field of MIL.

Michelle Betz is a senior media development consultant with 15 years of experience in assessment, project design, implementation, management and evaluation. Her areas of expertise include media in conflict and post-conflict, military-media relations, safety issues and rapid response interventions.

Tom Jacobson is professor of communication in the School of Media and Communication at Temple University in Philadelphia. He also serves there as director of the Master of Science in Globalization and Development Communication program. Dr. Jacobson is Chair of the Scholarly Review Committee for the International Association for Media and Communication Research.

Drew Sullivan is the editor and co-founder of OCCRP and served as the first director. He founded the Journalism Development Network, an innovative media development organization with programs worldwide.

Minna Aslama Horowitz is a visiting fellow at the Media Lab, LeGroup on educational technologies, at Aalto University, Finland. She taken part in several international research activities in the past decade, including comparative work based on the Open Society Foundation's global Mapping Digital Media project (2009–13).

Davor Marko is non-resident research fellow at the Analitika Center for Social Research and a PhD candidate at the Faculty of Political Sciences, University of Belgrade, in the domain of culture and communication.

Des Freedman is professor of Media and Communications at Goldsmiths, University of London. He was a founding member and recent chair of the Media Reform Coalition and was project lead for the Inquiry into the Future of Public Service Television.

Jonathan A. Obar is an assistant professor in the Department of Communication Studies. He also serves as a Research Associate with the Quello Center for Telecommunication Management and Law at Michigan State University, where he previously worked for four years.

Daniel O'Maley is the deputy editor and digital policy specialist at the Center for International Media Assistance at the National Endowment for Democracy. His policy portfolio includes internet policy, internet governance, and the implications of new digital technologies on media systems worldwide.

Michelle J. Foster is an international media management and marketing consultant who helps news media companies to improve business performance. She has worked with organizations throughout the United States and in China, Myanmar, SE Asia, the Balkans, Eastern Europe and Africa.

Tara Susman-Peña is a senior technical advisor in IREX's Center for Applied Learning and Impact and in the Information & Media practice. She is also a lecturer at the Elliot School of International Affairs, George Washington University.

Guy Berger is director for freedom of expression and media development at UNESCO. He is responsible for the Organization's global work on press freedom, safety of journalists, internet freedom, media pluralism and independence, gender and media, media and information literacy, and journalism education.

Mass Communication and Journalism

Lee B. Becker, *General Editor*

The Mass Communication and Journalism series focuses on broad issues in mass communication, giving particular attention to those in which journalism is prominent. Volumes in the series examine the product of the full range of media organizations as well as individuals engaged in various types of communication activities.

Each commissioned book deals in depth with a selected topic, raises new issues about that topic, and provides a fuller understanding of it through the new evidence provided. The series contains both single-authored and edited works. For more information and submissions, please contact:

Lee B. Becker, Series Editor | *lbbecker@uga.edu*
Erika Hendrix, Commissioning Editor | *erika.hendrix@plang.com*

To order other books in this series, please contact our Customer Service Department at:

(800) 770-LANG (within the U.S.)
(212) 647-7706 (outside the U.S.)
(212) 647-7707 FAX

Or browse online by series at www.peterlang.com